# THE HOLLYWOOD WAR FILM

# NEW APPROACHES TO FILM GENRE

## Series Editor: Barry Keith Grant

*New Approaches to Film Genre* provides students and teachers with original, insightful, and entertaining overviews of major film genres. Each book in the series gives an historical appreciation of its topic, from its origins to the present day, and identifies and discusses the important films, directors, trends, and cycles. Authors articulate their own critical perspective, placing the genre's development in relevant social, historical, and cultural contexts. For students, scholars, and film buffs alike, these represent the most concise and illuminating texts on the study of film genre.

1  *From* Shane *to* Kill Bill: *Rethinking the Western*, Patrick McGee
2  *The Horror Film*, Rick Worland
3  *The Hollywood Historical Film*, Robert Burgoyne
4  *The Religious Film*, Pamela Grace
5  *The Hollywood War Film*, Robert Eberwein

Forthcoming:
6  *Film Noir*, William Luhr
7  *The Fantasy Film*, Katherine A. Fowkes

# THE HOLLYWOOD WAR FILM

*Robert Eberwein*

**WILEY-BLACKWELL**

A John Wiley & Sons, Ltd., Publication

This edition first published 2010
© 2010 Robert Eberwein

Blackwell Publishing was acquired by John Wiley & Sons in February 2007.
Blackwell's publishing program has been merged with Wiley's global Scientific,
Technical, and Medical business to form Wiley-Blackwell.

*Registered Office*
John Wiley & Sons Ltd, The Atrium, Southern Gate, Chichester, West Sussex,
PO19 8SQ, United Kingdom

*Editorial Offices*
350 Main Street, Malden, MA 02148–5020, USA
9600 Garsington Road, Oxford, OX4 2DQ, UK
The Atrium, Southern Gate, Chichester, West Sussex, PO19 8SQ, UK

For details of our global editorial offices, for customer services, and for information
about how to apply for permission to reuse the copyright material in this book please
see our website at www.wiley.com/wiley-blackwell.

The right of Robert Eberwein to be identified as the author of this work has been
asserted in accordance with the Copyright, Designs and Patents Act 1988.

Wiley also publishes its books in a variety of electronic formats. Some content that
appears in print may not be available in electronic books.

Designations used by companies to distinguish their products are often claimed as
trademarks. All brand names and product names used in this book are trade names,
service marks, trademarks or registered trademarks of their respective owners. The
publisher is not associated with any product or vendor mentioned in this book. This
publication is designed to provide accurate and authoritative information in regard to
the subject matter covered. It is sold on the understanding that the publisher is not
engaged in rendering professional services. If professional advice or other expert
assistance is required, the services of a competent professional should be sought.

*Library of Congress Cataloging-in-Publication Data*

Eberwein, Robert T., 1940–
   The Hollywood war film / Robert Eberwein.
      p. cm.—(New approaches to film genre)
   Includes bibliographical references and index.
   ISBN 978-1-4051-7391-9 (hardcover : alk. paper)—ISBN 978-1-4051-7390-2
(pbk. : alk. paper)  1. War films–United States–History and criticism.  I. Title.
   PN1995.9.W3E245 2009
   791.43′6581—dc22

                                                                          2009010815

A catalogue record for this book is available from the British Library.

Set in 11/13pt Bembo by Graphicraft Limited, Hong Kong

Printed in the UK

For the Oakland University Department of English

# CONTENTS

| | | |
|---|---|---|
| List of Plates | | viii |
| Acknowledgments | | xi |
| Introduction | | 1 |
| 1 | Historical Overview | 14 |
| 2 | Critical Issues | 42 |
| 3 | *All Quiet on the Western Front* (1930) | 63 |
| 4 | *Destination Tokyo* (1943) and Retaliation Films | 76 |
| 5 | *Platoon* (1986) and *Full Metal Jacket* (1987) | 93 |
| 6 | *Glory* (1989) | 110 |
| 7 | The Iraq Wars on Film | 122 |
| 8 | Iwo Jima | 136 |
| Notes | | 152 |
| Index | | 172 |

# LIST OF PLATES

1   *Love and War* (James H. White, 1899). The soldier's return home.   6

2   *Birth of a Nation* (D. W. Griffith, 1915). "War's Peace" (David W. Griffith Corp./ Courtesy Photofest).   15

3   *The Best Years of Our Lives* (William Wyler, 1946). Peggy (Teresa Wright) tries to comfort Fred (Dana Andrews) (Samuel Goldwyn Company/ Courtesy Jerry Ohlinger's).   22

4   *The Steel Helmet* (Sam Fuller, 1951). Short Round (William Chun) and Sergeant Zack (Gene Evans) (Deputy Corporation/Courtesy Photofest).   25

5   *Apocalypse Now* (Francis Ford Coppola, 1979). Part of the helicopter fleet (Zoetrope Studios/Courtesy Photofest).   33

6   *This is the Army* (Michael Curtiz, 1943). One of the performers in drag (Alan Hale) complaining to a soldier in uniform (Tom D'Andrea) (Warner Bros./Courtesy Photofest).   49

7   *Saving Private Ryan* (Steven Spielberg, 1998). Captain Miller (Tom Hanks), the respected leader (Amblin Entertainment/Courtesy Photofest).   59

8   *All Quiet on the Western Front* (Lewis Milestone, 1930).
    The recruits forced to crawl through mud (Universal
    Pictures/Courtesy Photofest).                                    66

9   *All Quiet on the Western Front* (Lewis Milestone, 1930).
    Paul (Lew Ayres) and a buddy display longing for women
    and a world separate from the war (Universal Pictures/
    Courtesy Photofest).                                             68

10  *Destination Tokyo* (Delmer Daves, 1943). Pills (William
    Prince) about to operate on Tommy (Robert Hutton)
    as Captain Cassidy (Cary Grant) looks on (Warner
    Bros./Courtesy Larry Edmunds Bookshop).                          78

11  *Destination Tokyo* (Delmer Daves, 1943). The cramped
    mise-en-scène of the submarine. Wolf (John Garfield)
    and Tin Can (Dane Clark) are in front (Warner Bros./
    Courtesy Photofest).                                             81

12  *The Purple Heart* (Lewis Milestone, 1944). The heroic
    fliers, now prisoners of war, led by Captain Ross (Dana
    Andrews) subjected to a mock trial by their Japanese
    captors (Twentieth Century-Fox Film Corporation).                84

13  *Bataan* (Tay Garnett, 1943). The doomed men listen to
    the radio. Sergeant Bill Dane (Robert Taylor) is third
    from the right (MGM/Courtesy Photofest).                         86

14  *Platoon* (Oliver Stone, 1986). Sergeant Barnes (Tom
    Berenger) about to shoot an unarmed woman
    (Cinema 86 Hemdale Corp./Courtesy Photofest).                    98

15  *Platoon* (Oliver Stone, 1986). Chris Taylor (Charlie Sheen)
    before he finds and shoots Barnes (Cinema 86 Hemdale
    Corp./Courtesy Photofest).                                       100

16  *Full Metal Jacket* (Stanley Kubrick, 1987). Sergeant
    Hartman (R. Lee Ermey) engaged in a verbal tirade in
    the barracks (Warner Bros./Courtesy Photofest).                  104

17  *Full Metal Jacket* (Stanley Kubrick, 1987). Joker
    (Matthew Modine) on the way to Hue City. "Is that
    you, John Wayne, is this me?" (Warner Bros./Courtesy
    Photofest).                                                      106

18  *Glory* (Edward Zwick, 1989). Rawlins (Morgan Freeman),
    now Sergeant Major Rawlins, no longer a grave digger
    (TriStar Pictures/Courtesy Photofest).                           117

19  *Glory* (Edward Zwick, 1989). Trip (Denzel Washington)
    leading the hopeless charge (TriStar Pictures/Courtesy
    Photofest).                                                      118

20  *Courage Under Fire* (Edward Zwick, 1996). Serling (Denzel
    Washington) elicits the truth from Ilario (Matt Damon)
    (Fox 2000 Pictures/Courtesy Photofest).                          124
21  *Courage Under Fire* (Edward Zwick, 1996). Captain
    Karen Walden (Meg Ryan) defending her men
    (Fox 2000 Pictures/Courtesy Photofest).                          126
22  *Three Kings* (David O. Russell, 1999). The bullion hunters
    on guard (George Clooney, Mark Wahlberg, Ice Cube,
    Spike Jonze) (Warner Bros./Courtesy Photofest).                  128
23  *Jarhead* (Sam Mendes, 2005). Swofford (Jake Gyllenhaal)
    and Troy (Peter Sarsgaard) at the Christmas party
    (Universal Pictures/Courtesy Photofest).                         132
24  *Stop-Loss* (Kimberly Peirce, 2008). Sergeant Brandon
    King (Ryan Phillippe) given a warm welcome home
    from Iraq by his parents (Linda Emond, Cierán Hinds)
    (Paramount Pictures/Courtesy Photofest).                         135
25  *Flags of Our Fathers* (Clint Eastwood, 2006). The flag
    raising on Mount Suribachi (Dreamworks SKG/
    Courtesy Photofest).                                             138
26  *Flags of Our Fathers* (Clint Eastwood, 2006). Ira Hayes
    (Adam Beach), Doc Bradley (Ryan Phillippe), and Rene
    Gagnon (Jesse Bradford) talking in front of a flag poster
    (Dreamworks Skg/Courtesy Photofest).                             145
27  *Flags of Our Fathers* (Clint Eastwood, 2006). Ira Hayes
    (Adam Beach), Doc Bradley (Ryan Phillippe), and Rene
    Gagnon (Jesse Bradford) being served a strawberry sauce
    over ice-cream in the shape of the flag raising site
    (Deamworks SKG/Courtesy Photofest).                              146
28  *Letters from Iwo Jima* (Clint Eastwood, 2006). Saigo
    (Kazunari Ninomiya) reading (Amblin Entertainment/
    Courtesy Photofest).                                             148
29  *Letters from Iwo Jima* (Clint Eastwood, 2006). General
    Kuribayashi (Ken Watanabe) standing next to the flags of
    his country (Amblin Entertainment/Courtesy Photofest).           149

# ACKNOWLEDGMENTS

I am grateful to a number of kind individuals. Barbara Hall again offered her typically incisive and authoritative guidance through the wonders and treasures of the Margaret Herrick Library, Academy of Motion Picture Arts and Sciences. Sandra Joy Lee, Director of the University of Southern California Warner Bros. Archive, provided cartons filled with invaluable studio records and data. Derek Davidson of Photofest, Inc. helped once more to find appropriate stills. As usual, I'm grateful to Ronald Mandelbaum for his patience. At Oakland University, Virinder G. Moudgil, Senior Vice President for Academic Affairs and Provost, offered generous support for activities related to my research. Julie Voelck, Dean of Kresge Library, continued to make that unit's services readily available. Professors Mildred Merz and Dan Ring of the Library were helpful in a number of ways. Pat Clark and Dante Rance in Interlibrary Loans located everything I needed. Susan Hawkins, Chair of the Department of English, maintained a welcoming environment for a retired faculty member, as did Cynthia Ferrera and Becky Fernandez. Professor Jeffrey Insko helped with his masterful computer skills.

At Wiley-Blackwell, I have been fortunate to benefit from Barry Keith Grant's probing, invaluable editorial scrutiny and suggestions for revision. I have enjoyed working with Jayne Fargnoli, Executive

Editor of the Arts Division, and Margot Morse, Senior Editorial Assistant, Culture and Communication Studies, and appreciate their helpful suggestions and observations. Thanks to the anonymous reader for thoughtful and useful commentary and to Jack Messenger for his copyediting. I appreciate the encouragement and helpful suggestions of Dolores M. Burdick, Douglas Cunningham, Thomas Doherty, Peter Lehman, William Luhr, Brian Murphy, and Stephen Prince. Finally, thanks, as always, to Jane for making our lives so peaceful.

# INTRODUCTION

The narrative subjects of war films span human history, moving from a pre-literate past to an imagined future. Warring cave men appear in *One Million BC.* (1940). Pre-Christian epics about the Trojan War like the *Odyssey* and the *Iliad* provide the subject matter of *Troy* (2004), and historical figures and events are the focus of *300* (2007), an account of the Spartans' defeat by the Persians at Thermopylae. Films about later wars include the Crusades, *Kingdom of Heaven* (2005); the Hundred Years War, *The Messenger* (1999); England's wars with Russia, *The Charge of the Light Brigade* (1936, 1968), Scotland, *Braveheart* (1995), and Ireland, *Tristan and Isolde* (2006); the French Revolution and its aftermath, *Napoleon* (1927) and *War and Peace* (1956, 1967); the Spanish Civil War, *For Whom the Bell Tolls* (1943); Bosnia, *Behind Enemy Lines* (2004); and Israel and Lebanon, *Beaufort* (2007). Films about conflicts in American history include those on the French and Indian Wars, *The Last of the Mohicans* (1992); Revolutionary War, *The Patriot* (2000); War of 1812, *The Buccaneer* (1958); Civil War, *Gone With the Wind* (1939); Spanish-American War, *Love and War* (1899); World War I, *Wings* (1927); World War II, *Saving Private Ryan* (1998); Korean War, *The Steel Helmet* (1951); Vietnam, *Platoon* (1986); Gulf War, *Three Kings* (1999); and Iraq, *Redacted* (2007). Two other kinds of films about wars usually receive a different generic classification. Both *Die Nibelungen* (1924) and *The Lord of the Rings* (2001–2003) involve conflicts that take us to the mythic worlds of the fantasy genre. Those set in the distant future are classified as science fiction films: *Star Wars* (1977–2005) and *Starship Troopers* (1997). Obviously, some science fiction films about wars take place in the present, as occurs in *War of the Worlds* (1953, 2005) and *Independence Day* (1996).[1]

Although a complete history of war films is certainly needed, I have more modest aims for this book, which is designed to introduce the genre by focusing on the Hollywood war film. I comment briefly on war films from other nations as these are relevant. This Introduction looks at the first films about war made in 1898–1899 and uses them and information about conditions of reception to argue how they allow us to identify the foundations of the genre, its essential characters, and narrative conventions. It concludes by outlining the primary generic conventions that will be highlighted in the discussions of individual films. Chapter 1 presents an overview of the major films, trends, and cycles as it places the genre's development in relevant social, historical, and cultural contexts. Chapter 2 considers critical ideas and theoretical issues that inform the discourse concerning the genre by addressing three significant topics: the definition of a war film; the role of war films in relation to questions of history; and the concept of "realism" as a criterion in understanding and judging films in this genre. The chapter ends with guidelines for examining the films discussed in the rest of the book, stressing the importance of considering individual films in relation to the history and conventions of the genre, issues of production and reception, and the complex effects produced by the retrospective treatment of past wars.

The remaining chapters deal with particular films made over the last eight decades about major wars. Chapter 3 focuses on Lewis Milestone's film about World War I, *All Quiet on the Western Front* (1930). Regarded as one of the greatest anti-war films ever made, the film shows the impact of war on German soldiers. In addition to identifying some important conventions in the film, I connect it to other major films about World War I, many of them similarly anti-war. In contrast, Chapter 4 looks at the generic conventions of films made in the 1940s that were uniformly supportive of World War II, especially Delmer Daves' *Destination Tokyo* (1943), a film about sailors on a submarine acquiring information to be used in the bombing raid of the Japanese city. It also examines what I call "retaliation films," a kind of cycle or sub-genre of films made during World War II about Pearl Harbor and its immediate aftermath such as *Wake Island* (1942), *Air Force* (1943), and *Bataan* (1943). Chapter 5 considers two films about the Vietnam War, which was generally avoided by Hollywood until after its conclusion in the early 1970s. The first major wave of films about the war began in 1978, followed in the next decade by the films covered in detail here. Oliver Stone's *Platoon*, drawn partly from his experience in combat, revisits the horror of the war and includes a sequence that evokes the notorious My-Lai massacre. Brief consideration will be given to the other films that make up Stone's trilogy about the war, *Born on the Fourth of July* (1989) and *Heaven and Earth* (1993). Stanley Kubrick's *Full Metal Jacket* (1987) offers a very different perspective on the conflict. Divided into two parts, the film's first section shows life in basic training for Marine recruits; in the second, Kubrick focuses on combat, providing a complementary critique to his earlier examinations of the evil associated with power in World War I commanders, in *Paths of Glory* (1957), and the insanity of nuclear war, in *Dr. Strangelove or: How I Learned to Stop Worrying and Love the Bomb* (1964).

The focus of Chapter 6 is *Glory* (1989), Edward Zwick's film about an all-black regiment led by a white commander in the Civil War. Although this chapter on a Civil War film might seem to disrupt the chronology observed thus far in the book regarding particular wars, in addition to examining generic aspects of this film, I position its treatment of African Americans in relation to films about World War II and suggest a reading of it in light of films about the Vietnam War. The first phase of the Iraq War, which began in 1990, is the subject of three films examined in Chapter 7: *Courage Under Fire* (1996), *Three Kings*, and *Jarhead* (2005). Each is notable for different reasons: in *Courage*, focusing on a woman as a military commander and exposing the truth about military actions in Iraq; in *Kings*, confronting the effects of the United States' invasion on Iraqi citizens; and in *Jarhead*, conveying the actual experiences of a Marine whose autobiography serves as the basis of the work. The chapter concludes with consideration of the generic aspects of films about the next phase of the Iraq War, which commenced in 2003. Chapter 8 revisits World War II by examining Clint Eastwood's *Flags of our Fathers* and *Letters from Iwo Jima* (2006). While several films in the 1990s returned to World War II as a subject, these represent a first for the war film genre. Earlier films have sometimes approached World War II from more than one perspective, as occurs in *The Longest Day* (1962) and *The Battle of the Bulge* (1965), which look at battles through the eyes of the Allies and the German enemy. *Flags* and *Letters* are the first two films created specifically to encompass the experience of all the combatants in a specific battle. They present American and Japanese perspectives on the devastating bloodbath that occurred on Iwo Jima in 1945 when over 6,800 Americans and 20,000 Japanese soldiers died in the struggle over control of the island. The first explores the event's significance for the men who in raising the flag occasioned the most famous photograph in the history of war. The second looks at the battle for Iwo Jima through the eyes of the doomed Japanese soldiers charged with defending the island.

## The Earliest Films about War

In late December 2007, Adam B. Vary wrote an article in *Entertainment Weekly* titled "War Movies Tanked." It joined other essays devoted to the same subject, such as Diane Garrett's view on "B.O. Battle Fatigue? War is Hell as studios try to sell conflict pics." Richard Corliss and Christian Toto specifically identified the Iraq War as the one that had failed to sell. And in an article titled "The War Zone," Owen Gliberman observed: "Moviegoers, in case you haven't noticed, are in the midst of a siege of films about the war in Iraq and politics of the post 9/11 world (at this point the two are inseparable). So far, though, it isn't at all clear that moviegoers are interested."[2] Obviously, the writers agreed on the dismal box office chances and receipts faced by the films of late 2007 dealing with aspects of the Iraq War such as *In the Valley of Elah*, *Grace is Gone*, and *Redacted*. Perhaps less obvious but central to the reason for this book's existence is the critics' agreement about what they thought they were talking about: war films, specifically about the conflict in Iraq. *In the Valley of Elah* concerns a father's efforts to find out what really happened to his son, an Iraq veteran murdered in New Mexico. *Grace is Gone* focuses on a grieving widower who tries to prevent his young daughters from learning about the death of their mother, a soldier. And *Redacted* shows what happens to a group of soldiers in Iraq involved in the rape of a young girl and murder of her family. The primary narrative actions of these films do not evoke the "traditional" concept of a war movie that deals with American soldiers battling in specific locations in such works as *Bataan* or *Guadalcanal Diary* (1943). Still, for these critics, they are "war movies" dealing with a current military problem.

Flash back to the beginning of the Spanish-American War in April 1898. Although the rationale for that war is presented publicly as the result of Spain's oppression of Cuba, then part of the Spanish empire, and as revenge for the explosion that sank the battleship *USS Maine* in Havana Harbor in February, it's generally conceded that the war was largely the result of America's desire for international expansion. Even before war was declared, a 1:50 minute film was made in March for audiences eager to see *Burial of the Maine Victims* (1898).[3] A stationary camera records the procession of mourners honoring the victims who died when the ship exploded. Such records of events pertaining to the war were called "actualities" at the time. Some of the actualities made in June 1898 showed audiences what life was like in camp for the new soldiers. *Blanket-Tossing of a New Recruit* presented the initiation of a new man in the Ohio Volunteers; his comrades bounce the man up and down on a blanket. *Soldiers Washing Dishes* showed the men at KP. Americans anxious for information about military aspects of the ongoing war in a form other than newspaper accounts could see short actualities that recorded events such as *Troops Making Military Road in Front of Santiago* (1898), which displays soldiers engaged in preparing a road for equipment and vehicles, and *Wounded Soldiers Embarking in Row Boats* (1898), which shows an evacuation of casualties after a battle.

Equally welcome to the public avidly following the events of the conflict in 1898 were films that gave viewers back home "reenactments" of battles, especially those that featured men pretending to be part of Theodore Roosevelt's "Rough Riders" fighting the Spanish troops. This second kind of film provided the only way Americans could see scenes of combat, since no motion picture cameras were present to film the fighting that was occurring. All the reenactments were staged for waiting cameras and filmed in the United States. Photographers had recorded various aspects of other wars earlier in the nineteenth century. For example, as Beaumont Newhall explains, Roger Fenton went to the Crimea in 1855 and photographed "landscapes and portraits— battlefields and fortifications, officers and men."[4] Matthew Brady and others captured photographic images of the aftermath of the carnage in the American Civil War. But it wasn't until the Spanish-American War that the motion picture camera permitted photographers to capture *moving* images representing the war, even if they were reenactments.

One of the best-known of these, *Raising Old Glory Over Morro Castle* (1899), was actually made several months after the war in Cuba had ended. We see the Spanish flag being lowered and then replaced by the United States flag at the fortress in Havana Harbor. One battle reenactment appears in *US Infantry Supported by Rough Riders at El Caney* (1899). This opens on a road in a forest clearing. Soon foot soldiers carrying the American flag appear, fire their guns, and move on, backed by two cavalry soldiers. The scene is repeated, this time with more cavalry support, followed by the boisterous arrival of Rough Riders.

Over a year after the fighting ended in Cuba, a third kind of film about the war appeared, one that told a story, James H. White's *Love and War* (1899). This is the first narrative American film about war and the first to use the word "war" in its title, a fact that lends authority to conceiving of the "war" film in terms of its subject matter as understood by its creators and viewers. This 3-minute film has six scenes, each presented in a continuous shot from a stationary camera: (1) a youth leaves his anxious family to go to war; his brother holds the departing soldier's rifle, which is almost as tall as he is; (2) his mother, sitting next to his brother, reads the newspaper for accounts of him; (3) his father and another man come in with news that the soldier has been killed or wounded, producing anguish for all; (4) the brave soldier engages in battle, is wounded, and is rescued by his courageous comrade who dies saving him; (5) he is taken to a field hospital where a nurse prays over him; (6) he returns home and reunites with his family and girlfriend. Another version of the film was accompanied by songs and evidently suggested that the soldier's love interest is a nurse at the hospital. The message of the film is clearly that the hero is acting correctly as he fights for the United States in its war against Spain, thus initiating the country's internationalist expansion. His reward, after surviving, is union with a woman.

**PLATE 1** *Love and War* (James H. White, 1899). The soldier's return home.

## Foundations of the Genre

Unlike other genres such as westerns or gangster films, films about war have their roots in this specific, identifiable historical event. The genre grows out of a commercial impulse to provide information about events in Cuba, and later the Philippines, to Americans eager to learn about the war. The fact that the birth of a genre occurs in conjunction with a specific historical event underscores the relevance of Thomas Schatz's observations on the origins of genre in general. He uses a "structuralist" approach, drawing on the ideas of the anthropologist Claude Lévi-Strauss and his suggestion that myths arise as a culture tries to deal with the contradictions it experiences. Particular genres function like myths, becoming popular at a given time because their narratives and conclusions provide ways to understand and negotiate current experience. In them we see "a society collectively speaking to itself, developing a network of stories and images designed to animate and resolve the conflicts of daily life." "Genre films, much like the folk tales of primitive cultures, serve to defuse threats to the social order and thereby to provide some logical coherence to that order."[5]

With this in mind, it is important not to consider those viewers of the early films of the Spanish-American War as merely curious, wanting to get their news in a much more sensationalized form than that of the daily papers. Seeing films of the conflict can be said to have provided them a way to negotiate this new aspect of the American experience. As Lee Grievson and Peter Krämer have noted: "Audiences wanted to see realistic images of the conflicts. . . . Films came to fulfill an important role as visual newspaper and . . . as a propaganda tool and shaper of a sense of national identity."[6] In addition, as Jonathan Auerbach observes, the films could stimulate and encourage support for the war: "Whether the projection on the screen was the actual battleship *Maine* or another ship posing as the *Maine*, the phantom image was immediate, vivid, and powerful, capable of invoking immense patriotic responses from the cheering vaudeville audiences."[7]

Robert Allen comments on the popularity of the war films, which were being shown as parts of vaudeville programs: "By April 1898 war movies were, according to the *Dramatic Mirror*, 'the biggest sensation in the program' in vaudeville theaters across the country. Projectors were even given martial names; Edison dubbed his Projecting Kinetoscope the 'Wargraph' for the duration."[8] Charles Musser indicates that the programming practice in the Eden Musee, a specific venue in New York City for art and films rather than a vaudeville house, included a range of topics. He quotes the New York *Mail and Express* for 16 July 1898:

> The Musee's motion picture operators arranged the films as a chronology of the war: "The *Maine* sailors on parade are shown and then the *Maine* sailing into Havana harbor. Following this is the burial of the *Maine* sailors, General Lee at Havana, other scenes in and about Havana, the various camps, soldiers at drill, battleships at anchor and in action, troops leaving Tampa for Santiago and other equally vivid scenes up to the storming of Santiago." Audience response to the films was so enthusiastic than many of the pictures had to be shown a second time.[9]

It is important to contrast this practice with what had occurred earlier in the war. According to Musser, when it began, various films about it might be shown interspersed with unrelated films such as the *Annabelle Butterfly Dance* or *Storm at Sea*. But gradually more focus on the war figured in the total exhibition so that "by 1898 . . . programs that offered a much higher degree of continuity were very common."[10] As a result, audiences could see an extended assemblage of films about the war lasting much longer than any individual films.

In fulfilling the audiences' specific needs for information and encouraging patriotism and national pride, those first war films did more than merely satisfy those early viewers of silent film who were fascinated by what Tom Gunning identifies as "the cinema of attractions," one "that directly solicits spectator attention, inciting visual curiosity, and supplying pleasure through an exciting spectacle—a unique event, whether fictional or documentary. That is of interest in itself."[11] Moreover, possibly we can attribute to the early audiences a desire to find out about the war in a new medium that provided an enhanced form of experiencing the world, different in kind from newspapers as it offered unique spectatorial possibilities. David Levy points out that films actually provided more detailed photographic information than newspapers: "When the 'Maine' exploded in Havana harbour in February 1898, what were called the first published photographs of the event came out in the *New York World*. But they were in fact hand drawings based on photographs."[12] Here, Kristen Whissel's observation is relevant: "Not only did the Spanish–American War coincide with the rise of the moving pictures, it is also inseparable from the American experience of modernity."[13] To add to these suggestions, the new medium and genre serve as a way to *process* the experience of war—at once more immediate than still photographs and news print and simultaneously a source of distancing from the events by making it a spectacle viewed collectively in a common exhibition space.

The key ideas I will use in the rest of this book have to do with this historical situation involving the three kinds of films about the war and the way they were shown together. Early audiences knew nothing of "the war film," only that they were privileged to watch films about various aspects of war. While watching soldiers frolicking or washing dishes could not have been as exciting as seeing a battle, nonetheless for them all parts were elements in a larger "film" that recorded and documented what this war was like. Consideration of this verifiable historical reality about the birth of the genre justifies a broad conception of what we can call "war films" today, particularly in expanding the conception beyond those limited to combat alone.

All war films since 1898–1899 have continued to employ these three basic forms, usually in combination. The actualities, or records of events pertaining to an ongoing war, have their counterpart in documentaries such as William Wyler's *The Memphis Belle* (1944). Reenactments, in which actors take the part of military figures, have always been elements in war films from their beginning in 1898. More often than not, they serve as individual sections within war films (or in films belonging to other genres), such as in the battle scenes in D. W. Griffith's *The Birth of a Nation* (1915) in which both the central characters and nameless other soldiers engage in battle. Narrative films, the focus of this book, constitute the dominant form within the larger genre. These can include documentary material, practically always contain reenactments when presenting combat, and are primarily constituted by a sustained narrative. Beginning as early as Griffiths' *Hearts of the World* (1918), some narrative films have shown actual footage of the areas of conflict, or, most commonly, included documentary footage of battles and military operations supplied by the government, as, for example, in *Guadalcanal Diary*.[14] Such sections are sometimes recognizable as obvious documentary records when they are edited into war films since the quality of the film stock can seem inferior to that of the stock used in the commercially produced film. Even so, the authenticity of the added footage has a special kind of authority since it is "really" a record of the war, a point developed later. But the dominant mode of the war film is its narrative.

Taken as a whole, the three types of films about the Spanish-American War display documentary and narrative elements that will appear in subsequent films about war: raising the flag; departure from home to fight; a range of ages in those involved, from young to old; life at camp; the home front; battle; courage; wounding; death; hospitalization;

grieving; love; triumphant return home and reunion with family and girlfriend.

I have begun with this look back at the origins of the war film in order to respond to Andrew Tudor's thoughtful analysis of the problem facing all critics talking about a specific genre and its elements. Tudor asks how we can discuss a given film's display of the "principal characteristics" or conventions of its genre unless we have already determined what constitutes those characteristics. But to do so traps us in a logical impasse:

> To take a genre such as a western, analyze it, and list its principal characteristics is to beg the question that we must first isolate the body of films that are westerns. But they can only be isolated on the basis of the "principal characteristics" which can only be discovered from the films themselves after they have been isolated. That is, we are caught in a circle that first requires the films be isolated, for which purposes a criterion is necessary, but the criterion is, in turn, meant to emerge from the empirically established common characteristics of the films.

His solution is to "lean on a common cultural consensus as to what constitutes a western and then go on to analyze it in detail."[15]

Musser's description of programming practices used to show films about the Spanish-American War relates to Tudor's idea of a "common cultural consensus" since viewers knew they were looking at films about war, even if there wasn't a category in critical or popular discourse that identified the "war film." If we consider what has been understood historically by viewers as "a film about a war," perhaps we can avoid the logical problem. Even more to the point, suggesting that a particular film about war would not exist unless viewers understood what war involves may help us sort out issues. That is, viewers watching a film that shows battles or scenes with loved ones worrying on the home front realize that this content is a function of the existence of war. This kind of logic permits us to include war-related narratives that deal with the basic elements seen in the first films about war. On the one hand, the recruits engaged in horseplay or KP duties in the 1898 films are men about to go to war. On the other, those activities presented in the actualities anticipate aspects of service comedies. Displaying the anguish of the hero's family after hearing of his wounding or death looks ahead to films about the home front. Following a veteran's return and reunion can constitute the basis of a film in itself.

As an introduction to a general overview of the war film, the elements mentioned above, whether from actualities, reenactments, or the narrative film, can be thought of as a preliminary group of defining characteristics for that generic entity called the war film. The genre's conventions are grounded in those earliest films about war. While some of the conventions to be explored do not occur in these films from 1898–1899, they follow nonetheless from the existence of war. Using elements in the first films about war as guideposts, at a minimum it's clear that those films display the following, singly or in combination: factual records, staged events, and a fictional narrative about people whose lives are affected by war. Perhaps the overview that follows can be understood as grounded in a sense that a work can be considered as "belonging" to the war film genre if it focuses, with varying emphasis, directly on war itself (battles—preparation for, actual, aftermath/damage), on the activities of the participants off the battlefield (recruitment, training, leisure, recovery from wounds); and the effects of war on human relationships (home front, impact on family and lovers).

## Conventions

At this point, it will be helpful to provide an overview of the major elements that figure in our experience of war films. First, fully mindful of Tudor's concerns regarding the logical problems of defining a genre on the basis of the conventions that one derives from the genre itself, nonetheless, we can start by identifying the following essential features of the genre's conventions in regard to *characters* and *basic narrative elements*.[16]

## Characters

Some of the most familiar *males* are:

1   The older, seasoned leader: usually a sergeant, sometimes tough and apparently unfeeling, but often revealed to have a good heart; traits transferable to other older characters such as chaplain/priest, cook.
2   Young recruits: green, inexperienced, but matured by the experiences.
3   Camp/platoon clown—often a prankster, sometimes a needed scavenger for stolen supplies.
4   Ladies man—sometimes revealed to be merely a boaster.
5   Newly married or recent father—sometimes a guarantee of death.

6   Regional, ethnic, and racial types—New York (especially Brooklyn), midwestern, southern, Hispanic and Philippine (starting in World War II), African American and Asian (beginning with Korean War).
7   Examples of different social classes (starting with World War I films)—upper, middle, working (often tied to ethnicity).

Typical *female* characters are:

1   Loyal wife, girlfriend, nurse.
2   Prostitute, B-girl, floozie.
3   Wise, sustaining mother.
4   In combat/training/POW films—heroic, mutually sustaining, sometimes discriminated against.

In the categories of *youths/children/pets* are:

1   Eager brothers/boys wanting to be part of the war effort.
2   Younger sisters captivated by men in uniforms.
3   The child endangered or killed as a result of war.
4   Animals: dogs, sometimes smuggled along with missions; and, on occasion a cat or mule.

## *Basic narrative elements*

Preparation for combat begins with *basic training* where we often see:

1   A tyrannical squad leader/sergeant terrorizing recruits.
2   Demanding exercises, drills, physical challenges, tests of endurance.
3   Bonding, pranks (not limited to basic training); tormenting of problem recruits; revenge on cruel squad leaders.
4   Weekend passes as relief from training, sometimes leading to drunken brawls, but often the occasion for meeting girls.
5   For some, the opportunity for sexual initiation, although that can occur later in films.
6   Successful graduation after making it through the ordeals.

Once at war, certain activities are linked to *specific branches of the armed services*, although not exclusively, and to particular narrative situations:

1 *Army/Infantry/Marines*—water landings, patrols, ambushes, raids, digging in; combat in jungles, deserts, mountains; tanks, grenades, flamethrowers; dealing with heat/cold.
2 *Navy/Aircraft carriers*—shelling land; take offs and landings of planes, sometimes damaged; abandoning ship; storms.
3 *Submarines*—surfacing, descending; threatened by lack of air or flooding, depth charges and torpedoes; firing torpedoes, claustrophobic space.
4 *Army Air Force*—take offs and landings, dogfights, bombing missions; variety of vehicles (bombers, fighters, helicopters).
5 *Prisoner of war*—interrogation, merciless torture, atrocities, attempts at escape, liberation.
6 *Holocaust*—atrocities, attempts at escape, liberation effected when Allies discover camps.

*Elements common to all the branches*: writing letters; receiving mail from home (sometimes in the form of phonograph records or tapes), including birth announcements and "Dear John" letters; sharing, observing photographs; listening to the radio—baseball games, music from home or that presented by Tokyo Rose or Axis Sally, war reports—especially breaking news about the attack on Pearl Harbor or President Franklin Delano Roosevelt's announcement of war; spontaneous and improvised play to relieve tension, boredom; singing; prayers/church services/receiving communion; burials (at sea with flag-draped coffins, on land with makeshift crosses and sometimes with helmets put on rifles)—both accompanied by short, moving tributes and comments on heroism; leaves, sometimes the occasion for weddings; reflections on the nature of the enemy, ranging from outright demonization to recognition of common humanity.

Films dealing with the *aftermath of war* focus on the following:

1 Recovery and rehabilitation for physical and psychological injuries in hospitals and at home.
2 Difficulties adjusting to life after war.
3 Reunion with wife, girl, family, and friends.

# CHAPTER 1

# HISTORICAL OVERVIEW

This chapter presents an overview of the genre's development in relevant social, historical, and cultural contexts. Without pretending to offer a comprehensive history of the genre, I focus on films about those wars that have prompted significant creative activity and critical interest. Rather than simply offering a list of films, I hope to suggest a framework that will give direction and organization to understanding the persistence of the genre over time.

## Major War Films, Trends, and Cycles: The American Civil War

Although the Spanish-American War remained a subject for the burgeoning film industry in the early twentieth century, the American Civil War eventually supplanted it, specifically in Thomas Ince's *Drummer of the Eighth* and *Grand-dad* (1913), and most notably in the first American film epic, D. W. Griffith's *Birth of a Nation* (1915). The importance of *Birth of a Nation* for the war film genre and American culture is immense.[1] It follows the interactions before, during, and after the war of two families, the Stonemans from the North and the Camerons from the South. Friends before the war, they find themselves on opposite sides during the conflict, a situation highlighted when former pals Tod Stoneman and Duke Cameron end up fighting opposite one another and dying in each other's arms. Love develops between the younger members of both families but is thwarted by the military and political effects of the war, especially by Reconstruction.

Some of the generic conventions identified in the Introduction appear in the film: youthful, immature soldiers; emphasis on the love of soldiers for the women back home; the effects of war on the home front; and displays of courage and heroism in battle. One of the most memorable battles in any war film climaxes when Ben Stoneman stuffs the Confederate flag into the barrel of a Union cannon. The conclusion of this battle is followed by a famous shot in which Griffith shows scores of dead soldiers from both sides, and provides an ironic comment in the intertitle: "War's Peace." But many of the conventions identified earlier are not present here. Actually, a great deal of the film does not occur in connection with fighting on the battlefield but on the home front, since Griffith's most important focus is on the effects of the war and Reconstruction on the South.

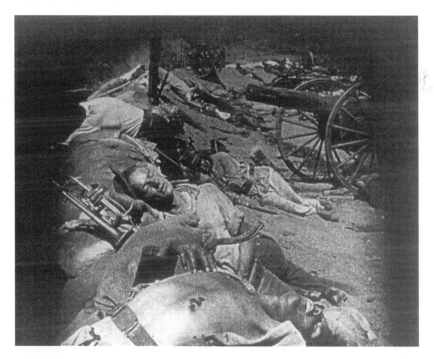

PLATE 2 *Birth of a Nation* (D. W. Griffith, 1915). "War's Peace" (David W. Griffith Corp./Courtesy Photofest).

Besides its technical achievements, which include stunning shots of warfare and well-edited cross-cutting to build suspense at the film's climax, its greatest importance has to do with the notoriety created by the film's depiction of African Americans and race relations. The film quite unambiguously supports the Confederacy's position in the Civil War. Led by the rhetorical power of W. E. B. DuBois, who edited *The Crisis*, the primary publication of the National Association for the Advancement of Colored People (NAACP), thousands protested the racism of the work, probably the most censored in American film history. African Americans, played by whites in blackface, appeared either as passive, faithful servants or as oversexed and threatening villains. The worst of these are Gus, whose overtures to Flora Cameron (Mae Marsh) result in her death as she jumps off a mountain trying to escape from him; and Silas Lynch, a mulatto given ruling power over the southern community during Reconstruction as a result of the misguided efforts of Elsie's father. Emboldened by his rise in white society, he seeks to marry Elsie, who is in love with Ben, and overpowers her and her father. To counter the acts and rising power of the blacks, Ben Cameron founds the Ku Klux Klan, which murders Gus and stops Lynch's "marriage" to Elsie.

The film's opening coincided with a resurgenge of Klan activity in the country. Its depiction of racial tensions after the Civil War clearly affected contemporary audiences throughout the nation. According to historian Leon Litwack, the film "appeared during the most repressive and violent period in the history of race relations in the South."[2] Contributing to the controversy was the infamous approving comment on the film by President Woodrow W. Wilson, a classmate of Thomas W. Dixon who wrote *The Clansman* on which the film is based: "it is like writing history with lightning."[3] In contrast to the favorable response of the American public to films about the Spanish-American War, which was widely supported, the divided reaction along racial and political lines to *Birth of a Nation* illustrates the phenomenon discussed throughout this book: the way films based on a past historical moment can speak to the times in which they are produced. In this case, the tensions attending the growth of African Americans' status in American society figured in the negative contemporary response. Evidently sobered by the hostile reaction to the film and accusations of racism, Griffith, who was a southerner, next made *Intolerance: Love's Struggle Throughout the Ages* (1916). Its thematic emphasis on advocating acceptance of others can be seen as a redemptive corrective to the earlier film.

The best-known silent film about the Civil War made after *Birth of a Nation* is *The General* (1927), Buster Keaton's hilarious comedy about a southern railroad engineer who, although not a soldier in the Confederacy, manages to foil the Union forces and win the woman he loves by rescuing her from the enemy. It certainly can be said to fit the definition of a war film mentioned in the Introduction since it focuses directly on elements of war itself. As noted there, humorous subject matter, such as the blanket tossing, was among the activities and elements shown in 1898–1899 films about the Spanish-American War. Just as the total range of films included everything from battles to horseplay, so too here, Keaton's film shows soldiers being shot and dying during battle and also classic comic scenes, including one in which Keaton's character manages to avoid detection while hiding under the dining room table of his enemies, and another in which he discovers he's forgotten to attach cars to his stolen engine.

The most famous film ever made about the Civil War after *Birth of a Nation*, *Gone with the Wind* (1939), was based on the best-selling novel of 1936 by Margaret Mitchell. It remains the highest grossing film domestically in American history: $1,450,680,400 (gross adjusted for inflation, per Box Office Mojo.com). Even though it had no combat scenes, it presented a telling depiction of the destruction of an apparently stable and secure world, especially in the indelible images of the burning of Atlanta and the depiction of the Confederate wounded and dead lying in the sun. The enormous popularity of the film was overwhelmingly driven by the success of the novel; the national interest in the competition among actresses over who would play Scarlett O'Hara; the masterful technical achievements, especially with color; and the question of censorship. A controversy ensued whether Rhett Butler's famous last line to Scarlett, "Frankly my dear I don't give a damn," could be used, given the restrictions of the Production Code Administration at that time.

Another reason for the popularity of the film on its first release in December 1939 may have to do with World War II, which had begun on September 1. One element operating in viewer response could have been the way the film spoke indirectly to a country aware of the conflagration that was now beginning to engulf Europe. Even though the United States had started to emerge from the effects of the Depression, the world itself had again become unstable, and a massive epic was opening that provided a chronicle of how vulnerable an apparently stable society is to dissolution.

## World War I

Early films about World War I, or the Great War as it was called then, present complex responses to a conflict whose immensity had never before been experienced. The first ones appeared during or soon after the war itself and thus have a historical immediacy unlike that of the Civil War films, which are in a retrospective position in relation to the war depicted. *Civilization* (1916), although not specifically about the war occurring in 1916, is clearly anti-war. It concerns a submarine captain whose remorse over the destruction and death his ship inflicts on innocent passengers on another ship is followed by a kind of religious and physical rebirth, as well as recognition by the chief combatant in the story that war is wrong. In contrast, D. W. Griffith's *Hearts of the World* (1918) is completely supportive of the war. He made it at the behest of the British government, which hoped the film would encourage the United States' entrance. Set in France, the film follows the fortunes of two families torn apart by the war, the hero's battle experiences, and the threats faced by the heroine and the hero's mother and brothers. By the time of the film's release, the US had already joined Great Britain and France against Germany. Griffith deploys various strategies to demonize the German enemy, including emphasizing the pathos of young children whose mother dies as a result of the war, and presenting a vicious Hun intent on raping Marie Stephenson (Lillian Gish). The film was popular with audiences.[4]

In *Shoulder Arms* (1918), another comedy, Charlie Chaplin plays a private in the army who falls asleep and dreams he single-handedly overcomes a number of German soldiers, who are portrayed simultaneously as both threatening and oafish. The moral question of accepting or rejecting war as such never becomes an issue. In contrast, Abel Gance's *J'Accuse* (1919) clearly attacks war, using various characters and images to underscore its evil. The heroine is raped by a German soldier (an act seen twice in silhouette); one of the two principal heroes is killed in battle; the other goes mad and dies. A recurring surreal visual motif has skeletons dancing in a circle. The last fifteen minutes of the film present a remarkable surrealistic sequence in which the deranged soldier envisions the dead rising from their graves and coming back to haunt those at home who have survived.

Anti-war sentiments pervade some major silent war films of the 1920s: *The Four Horsemen of the Apocalypse* (1921), *The Big Parade* (1925), and *What Price Glory?* (1926). With the coming of sound, other anti-war films appear. While none of the famous aviation films of this period celebrate war, they nonetheless offer often breathtaking sequences of aerial combat. William Wellman's *Wings* (1927) won the first Academy Award for Best Picture. Howard Hughes' *Hell's Angels* (1930) began as a silent film and then was turned into a sound film. Although in black and white, it has a well-known explosion of a zeppelin presented in a two-color process. Howard Hawks' *The Dawn Patrol* (1930) focuses on the problems facing aerial commanders and the psychologically damaging effects on them of sending men off to certain death. These strongly anti-war films reflect the disillusionment of the 1920s and 1930s about the Great War, its terrible destruction, and its failure to resolve the conflicts that caused it.

Other nations also produced anti-war films. From Germany, which was obliterated by its defeat and economic suffering throughout the 1920s, came G. W. Pabst's *Westfront 1918* (1930). This powerful film with impressive combat scenes introduces us to the lives and loves of four young men who all die as a result of the war. French filmmaker Jean Renoir's classic *La Grande Illusion* (1937) focuses on the French prisoners of war in a German camp. The commander, Captain von Ruffenstein (Erich von Stroheim), an aristocrat, gives special attention to one the prisoners, Captain de Boeldieu (Pierre Fresnay), who is also an aristocrat. Nonetheless he shoots the Frenchman when he realizes that the latter has helped prisoners to escape. The depth of his grief at his action points to the disillusion of the prewar social structure, as Roger Ebert notes: "it's a meditation on the collapse of the old order of European civilization."[5]

As the decade ended, clearly responding to the threats posed by the onset of World War II, Hollywood began to make films supportive of the United States' role in World War I. Warner Bros., having already produced *Confessions of a Nazi Spy* (1939), a cautionary warning about the current dangers posed by Hitler and the rise of Germany in the 1930s, made two pro-war films based on historical figures drawn from World War I: William Keighley's *The Fighting 69th* (1940) and Howard Hawks' *Sergeant York* (1941). The first concerns a famous all-Irish regiment from New York City, which included the poet Joyce Kilmer. The second depicts the life of Alvin York, who began life as a pacifist but gradually came to accept the need for killing in war. He single-handedly knocked out a German machine-gun nest, killing many and capturing over 100 men. Interestingly, as one measure of how films may be usable as an index of sentiment about war in general, the anti-war *All Quiet on the Western Front* won the Oscar for best picture in 1930. Eleven years later, with America recently engaged in war, Gary Cooper won the Best Actor Oscar for playing the heroic soldier Sergeant York in a pro-war film.

Practically no films about World War I were made during World War II, and only a small number after 1945. With a few exceptions, their ideological positions reflect a return to the anti-war sentiments of the 1920s, whether displaying the disillusionment of Stanley Kubrick's *Paths of Glory* (1957), made a few years after the Korean War, or serving as a vehicle to criticize the war in Vietnam, as happens in *Johnny Got His Gun* (1971) and the Australian film *Gallipoli* (1981). While William Wellman's *Lafayette Escadrille* (1958) and Tony Bill's *Flyboys* (2006) return to the focus on aviation and the famous division that fought in France, the films are not political. In contrast, the love story in French filmmaker Jean-Pierre Jeunet's *A Very Long Engagement* (2004), which concerns a woman's search for her soldier lover who is presumed to have died in No Man's Land during the war, is part of a larger study of war. Cynthia Fuchs suggests the film speaks to contemporary concerns since it "arrives in theaters at the same time that real life war images appear nightly on television . . . the thematic and political connections are impossible to resist."[6]

## World War II

Films about World War II began appearing in 1942 and had an immediate relationship to the ongoing conflict and to audiences akin to that seen earlier in films about the Spanish-American War. This period saw the greatest attendance figures in the history of film, with some 80 million Americans per week attending the movies. Several exemplary combat films to be discussed in Chapter 4 were about the war in the Pacific: *Wake Island* (1942), *Air Force, Bataan, So Proudly We Hail!*, and *Destination Tokyo* (all 1943). All belong to what I call a retaliation subgenre, in which films focus on how the United States is affected by and responds to the Japanese attack on Pearl Harbor. John Ford's *The Battle of Midway* (September 1942), an Oscar-winning documentary, chronicles the first decisive victory of America in the Pacific, a major turning point in the war. Ford, a member of the Naval Reserve since 1934, was now an officer and filmed some of the action himself, during which he was wounded. In terms of the three kinds of war film to come out of the Spanish-American War, Ford's film bears noting. It is simultaneously an actuality, since the battle sequences are in fact real, but also a semi-fictionalized film in that a quasi-narrative element is provided by the voiceovers of Jane Darwell and Henry Fonda who comment on the soldier as if they knew them. As such, the film offers an interesting example of the kind of genre hybridization mentioned earlier in the Introduction.

Europe, the other major theater of war, was represented by a number of films, such as *Desperate Journey* (1942), about the successful escape efforts of a multinational group of fliers shot down and imprisoned after a bombing raid in Germany; *Action in the North Atlantic* (1943), about a Merchant Marine ship evading German submarines as it brings supplies to Russia; *Passage to Marseille* (1944), an extremely complicated narrative (containing a flashback within a flashback) about French resistance to the Nazis before and during the war; and *The Story of G. I. Joe* (1945), about an Army company's progress from Africa to Italy as witnessed and chronicled by war correspondent Ernie Pyle. Africa was the setting of combat films such as *Immortal Sergeant* (1943) and *Sahara* (1943), and the classic Oscar-winning love story about those caught up in the Nazi occupation, *Casablanca* (1942).

Joining these films made during the war are home front films such as *Tender Comrade* (1943), *The Human Comedy* (1943), *The Sullivans* (1944), and *Since You Went Away* (1944), which all focus on the trials faced by the women and families of servicemen. In the first, working wives pool their money and resources to share a house. At the end of the film, the heroine, who has recently had a baby, receives a telegram announcing the death of her husband. The second concerns a widow and her children. One son, a high school boy, delivers telegrams in order to help support the family since his brother is at war. In one of the film's many heartbreaking moments, he discovers the dreaded telegram announcing his brother's death. The convention of breaking the bad news to family members is a staple of these films, and figures most agonizingly in *The Sullivans*, in which a Naval officer has to tell the Sullivan family that all five of their sons have been killed at sea. Everyone watching the film in 1944 knew that this true story had effectively prompted a change in policy about family members serving together. The circumstances served as one of the inspirations for *Saving Private Ryan* (1998). In *Since You Went Away*, a mother works to provide for her family while her husband is at war. One of her daughters falls in love with a soldier who is killed. Also popular during the war were service-comedies such as *See Here, Private Hargrove* (1944) and entertainment-musicals centered on the war such as *This Is the Army* (1943). The range of narrative interests represented in the films from 1942 to 1945 takes us back to the variety of viewing experiences available to audiences watching films about the Spanish-American War. These also provided audiences with different perspectives on the conflict, ranging from the comic to the serious.

Some films released in the 5–6 year period after the end of the war focus on problems of adjustment faced by returning veterans, such as William Wyler's *The Best Years of Our Lives* (1946), which won seven Oscars, including Best Picture and Director, and was the highest grossing film of the entire decade. Its financial success indicates how much its themes and concerns hit a collective nerve in the American public. Three veterans—Al (Fredric March), an upper-middle-class banker from the infantry, Fred (Dana Andrews), a former soda-jerk who was a bombardier, and Homer (Harold Russell), a sailor who lost both his hands—meet by chance on their way home. They and their loved ones interact in ways that underscore the emotional toll of the war and the economic problems faced by all as the nation tries to return to normal. Al, uneasy in his new civilian role, drinks too much. Fred falls in love with Al's daughter Peggy (Teresa Wright) after his marriage dissolves; she offers support for the veteran who is still troubled by his experiences at war. Homer has to overcome his initial reluctance to marry his high school sweetheart because of his condition.

**PLATE 3** *The Best Years of Our Lives* (William Wyler, 1946). Peggy (Teresa Wright) tries to comfort Fred (Dana Andrews) (Samuel Goldwyn Company/Courtesy Jerry Ohlinger's).

Two other films explored the difficulties faced by wounded and disabled soldiers. Fred Zinnemann's *The Men* (1950) features Marlon Brando in his first film role as Bud, a paraplegic who has to accept the fact he will never walk again. Teresa Wright plays his wife Elly, who helps him adjust. *Bright Victory* (1951) shows the rehabilitation of blinded veterans and introduces the theme of racial bigotry to the complex problems of adjustment. A blind white southern soldier who befriends an African American at a rehabilitation hospital crudely uses a racist epithet, not realizing he is black. Eventually, their friendship is renewed. The emphasis on individual physical and emotional problems of veterans during this period may well have been a way of commenting on the national postwar malaise in general.

Several films provided a retrospective return to the war itself in *Fighter Squadron* (1948), *Command Decision* (1949), and *Battleground* (1949). Although certainly not parallel to what happens in the 1920s, when most films are strongly anti-war, these films display a marked change of tone, compared to those produced during the war. Some, like the three mentioned here, involve complicated examinations of leadership and authority, issues that were not raised in combat films made during the war. Others, like the western *Fort Apache* (1948) and gangster film *White Heat* (1949), display a greater interest in the psychology of the hero, as occurs in *Sands of Iwo Jima* (1949) and *Twelve O'Clock High* (1949). Heroic leaders in those films, played by John Wayne and Gregory Peck, are shown to be psychologically troubled men in a manner that was not typical of films made during the war, with the exceptions of *I'll be Seeing You* (1944) and *A Walk in the Sun* (1945).

This shift in tone can also be linked to films appearing in another genre of this period, film noir. The dark, brooding worldview in works such as *Detour* (1945) and *Out of the Past* (1947) makes explicit what is implicit in post-1945 films about the war, a sense of unease, hopelessness, and disillusionment now that the great battle that had united everyone in a common purpose was over. Even more telling in this regard are two films noir about veterans involved in complex narratives about crime: *Crossfire* (1947), which explores the investigation of a Jewish soldier's murder by an anti-Semitic sergeant; and Zinnemann's *Act of Violence* (1949), which concerns a wounded veteran's revenge on his officer who betrayed him and others in a Nazi prison camp.[7]

One topic introduced at this time becomes increasingly more dominant in films: the Holocaust and survivors of prison camps. The few films about escapes from concentration camps that appeared before the end of World War II, such as *The Mortal Storm* (1940) and *The Seventh*

*Cross* (1944), were made before people had knowledge of the evil genocide that had occurred in them. Orson Welles' *The Stranger* (1946), the first narrative film to show concentration camps, concerns a German director of a camp who has escaped to the United States where he has been living undetected. Zinnemann's *The Search* (1948) shows the ultimately successful efforts of an American serviceman played by Montgomery Clift to reunite a little boy separated from his mother during their time in camps.

The first commercially released film to expose the utter horror of concentration camps was French director's Alain Resnais' *Night and Fog* (1955). In this short documentary he alternates between scenes in Technicolor showing the empty camps as they appear in the present with unbearably graphic shots of the evil and inhuman atrocities that occurred during their operation. Sam Fuller's *Verboten!* (1959) was the first American film to show actual footage of the atrocities that occurred in concentration camps. Other films that address the topic include *The Diary of Anne Frank* (1959), based on the true account of how she and her family hid in Amsterdam during the Nazi occupation; *Judgment at Nuremberg* (1962), about the trials of Nazi war criminals; *Sophie's Choice* (1982), for which Meryl Streep won an Oscar playing a mother who has to choose which one of her children will be sent to a camp to die; *Europa, Europa* (1990), the true story of Simon Perel, who escaped detection by posing as an Aryan; and Steven Spielberg's *Schindler's List* (1993), which shows how a businessman saved 1,200 lives (seven Oscars, including Best Picture and Director). Most recently the Holocaust has been the subject of Roberto Begnini's *Life is Beautiful* (1997), for which he won an Oscar as Best Actor, depicting a father trying to protect his son; Roman Polanski's *The Pianist* (2005) (Best Director Oscar), about someone who hides from the Nazis for several years; *The Boy in the Striped Pyjamas* (2008), about the son of a German commandant who befriends a boy in a concentration camp; *Adam Resurrected* (2008), about the psychologically damaging long-range effects of incarceration in a camp; and *The Reader* (2008), which examines the effects of a love relationship between a woman, formerly a guard at a camp, and the young boy whom she seduces after the war.

## The Korean War and the Cold War

Over 30,000 Americans were killed in the Korean War, which began in June 1950 when North Korea crossed the 49th Parallel to invade the South, and lasted until July 1953. The Korean War was the first military manifestation of the Cold War that began at the conclusion of World War II, when the Soviet Union and countries dominated by it squared off against the United States and other countries that would become part of the North Atlantic Treaty Organization (NATO) in 1949. The conflict generated war films that were different in several ways from earlier films about World War II.

Sam Fuller wrote, produced, and directed *The Steel Helmet* (1951), the first combat movie made about the Korean War. It makes important contributions to the genre on a number of levels. First, the main platoon consists of a historically accurate amalgam of race and ethnicities. Fuller specifically excluded the typical New Yorker/Brooklynite, having earlier inveighed against the stereotypical inclusion, asking: "Why is it that every movie has to have a rifleman talk about Brooklyn or Coney Island?"[8] Instead of the typical American melting pot, it includes an African American, who since President Harry S. Truman's 1948 order, really could be integrated into the armed services rather than placed in a combat role inaccurately, as had occurred in *Bataan*. It also has a Japanese

**PLATE 4** *The Steel Helmet* (Sam Fuller, 1951). Short Round (William Chun) and Sergeant Zack (Gene Evans) (Deputy Corporation/Courtesy Photofest).

American, who had earlier fought in World War II for the United States. Moreover, Fuller foregrounds these issues when a North Korean prisoner of war verbally attacks both the African American and the Japanese American for their stupidity in serving in their oppressor's army.

Second, it introduces the character of an innocent child as a more active participant in the war. While children had appeared in American war films as early as D. W. Griffith's *Hearts of the World*, and in Italian neorealist war films such as *Rome, Open City* (1945) and *Paisan* (1946), this is the first American film in which a little child who plays a significant role is killed by enemy gunfire. Short Round (William Chun), the South Korean child who saves the life of the hero Sgt. Zack (Gene Evans) and tags long with the platoon, is shot by North Koreans attacking the temple where the platoon is housed.

Third, Fuller consistently employs a bitter, hard-edged tone. Sgt. Zack quotes approvingly his commander from World War II: "There are two kinds of men on this beach, those that are dead and those that are going to die." A soldier ordered by Zack's current officer to check a dead body for dog tags (against the latter's advice) is blown to bits, prompting Zack to observe realistically on the nature of death in war: "A dead man's nothing but a corpse." When their North Korean prisoner makes a disparaging comment about the recently killed Short Round, Zack shoots the wounded man in cold blood, then threatens him (in the film's most famous line): "If you die, I'll kill you."

Of interest in terms of the genre is the number of prisoner of war films that appear in the postwar period. While there had been films about this subject during World War II, for example *The Purple Heart* (1944) and at least one about rescuing POWs, *Back to Bataan* (1945), such works stressed the heroism and invincibility of prisoners. But in *Act of Violence*, the postwar film mentioned above, and those that come out of the Korean War, the issue is much more complicated. In varying degrees *Prisoner of War* (1954) and *The Rack* (1956) foreground the men's vulnerability and the terrible pressures on them to survive the torturous behavior of their North Korean–Soviet captors. Sometimes soldiers who break down are perceived as traitorous, even when they are working undercover for the United States, as occurs in *Prisoner of War* in which Webb Sloane (Ronald Reagan) is vilified for appearing to conspire with the enemy.

The issue of brainwashing occurs in its most chilling form in John Frankenheimer's *The Manchurian Candidate* (1962). While the Korean War was long over by the time of this film, it appeared in the midst of the now prolonged and increasingly tense Cold War. Although the United

State entered the war as part of a United Nations force to defend South Korea, the North was receiving support from both Russia and China, the ultimate antagonists in the conflict. In the film, Chinese communists, acting on orders from an evil married communist couple in America, who appear to be super patriots, brainwash a troop of POWs. The wife, Mrs. Iselin (Angela Lansbury), has her son Raymond (Laurence Harvey) programmed by the Chinese to follow commands she gives him to assassinate various people, most importantly the winner of their party's convention nomination for president. Her husband will then be able to snag the nomination and, presumably, win the election, thus allowing communist domination of the country. Ben Marco (Frank Sinatra), a fellow prisoner, discovers the plot and is able to thwart the plan, which comes unraveled as Raymond kills his mother and her husband before committing suicide. Ironically, the film's October 24 release date put it in the midst of the Cuban Missile Crisis, which occurred between October 12 and 28. For several days, the entire world wondered if there would be nuclear war because of the United States' demand that Russia eliminate its missiles in Cuba.

The lingering bitterness about a war that stopped rather than ended, coupled with increasing international tensions between western and communist countries, created a climate in which films about World War II can be seen to reflect the tenor of the times. For example, two famous POW retrospective World War II films of the 1950s are Billy Wilder's *Stalag 17* (1953) and David Lean's *The Bridge on the River Kwai* (1957). The first follows the story of Sefton (William Holden, Best Actor Oscar), a cynical operator within the camp suspected of being a collaborator with the German captors, partly because he makes such advantageous deals for presumably unavailable contraband and comforts. He is vindicated when the actual agent is discovered, but not before Sefton is beaten. One contribution of this film to the genre is the introduction of the savvy operator like Sefton who manages to acquire stuff. George Segal plays a similar type of character in another retrospective World War II POW film, *King Rat* (1965).

Although set in World War II, in a Japanese prison camp, Lean's Oscar-winning masterpiece *The Bridge on the River Kwai* very much speaks to the mood of the country caught up in the Cold War. The film shows how the Japanese force British prisoners led by their commander Colonel Nicholson (Alec Guinness, Best Actor Oscar) to build a bridge. William Holden plays an American commander who works with British soldiers to sabotage the bridge. The film's conclusion in which most of the principal characters are killed, including the Japanese leader of the camp, prompts one survivor to utter the famous last words: "Madness, madness." It is interesting in this regard to think about possibly the most famous prisoner of war film after *Kwai*, John Sturges' *The Great Escape* (1963). Even though celebrating the heroism of a unified group of soldiers in a German POW camp, it ends with the deaths of most of those trying to escape, a melancholy defeat, another symptom of the ongoing and dispiriting Cold War.

Although they are not about POWs, some other films about World War II display a similar dark mood. In *Attack!* (1956), an inept commander, having lost the confidence of his men because of repeated blunders, some leading to American deaths, is murdered by his second in command, who then confesses his crime to his superiors. Also of interest is the first film version of *The Thin Red Line* (1964). This retrospective film about World War II that appears at the height of the Cold War is a profoundly unsettling work that destabilizes many of the values associated with the World War II combat film: the unity of the group, the common shared goals, and the ability of American soldiers to survive the onslaughts.

Several notable foreign films made during the Cold War should be acknowledged since they also provide equally troubled retrospective views of World War II. Réne Clément's *Forbidden Games* (1952), which won the Oscar for Best Foreign Film in 1953, shows how two little French children adjusting to the bleak world of war and death by making a cemetery for animals. The hero of Andrzej Wajda's *Ashes and Diamonds* (1958) is a Polish resistance fighter who dies in the process of trying to eliminate a communist leader, whose ominous presence signals the post-war domination of the country. Bernhard Wicki's *The Bridge* (1959) exposes the misery and horror faced by a group of young German boys who are responsible for holding a bridge at the end of the war. Its searing depiction of their hopeless situation invites comparison with *All Quiet on the Western Front*, discussed in Chapter 3.

An important Civil War film also appeared during the Korean War. Just as World War II films made during the height of the Korean conflict show a different tone, so too does John Huston's *The Red Badge of Courage* (1951), which concerns a young soldier who runs away from battle but eventually rejoins his troop. A member of the Signal Corp., Huston had made important documentaries during World War II. According to Guerric DeBona, his film version of *The Red Badge of Courage* was cut mercilessly by MGM not because it was really "about" the Korean War, but because Huston had questioned the power of the hero's masculinity, emphasizing his cowardice too much at a time when the United

States was at war in Korea.[9] Interestingly, the next film Huston made was about World War I, this time outside the studio system, *The African Queen* (1951). Humphrey Bogart won an Oscar playing Charlie Allnut, a rugged skipper of a boat who, with Rose (Katharine Hepburn), succeeds in destroying a German war ship. This film focuses on heroic behavior in a much earlier war and shows both the principal actors winning decisively over the enemy, perhaps a gesture of turning away from the frustrating lack of closure then current with the Korean War. In its way, the film's emphasis on individuals outside any organized military force triumphing over evil may be saying something about the national sense of malaise with the lack of progress of the war that involved multinational forces.

A number of films made during the Cold War that continue to reassert the values of World War II do so in a context that very much privileges historical truth, an issue to be explored in more detail in Chapter 2: *Three Came Home* (1950), *Battle Cry* (1955), *To Hell and Back* (1955), and *Strategic Air Command* (1955). The first draws on the factual account published in 1947 by Agnes Newton Keith (Claudette Colbert) of her imprisonment by the Japanese from 1941 to 1945 in a camp on Borneo. The film presents her harrowing experiences: separated from her husband, a prisoner in another part of the camp, she and her little boy withstand horrible deprivations.[10] The second, based on the immensely popular bestselling novel (1953) by Leon Uris, foregrounds the toughness and stamina of Marines, interlaced with various romantic subplots. Uris had fought with Marines in World War II, and adapted his own novel for the screen. The authenticity associated with his creation and its celebration of the Marines certainly factored into the appeal of the film. The third unqualifiedly celebrates the heroism of its star and subject, Audie Murphy, on whose autobiography the film was based. Murphy was the most highly decorated soldier in all of World War II. Perhaps these films, which did very well at the box office, indicate that spectators, weary from the Korean War's casualties and inconclusiveness, were anxious to welcome back films that showed the country successfully waging war. Murphy's film in particular is important in that the iconic star was "really" the subject; that is, the film performs an interesting act that takes us back to the three kinds of films about the Spanish-American War. It has elements of the actuality (Murphy himself, the real hero), the reenactments of the battles some eleven years after he fought, and narrative.

While not a war film that depicts combat, the last, *Strategic Air Command*, certainly connects to *To Hell and Back*. This very successful film concerns a former Air Force pilot, now a baseball player with the St. Louis Cardinals, who is brought back into the Air Force to fly the newest bombers. According to the American Film Institute notes, "Modern sources state that James Stewart, who, like his character 'Dutch,' was a World War II bomber pilot and was still active in the Air Force Reserve in the 1950s, achieving the rank of brigadier general in 1959, persuaded Paramount to make a picture about the SAC, arguing that it would be patriotic and financially sound."[11] That is, another "real" serviceman, James Stewart, who flew during World War II and who was the narrator of *Winning Your Wings*, a recruiting film directed by John Huston for Warner Bros. and the First Motion Picture Unit of the Air Force, plays a flier of the newest aviation weapon, the B–36 bomber, which is a key part of SAC that will be defending America in the *next* war.

Probably the most extreme example of authenticity as a factor in generating a positive retroactive World War II film occurs with Darryl F. Zanuck's *The Longest Day* (1962). While Zanuck was responsible for producing the film and directing some sequences, the principals in this regard were Andrew Marton, Ken Annikin, and Bernhard Wicki, who directed the American, English, and German sections of the film, respectively; all were from the countries represented in their responsibilities. A three-hour chronicle of the D-Day landing, the black and white film strives for an authenticity rooted in honoring the actual historical records, even when the facts are horrible in regard to deaths, as occurred with the fate of paratroopers who were killed when they landed in St. Eglise d'Mer by mistake. The film is one of the first epics to use dozens of name actors, familiar to audiences from many other war films, like Henry Fonda, Robert Ryan, Robert Mitchum, and John Wayne. This retrospective film about the greatest allied invasion in history thus benefited from its own honoring of generic history since so many of the actors were familiar as war heroes in earlier films. Wayne in particular, although he never was in the armed services, had by this time achieved iconic status as an actor in war films, particularly in *Flying Tigers* (1942), *The Fighting Seabees* (1944), *Flying Leathernecks* (1951), and above all, *The Sands of Iwo Jima* (1949), for which he was nominated for an Oscar. Use of the immense list of previous stars of World War II films has the curious effect of reviving their roles as heroes of the genre and bringing with them the values associated with the earlier films.

The impact of the Cold War on other genres appears in science fiction and horror films. As Susan Sontag has demonstrated in her famous essay "The Imagination of Disaster," the prevalence of movies about invasion from outer space speaks to the nation's anxieties about the Cold War. In the bonding together of warring nations to fight a common external enemy, she sees a longing for unity with one's enemy. Correspondingly, the rash of monster movies that begins around the time of the Korean War and continues to flourish reveals anxieties about the fear of nuclear warfare, particularly after both Russia and China acquire nuclear weapons.[12]

One retrospective movie about the Korean War speaks to the time of its production. Although set during the Korean War, Robert Altman's *M★A★S★H* (1970) was perceived as a stinging condemnation of the Vietnam War, which by 1970 had escalated into an increasingly hopeless conflict. This unsettling mixture of hilarious comedy (some of it highly sexist) and gruesome images (in the operations), focuses on Hawkeye (Donald Sutherland), who runs the mobile army surgical hospital that gives the film its title.[13]

## Vietnam

The war in Vietnam, which the United States lost in 1974 after over 58,000 Americans were killed, extended the Cold War into a different realm in Asia. The civil war between North and South Vietnam, eerily replicating the enmity between North and South Korea, played out as a conflict between Chinese and Russian communism and American democracy. Unlike any of the wars discussed in this overview, practically no films were made about it while it was occurring. The primary exception was *The Green Berets* (1968), directed by and starring John Wayne. Possibly the most reviled war film in American history, it was made in support of the US policy of sending "military advisers" to defend South Vietnam against the Viet Cong and communism. Although much less known, *The Losers* (1970, known as *Nam's Angels*), an exploitation film about American bikers in Cambodia, also supports the war.

Only after the war ended did Vietnam become a major subject of films, starting with Peter Davis' Academy Award winning documentary *Hearts and Minds* (1974), a searing attack on US policy. It presents agonizing film records of atrocities, including the famous shots of the little girl who has been burned by napalm and the shooting of the Viet Cong soldier in the head. Davis combines these with painful monologues by veterans and interviews with governmental figures, including a horrifying commentary from General William Westmoreland defending US policy.

Beginning in 1978, a number of narrative works about American involvement appeared, many of them characterized by a complex mix of sadness and devastating depictions of the horrors of war. *Go Tell the Spartans* (1978) examines the futility of the war by concentrating on the bitter disillusionment of its main star, Burt Lancaster. *The Boys in Company C* (1978) shows the absurdity of the war by castigating most of the military officers. Michael Cimino's *The Deer Hunter* (1978) achieved fame because of its extreme violence, particularly in a lethal game of Russian roulette that American POWs are forced to play by their Viet Cong captors, a form of torture that was not in fact documented. As if to confirm the continuing tensions and resentment in the United States about involvement with the war, the film's controversial ending produced sharply divided interpretations. Some saw its conclusion, in which a group of mourners for a suicidal veteran sing "God Bless America," as supportive of United States policy. Others, in contrast, interpreted the scene as a poignant reflection on the sadness of war and its effects.[14] The film won five Oscars, including Best Picture and Director, and set a new standard for "realism," discussed in Chapter 2.

Although the issue of whether *The Deer Hunter* is ultimately pro or anti-war remains unresolved in the criticism, no such debate exists about Hal Ashby's *Coming Home* (1978), a powerful anti-war film that combined two narrative situations familiar from World War II films: the home front and problems faced by returning, wounded veterans. In depicting the affair that develops between a housewife (Jane Fonda) and a paraplegic vet (Jon Voight), the film went far beyond anything ever seen in World War II films, not just in the explicitness of the sexual relationship but in its condemnation of the war. It won three Oscars, for its two stars and for the writing. Thus, two of the four major war films of 1978 accounted for eight Oscars, six in major categories. This suggests something about the anguished mood of the country in regard to the Vietnam War close to the time of US defeat. These films do not bear the same retrospective relationship to the war as those made shortly after World War II. They are, in effect, the repressed of the Vietnam War, the films that didn't get made during the conflict.

Francis Ford Coppola's *Apocalypse Now* (1979) epitomizes the various complex impulses detectable in the first wave of Vietnam films. Winner of two Oscars and many other awards, it adapts Joseph Conrad's novel *Heart of Darkness*, which follows its narrator's discovery of the extent of human evil, in order to condemn US involvement and military policy. Marlon Brando plays Colonel Kurtz, a totally insane embodiment and extension of US military policy. A line from Conrad's novel used

**PLATE 5** *Apocalypse Now* (Francis Ford Coppola, 1979). Part of the helicopter fleet (Zoetrope Studios/Courtesy Photofest).

in the film, spoken by Kurtz, "the horror, the horror," epitomizes US folly in the war. Matching it in intensity is the sentiment expressed by Lt. Col. Kilgore (Robert Duvall), who states: "I love the smell of napalm in the morning." Some of the film's famous sequences underscore the madness of Kurtz and the war. In one, Coppola shows a large contingent of helicopters about to drop Agent Orange and accompanies their flight with "The Ride of the Valkyrie" from Richard Wagner's opera *Die Valküre*. Because of Hitler's fondness for Wagner operas, this music has a particularly ironic function. An evening's entertainment for soldiers consists of a show put on by Playboy bunnies flown in for their amusement, but the show is cut short when the men become unruly and swarm around the bunnies.

Films in the 1980s about Vietnam display quite contradictory trends. On the one hand, some combat films such as *Hamburger Hill* (1987) and *84C Mopic* (1989) do not specifically condemn its politics. The first offers an agonizing account based on an actual event of an attempt to take a hill during 1969. In a manner that recalls Albert Camus' use of the myth of Sisyphus as an exemplum of the absurdity of human life, the soldiers try to capture the hill, are beaten back with losses, try again, with more losses, and do so for ten days, until they succeed. The second provides an interesting experiment in which the "narrator" is a camera man with the Army's motion picture unit making first-hand accounts of life with his platoon, including battles. His death at the end of the film is signaled by the obvious loss of control over his camera. While obviously not sympathetic to the war, Barry Levinson's *Good*

*Morning, Vietnam* (1987) offers a different kind of perspective on it in this film based on Adrian Cronauer's experiences as a disk jockey in Saigon. The film mixes comedy, Robin Williams' typical non-stop verbal barrages, with a moving story of his attempts to befriend what he believes to be friendly Vietnamese citizens. He learns, though, that he has been involved with a Viet Cong operative, whom he thought was his friend. The film had the fourth highest domestic gross in 1987: $123,922,370.

A second kind of film revisits the war, literally from a later time period. Characterized by Thomas Doherty as "extraction films," they depict attempts to rescue prisoners of war long after the ending of the conflict, as in *Missing in Action* (1984) and *Rambo: First Blood Part II* (1985).[15] In the first, Chuck Norris plays a Vietnam veteran, himself a former POW, who returns to Cambodia to rescue prisoners still held by the North Vietnamese, even though they deny having them. The second, the most famous of such films, features Sylvester Stallone as John Rambo, reprising his role from *First Blood* (1982) in which he played a returning veteran assaulted by hostile Americans who scorn his service to the country during the war. In the sequel, he is released from prison, where he was sent because of his actions in the earlier film, and sent to Vietnam, presumably to take photographs that will prove no prisoners are being held. But he discovers the opposite and rescues them. The violence in the film is striking, most of it directed against the seemingly invincible hard body of Stallone, whose masculinity is the subject of a study by Susan Jeffords. She links him persuasively to President Ronald Reagan. Rambo's line to his superior upon being released from prison—"Do we get to win this time?"—is very much in line with the militarism of President Reagan, who, after watching *Rambo: First Blood* at a time when the US had suffered an embarrassing defeat by Libyan terrorists, said: "Boy, I saw *Rambo* last night. Now I know what to do the next time this happens."[16] Rambo's characters and the film itself can be seen as ideological instruments that use his body, and by extension that of President Reagan who survived an assassination attempt, to reassert America's power in the world. The film was successful, earning $150 million domestically, second only to Robert Zemeckis' *Back to the Future* ($210 million). In both of the extraction films the war gets fought again with a different resolution. In terms of our interest in contextualization, it's worth noting that *Rambo* and *Back to the Future* deal with somehow rewriting the past: in one case by sort of winning at least part of the Vietnam War, in the other by guaranteeing that errors in the past can be negated.

Yet another category of Vietnam films from the 1980s offers probing analyses of the impact of war on men, complete with harrowing violence and disturbing depictions of evil. The two most searing examinations occur in Oliver Stone's *Platoon* (1986) and Stanley Kubrick's *Full Metal Jacket* (1987), discussed in Chapter 5. One of the most disturbing is Brian DePalma's *Casualties of War* (1989). Based on a report by Daniel Lang of an actual incident in 1968, it shows how a small platoon led by Sean Penn kidnaps, rapes, and kills a young woman, and the efforts of one member of the group who does not participate (Michael J. Fox) to bring the others to justice.

As was the case with the Korean War, retrospective films about World War II appear during the Vietnam War. Again, as we saw earlier, the current conflict provides a context for considering them. Three key films in 1970 appeared at the height of the war and violent protests against it, most horribly at Kent State University, where the National Guard killed four students during a rally against President Richard Nixon's escalation of the war by bombing Cambodia: *Catch-22* (June), *Patton* (September), and *Tora! Tora! Tora!* (September).

*Catch-22*, set in the Pacific, attacks the insanity of war by focusing on the attempts of Yossarian (Alan Arkin) to be relieved from his bombing duties in order to escape the mental stress they create. But the "catch" in the title refers to the fact that only a sane person would wish to be relieved; hence, he can't claim mental pressure. He would have to be insane to want to continue. The film's bitter treatment of various conventions of the World War II film such as heroism and the value of war undercuts all their positive aspects. Its tone of despair speaks much more of Vietnam than of World War II. For example, the unconscionable Lt. Milo Minderbinder (Jon Voight) controls a prostitution and blackmarket operation. By mistake, an American soldier standing on a raft is literally (and bloodily) cut in half by a plane that passes too low over him.

*Patton* won seven Oscars, including Best Picture, Best Director (Franklin J. Schaffner), Best Writing (Francis Ford Coppola), and Best Actor (the latter refused by George C. Scott). While not an anti-war film in any traditional sense, it offers a remarkable examination of a military mind and the way that personal ambitions can affect or subvert military responsibilities. Beginning with a stunning monologue in praise of war delivered by Patton in front of an enormous flag, the film follows his ambitious and contentious relations with his cohorts, especially the personal contest with Viscount Montgomery, who leads the British forces in Europe, as to who will get more credit quickly for achieving certain strategic goals. For an audience enduring an unpopular war in the present, this picture of a powerful and deeply flawed military commander fighting for a noble cause certainly captures the complexity of the period. Interestingly, the film was a favorite of Richard Nixon's. According to Robert C. Toplin, Nixon made his decision to invade Cambodia after watching the film twice.[17]

Like *The Longest Day, Tora! Tora! Tora!* was also produced by Darryl F. Zanuck, who repeated his practice of using directors from the different countries depicted in the conflict, in this case from America (Richard Fleischer) and Japan (Kinji Fukasaku). Like its predecessor, it aims for minute accuracy in its detailed examination of the events preceding the attack on Pearl Harbor. In sharp contrast to films about the attack and its aftermath made during World War II, the film doesn't demonize the Japanese enemy, but, rather, offers a reasonably balanced depiction of both sides and the way the attack unfolds. The film failed at the box office, earning only $14.5 million, against a production budget of $25 million. Part of the problem was its perceived dullness. Vincent Canby of the *New York Times* compared it to the Spanish-American War actualities discussed earlier: "The cinema of actual event is a very old film genre that has its roots in ancient newsreels that, in 1898, passed off re-creations of the Battle of San Juan Hill as recordings of the real thing. As it has become more respectable over the years, it has also become more pious and dull."[18] Another problem may have been the absence of major stars from earlier war films. Even more, its failure to win audiences probably had to do with its actual evenhandedness. In its attempt to offer a reasonably objective depiction of how World War II begins, the film's explanation of both sides' experiences might seem to suggest the possibility of a rational reading of the conflict. But such a project actually runs counter to the mood of a country torn apart by those who disagreed totally on the value and reason for the Vietnam War: some justifying it in terms of the domino theory, which held that defending Vietnam would prevent the spread of communism even more, as opposed to those who saw the war as a hopeless, unwinnable conflict achieving nothing but destruction. Even more, a spectator in 1970 might be struck by the powerful ironies in the film, which demonstrates again and again how human blunders, frailty, and incompetence make catastrophic conflicts inevitable. In short, a movie offering a balanced perspective on a major conflict had little or no appeal.

Another retrospective film about World War II released before the wave of anti-Vietnam War films in 1978 spoke very much to the post-Vietnam anger and disillusionment. Richard Attenborough's *A Bridge Too Far* (1977) was a decided success, the third-highest grossing film of the year, earning $50 million. It concerns a disastrous failure by the

Allies to capture and secure three bridges in Holland in Operation Market Garden. In contrast to *Tora*, this film had a huge cast of internationally famous actors, including Dirk Bogarde, James Caan, Michael Caine, Sean Connery, Gene Hackman, Laurence Olivier, Ryan O'Neal, Robert Redford, and Maximilian Schell. By no means is its treatment of the failure even handed, for it pointedly exposes the way sheer ego and arrogance in the coordinator Lt. Browning (Bogarde) doom the endeavor. Very much in keeping with the post-Vietnam malaise, it examines a major loss from the later stages of a war we ultimately won.

While the next major retrospective World War II film, which celebrates the United States' role, did only modest box office business, Sam Fuller's *The Big Red One* (1980; restored by Richard Schickle, 1994) represents a decided turning away from post-Vietnam disillusionment in war films and a return to the heroic values of films made during the conflict. This highly autobiographical film follows an unnamed sergeant (Lee Marvin) and four men in his unit from Africa in 1942, Sicily, and Omaha Beach on D-Day, through France, Belgium, and ultimately to Czechoslovakia where they discover a concentration camp. Many of the familiar conventions of the war film appear (gruff, loving sergeant; untried soldiers) along with one that Fuller had introduced in *The Steel Helmet*, the way war grinds down innocent children, in this case a little boy discovered in the camp. Although he cannot speak when liberated by the heroes, prompted by the sergeant, he does take some food, and, for a moment, enjoys the companionship of his rescuer. But in one of the most heartbreaking scenes in all war films, having bonded with the sergeant at a kind of picnic, he dies as he's being carried on the sergeant's back, another child who dies as a result of war in Fuller's films.[19]

It's fascinating to view this film that turns aside entirely from Vietnam when one knows that Fuller died before being able to fulfill his desire to make a film about that war. The very first filmmaker to treat the subject of the hostilities in that area in *China Gate* (1957), he would certainly have offered a significant variation to the war film genre's conventions:

> I'd finished my own Vietnam protest, a terrific yarn called *The Rifle*. . . .
> The story was centered on an old M1 rifle, a World War II relic, which
> passed through the lives of my main characters, a legendary colonel with
> a death wish, a 14-year-old Viet Cong murderer, an insane French nun,
> and a crazed soldier who steals blood from the wounded. The movie
> would show the war from the perspective of the "little people" who are
> most affected by violence. My dream was to shoot the picture from the
> viewpoint of the rifle, in continuous ten-minute takes.

He described John Wayne's *Green Berets* (1968) as a "blundering movie. . . . Americans lost the real-life war because we couldn't comprehend Vietnam, its people, or its goals. We pursued our own aims, regardless of realities. So did John Wayne."[20]

## Operation Desert Storm, Iraq, and the War on Terror

Conflict with Iraq began formally in 1990 as President George H. W. Bush initiated the Gulf War with Operation Desert Shield and Operation Desert Storm, an attack motivated by Saddam Hussein's incursion into Kuwait. The multinational assault resulted in Iraq's defeat and a cessation of hostilities early in 1991. Since the Gulf War ended so quickly, there was hardly time for a corpus of films to be greenlighted. Some television documentaries came out quickly after the invasion, but the first major films about the Gulf War appeared later: *Courage Under Fire* (1996), *Three Kings* (1999), and *Jarhead* (2005), discussed in Chapter 7. A period of political tensions ensued, unsettled most violently by Al-Qaeda's 9/11 attack on the World Trade Center, leading to the US invasion of Afghanistan and then Iraq in March 2003, justified by the never-substantiated claim that Hussein had weapons of mass destruction. It was followed swiftly by Hussein's fall from power in April and execution in December 2006.

The post-9/11 war in Iraq and Afghanistan has resulted in documentaries such as Michael Moore's *Fahrenheit 9/11* (2004), which exposes the Bush administration's complex connection to Saudi Arabia and the Bin Laden family, and Charles Ferguson's *No End in Sight* (2007), another probing examination of the causes of the war; films about combat such as *American Soldiers* (2005), returning veterans, *Home of the Brave* (2006) and *Stop-Loss* (Kimberly Peirce, 2008); those from 2007 mentioned in the Introduction: *In the Valley of Elah*, *Grace is Gone*, and *Redacted*; and three films about 9/11, *The Guys* (2003), *United 93* (2006), and *World Trade Center* (2006). More will be said about films dealing with the Iraq War in Chapter 7. As will be seen, the changed nature of warfare in the Gulf and Iraq Wars and the War on Terror has affected the way some of the common conventions of the genre are used, specifically an increased emphasis on battles within civilian space, and the nature of combat, which so often now involves defending against suicide bombers and small groups of militants in cars and trucks.

A new kind of war film cycle appears in the remake of *The Manchurian Candidate* (2004), *Syriana* (2005), and *The Kingdom* (2007). We need to see films in this group in relation to the concept introduced by President Dwight D. Eisenhower in 1961 when he warned of "the military-industrial complex":

> In the councils of government, we must guard against the acquisition of unwarranted influence, whether sought or unsought, by the military-industrial complex. The potential for the disastrous rise of misplaced power exists and will persist. We must never let the weight of this combination endanger our liberties or democratic processes. We should take nothing for granted. Only an alert and knowledgeable citizenry can compel the proper meshing of the huge industrial and military machinery of defense with our peaceful methods and goals, so that security and liberty may prosper together.[21]

The films I put in a cycle of the military-industrial-complex conflict provide frightening demonstrations of how the huge corporations tied into or heavily dependent on the oil industry, which benefits from the United States' spending on war, are succeeding in a "disastrous rise" connected with their acquisition of international power.

The remake of *The Manchurian Candidate* keeps the basic plot device of the earlier film, programming someone to be an assassin, but updates it by making Raymond Shaw (Liev Schreiber) a veteran of the Gulf War. He becomes the nominee for vice-president, given the machinations of his mother Eleanor (Meryl Streep), who has arranged for scientists to implant a chip in him so that he becomes a conscienceless assassin who follows directions to kill unquestioningly. Ben Marco (Denzel Washington) also has a chip implanted in him to make him an assassin. Instead of being a communist, Eleanor is a United States senator working in conjunction with the Manchurian Corporation in order to take over the country. In fact, she is the ultimate force behind the Manchurian Corporation, which deals in oil and power. One scene at the Shaw home underscores the linkages as it shows a reception populated by corporate leaders, some of whom seem to be in on the ultimate plot. Much darker than the 1962 version, the remake indicates that Ben has probably killed people in the past. Unlike the original in which the assassin kills his mother and stepfather and then commits suicide, Ben kills both Raymond and Eleanor but is never charged because the Secret Service protects him.[22]

The extremely complicated plot of *Syriana* focuses on a CIA operative past his prime (George Clooney) being used by the government to aid it in killing a progressive Arab prince. The latter is undesirable to the government because he represents a change from the status quo that supports the link of government and industry. At the end of the film both he and the operative die in a car bombing set up by the US government. *The Kingdom* begins with a suicide bombing killing a number of families all connected with a US corporate installation in Arabia. The particular significance of the link between the government and the corporation is never raised as an issue. Rather, the focus is on the successful efforts of Jamie Foxx and his team of investigators to root out the terrorists who killed the Americans.

While these war films display somewhat different kinds of conventions than those outlined thus far, each demonstrates what Eisenhower warned about in his speech. Still, the destruction in *Syriana* and *The Kingdom* shows the kinds of terrorist attacks and car bombings seen in actual war films about Iraq like *Home of the Brave*. All have done reasonably well at the box office domestically: *Candidate*, $65 million; *Syriana*, for which Clooney won the Oscar for Best Supporting Actor, $50.8 million; and *Kingdom*, $47 million. In contrast, actual combat films about the Iraq War have done poorly. *American Soldiers* had no release. Several had dismal grosses below $100,000: *Home of the Brave*, $51,708; *Grace is Gone*, $45,213; and *Redacted*, $65,388. Although the domestic gross of *In the Valley of Elah* was better, its mixture of combat and domestic crime investigation yielded only $6.7 million. In contrast, two of the three films about 9/11 have done quite well domestically: *United 93*, $41.383 million and *World Trade Center*, $70.278 million.

The fact-based comedy *Charlie Wilson's War* (Mike Nichols, 2007) has been the most successful film thus far to deal with United States foreign policy, making over $66 million domestically and over $31 million internationally. But unlike the other films, it takes place in the 1980s *before* the Gulf War begins. It focuses on the actions of Charlie Wilson, a Texas congressman, who is instrumental in supplying Afghanistan with weapons that will allow it to defeat the Russians whom they are fighting. Their success led to the expulsion of the Russians and a softening and change in that country's foreign policy and status, signaled most dramatically by the tearing down of the Berlin Wall in 1989. Wilson is played by Tom Hanks. Even though a hard-drinking womanizer, he is, nonetheless, once again the hero who helps the United States fight its enemies. In one sense, the film is a curious analog to *Saving Private Ryan* in that it looks back to a period when the United States was in a position to make positive changes in the world.[23]

During the period of the wars beginning in 1990, there have been many films that revisit a number of earlier wars retrospectively, many of them positively. These include the French and Indian Wars, *The Last of the Mohicans* (1992); the American Revolution, *The Patriot* (2000); World War I, *Flyboys*; Vietnam, *We Were Soldiers* (2002), *Rescue Dawn* (2007); and Somalia, *Black Hawk Down* (2001). But by far the most significant revisiting of an earlier conflict has occurred with films about World War II: *Memphis Belle* (1990), *A Midnight Clear* (1992), *Saving Private Ryan*, *The Thin Red Line* (1998), *Pearl Harbor* (2001), *Hart's War* (2001), *Band of Brothers* (2001, the major HBO series co-produced by Steven Spielberg and Tom Hanks), *To End All Wars*, and *The Great Raid* (2005). I will discuss *Flags of our Fathers* and *Letters from Iwo Jima* (2006) in Chapter 8. As I suggest in the next chapter, the reasons for the most recent return to World War II as a subject in the late 1990s in particular are complex, ranging from disillusionment with recent foreign policy debacles to, most profoundly, a desire to memorialize what Tom Brokaw calls "the Greatest Generation," those soldiers who fought in World War II, which is for many the last "good war" in which the United States engaged.

But even a cursory look at this list suggests that those retrospective war films dealing with the United States' earliest history and achieving independence, and those about US involvement in foreign wars that it wins, deserve consideration along the lines I've suggested throughout this chapter. They are made and released during a period when the wars in which the US is engaged have nothing like the support that existed for the wars depicted on screen. Significantly, even two of the films that deal with Vietnam have positive elements in them. *We Were Soldiers*, which focuses on the very first battle of the Vietnam War, emphasizes the nobility of both sides in the conflict and suggests that all the combatants are caught up in ways beyond their control in historical carnage played out on a battlefield that is indeed a level playing field. *Rescue Dawn* presents the true story of the escape of Dieter Dengler, a German-born US pilot, from a prison camp in Laos. The focus is not on the war itself but on individual heroism.

**CHAPTER 2**

# CRITICAL ISSUES

This chapter provides an overview of the critical ideas and theoretical issues that have informed the discourse concerning the war film genre. Specifically, it considers what we mean by a "war film" and explores its relationship to "history" and to concepts of "realism." The quotation marks around these terms should signal in advance that these complicated issues resist easy definition and analysis. The chapter concludes by offering guidelines for considering individual genre films, using *Saving Private Ryan* (1998) as a model.

## *Questions of Definition: What is a "War Film"?*

The answer to this question depends on whom one is reading. Some writers define it in relation to particular wars and narrative situations, while others position it in terms of different genres. Kathryn Kane offers an example of the first approach when she suggests that by "war films" we mean "those films that depict the activities of uniformed American military forces in combat with uniformed enemy forces during World War II." In defining it this way, she "eliminates . . . costume dramas with major battle scenes, all other wars, spy dramas, films made during the war years which may refer in passing to those historical events but do not take them as the basic narrative structure."[1] She argues that combat films are structured by "dualities, or oppositions . . . the forces of good and evil, civilization and savagery" and "War and Peace." Specific narrative elements include a positive theme about unity within the forces, combat settings, representative characters, and a typical plot that leads to "victory or defeat."[2]

Jeanine Basinger identifies the quintessential generic features of the American combat film during World War II, explains its prehistory and subsequent developments, the way one story can move from genre to genre, and variations in genre such as war musicals and comedies: "World War II gave birth to a story pattern which came to be known and recognized as the combat genre, whether it is ultimately set in World War II, the Korean War, or in Vietnam, or inside some other genre such as the Western."[3] The story pattern refers to the kinds of characters, specifically an ethnically and geographically mixed group of soldiers and the hero distanced by virtue of his leadership responsibilities; a particular objective; internal conflict within the group; a faceless enemy; few if any women; reminders of home; a last stand; propaganda; common behaviors (writing letters, singing); and death. She illustrates the genre's attributes with extensive commentaries on films such as *Bataan* (1943) and explains the complex challenges presented by comedies and musicals that are set in wartime or contain elements of combat.

Although using a similar kind of historical conception, Steve Neale excludes certain types: "war films are films about the waging of war in the twentieth century; scenes of combat are a requisite ingredient and these scenes are dramatically central. The category thus includes films set in the First World War, the Second World War, Korea and Vietnam. And it excludes home front dramas and comedies and other films lacking scenes of military combat."[4] Like Basinger, he acknowledges that a particular kind of story can move from the war film genre to another, such as a western or prison film, and points to "the extent to which generic overlap can occur, of the extent to which a service comedy like *The Wackiest Ship in the Army* (1960) can culminate in scenes of serious combat or to which a 'combat film' like *Battle Cry* (1955) can include scenes of personal drama."[5] Lawrence Suid defines "a war movie as one in which men appear in battle or in situations in which actual combat influences their actions. A military movie portrays men in uniform in training situations during peacetime or performing duties intended to preserve the peace." Unlike Neale, he also includes "the Vietnam home front movie" because it shows "the impact of war on the civilian population."[6]

Lenny Rubenstein expands the definition more broadly than Neale, even though he too uses historical considerations in his definition:

> Most war films deal with the events or methods of World Wars I and II, the Korean War, and the Vietnam War. These were the first fully modern wars, including combat cameramen from whose footage Hollywood filmmakers could model their feature films. The basic categories into which most war films fall are the Embattled Platoon, the Battling Buddies, the POW Escape, the Preparedness Film, the Service Comedy-Musical, the Battle Epic, the Strain of Command, and the Antiwar Film.[7]

Thomas Doherty provides the most expansive conception. While his primary focus is on World War II films, he also explores those that precede and follow them, defining "the war-minded motion picture" as one that includes "military education and civilian orientation, combat films, home front melodramas, wartime comedies, martial musicals, and the newsreels, combat reports, and documentaries chronicling the front-line action."[8]

A second approach to war films involves positioning them in relation to other genres. Thomas Sobchack includes them implicitly as he suggests that "the fictional genre film" is "a single category that includes all that is commonly held to be genre film—i.e., the western, the horror film, the musical, the science fiction film, the swashbuckler—in order to show that all of these films have a common origin and basic form." Drawing on Aristotle's *Poetics*, he argues that all genre films share the same basic elements and are all "made in imitation not of life but of other films."[9] He acknowledges that there must be a "first": "True, there must be a first instance, in a series or cycle, yet most cases of the first examples of various film genres can be traced to literary sources, primarily pulp literature. Even the gangster films of the thirties derive not from life itself but from newspaper stories; the musical film, from the musical stage."[10] But one could argue that the newspaper stories were indeed about "life itself" and are certainly different in kind from musical films and their origins in theatrical performances. Moreover, such a view does not address what we have seen in the origins of the war film, specifically the multiple *formal* perspectives of actualities, reenactments, and narratives that arose in direct association with the nation's experience of war. While the narrative elements of war films relate to other stories that go back to the *Iliad*, they begin as a way of recording and organizing the experience of people at an ongoing historical moment during the Spanish-American War. If there is "imitation," as in the reenactments, it is because the technology and filming conditions do not yet permit a more intensely accurate record of the experience of war.

In contrast to Sobchak's idea that individual film genres can be understood as particular manifestations of one originating fictional genre, Robert Burgoyne sees the American historical film as "a specific genre, one that emerged in the earliest days of American filmmaking. . . . Like many genres, the historical film has developed several different variants, branching off into distinct subtypes, such as the war film, the epic, the biographical film, the topical film, and . . . the metahistorical."[11] So, for Sobchak, the fictional narrative film includes all other genres; for Burgoyne, the historical film serves as the basis for a number of other kinds of genres, including the war film.

## Generic History as a Basis for Defining the "War Film"

My definition adapts itself to the more inclusive of these conceptions mentioned above, for I think that a film belongs to the genre if it focuses, with varying emphases, (1) *directly on war itself* (battles—preparation, actual, aftermath/damage); (2) on the *activities of the participants off the battlefield* (recruitment, training, leisure, recovery from wounds); and (3) the *effects of war on human relationships* (home front, impact on family and lovers). While some films easily meet all three criteria, others are notable for qualifying on the basis of one in particular.

I base this conception on generic history and the earliest actualities, reenactments, and narrative films that pictured a range of experiences during the Spanish–American War such as horseplay, combat, death, home front, and return. Recall the experience of patrons at the Eden Musee described in the Introduction. They saw a projected accumulation of films that included separate works about different aspects of war. In a way, it's analogically as if viewers were looking at the canvas of a vast painting or diorama that contained various aspects of the war. After looking at one part of this canvas, viewers could look at another part, distinct from the first but still part of the whole. Audiences seeing a short film about a training camp in the compilations at the Eden Musee would in close succession also be watching films showing troops and battles. There were no genre distinctions as yet to provide categorical distinctions among these films. Those that succeeded each other were all part of a series of films about war. That is essentially the viewing position I propose for us as we watch any one war-related film. Whatever kind of film about an aspect of war one is watching, one could also be viewing some other kind of film about another aspect. But they're all parts of the constitutive generic body the "war film."

The logic of turning to the genre's history can accommodate the categorical problems in presenting such a broadly based definition. For example, consider a film that focuses on recruitment and training. *Buck Privates* (1941), an Abbott and Costello comedy released in January 1941, concerns the antics and escapades of the team after they find themselves in the army. On the surface it seems difficult to justify calling this a "war film." For one thing, the United States was not at war. Second, such military values as discipline and regimentation are humorously negated. On the other hand, though, the film begins with confusion regarding the team's proximity to a draft board station. The peacetime draft had been authorized by the Selective Service Act of September 1940 in response to the tensions caused by World War II. The war game exercises they participate in during basic training are similar to what real recruits would have encountered. One option is to call it a comedy set in peacetime that acknowledges the existence of actual and deadly combat directly by its plot, which has recruits training for it. During the course of the film, that remains an unrealized but potential narrative possibility, one element of the vast "war film" of which this comedy is part, just as combat is for the young men seen tossing the blanket or washing themselves and dishes in the earliest films about war.

*See Here, Private Hargrove* (1944), a comedy set during World War II, focuses on the training activities of the hero, a journalist drafted into the service, his initial ineptness meeting training requirements, and his romantic quest of a woman. The film ends as he prepares to leave for his war assignments. So, two comedies with lots of laughs: one set before, one during the war. The second is more closely connected to the war film genre, but the first is certainly not excluded, since a country drafts men because it needs a standing army in the event of war.[12]

Several years later, within eighteen months Dean Martin and Jerry Lewis starred in three training film comedies: *At War With the Army* (January 1951), *Sailor Beware* (February 1952), and *Jumping Jacks* (July 1952). The first is set during World War II, the others in some vague time frame that does not acknowledge the presence of the Korean War, which is ongoing when the films are released. *At War With the Army* can serve as a key text in thinking about this issue. Setting the narrative in World War II has the effect of turning away from the existence of the present conflict in Korea and revisiting a past triumphant war as the site of comedy. Audiences can look back at the earlier war we won and have some laughs, made all the funnier by not having to confront combat and death, which are in fact occurring at that time. The Korean War is off screen in a way that positions the Martin and Lewis comedy as one option in the possible treatments of war. And that's the case in *all* war films. Some of the events we associate with war are present at some point during any individual film; some remain narratively out of sight or off screen for part or all of the duration of a particular work. To that extent, any individual narrative moment or action signals a choice by the filmmaker to include a particular dimension of the vast array of potentialities that might have been included.

There are actually more war films off screen to consider in relation to *At War With the Army* and the other comedies. Sam Fuller's *The Steel Helmet* opened within a month of *At War With the Army*. The first combat film about the Korean War presents several characters that have fought in World War II, including the hero Sergeant Zack (Gene Evans). The earlier conflict remains in the diegetic past of the narrative. Fuller incorporates stock footage of actual combat supplied by the United States government, thus evoking the "real" war that is off screen from this fictionalized representation of it. John Huston's film about the Civil War, *The Red Badge of Courage*, opened in March. In it a young soldier redeems his cowardice in battle. *Up Front*, which opened in April, is a comedy based on Bill Mauldin's famous characters Willie and Joe, who appeared regularly in cartoons in *Stars and Stripes* during World War II. This was a military publication distributed to American troops beginning in 1942. Mauldin won a Pulitzer Prize for his depictions of the infantryman's travails. Like Buster Keaton's *The General* (1927), this comedy includes actual moments of combat and death. While *Up Front* also looks away from the Korean War, unlike *At War With the Army*, it acknowledges the darker elements of war.

In a sense, these films from 1951 can be said to offer an experience of war analogous to that available to audiences watching films about the Spanish-American War in 1898–1899. "War" as a historical reality exists for the audiences in the first part of 1951 because of our presence in Korea. Those at the Martin and Lewis comedies can laugh about men who haven't yet gone to another war, one that was successfully ended six years earlier. Audiences for *Up Front* could experience beloved cartoon characters brought to life in ways that acknowledge both the comic and the serious in the earlier war. Audiences watching Huston's film were seeing an adaptation of a famous novel about war. And those at *The Steel Helmet* received a narrative treatment depicting the current conflict.

Adding to the collection were combat films about World War II. Lewis Milestone's *The Halls of Montezuma* (January) depicted the experiences of a Marine captain in the South Pacific fighting physical problems as well as the Japanese. *The Frogmen* (June) concerned Navy divers who have to set up and explode bombs at a Japanese port. *Flying Leathernecks* (August) followed the rivalries of two Marine pilots. The first in particular is of note since it was a prestige film by a major director given massive benefit premieres in Los Angeles and in New York at the Radio City Music Hall, with the proceeds going to Marine Corps charities. Thus audiences could see films about wars from the distant past to the immediate present.

Michael Curtiz's *This is the Army* (1943), the most financially successful war-themed film of *any* kind made during World War II, displays a number of generic elements, including ground and aerial combat, recruitment, training, and marching, as well as comedy, romance, song, and dance.[13] Its immense popularity suggests audiences' interest in seeing a war film that served as a kind of matrix for all the other genres in 1943. Based on the successful theatrical review that had opened on Broadway in 1942, it opens with a patriotic song and then follows a group of soldiers fighting in World War I. We witness a battle scene and the wounding of Jerry Jones (George Murphy), a dancer turned soldier who has been part of a musical group within their unit. The movie then moves to the beginnings of World War II in Europe, introduces "God Bless America," sung by Kate Smith, and then has shots of the attack on Pearl Harbor. Now a producer, Jerry decides to revive the musical show he and his buddies were in during World War I. Using his son Johnny (Ronald Reagan) as the director, he recruits performers from the service. Practically all the male performers in the film were actually in the armed forces, thus double draftees—into the army and a show. Engaged to Eileen (Joan Leslie), Johnny doesn't want to marry yet because of his fear of leaving her a widow, as has happened with his friend who was killed at Pearl Harbor when his plane is shot down, an event which we see. After showing the recruiting and training of performers, the film presents a number of elaborate musical production numbers, some involving men in drag, some emphasizing the power of the military. It concludes with the troop ending its stateside shows by marching out of the theater to take the review to servicemen, as indeed happened. Johnny marries Eileen. When the show goes on the road to various cities, we could be watching a group of entertainers in a Hollywood musical, given the typical montage sequence of railroad shots followed by indications of the cities at which they're arriving.

**PLATE 6** *This is the Army* (Michael Curtiz, 1943). One of the performers in drag (Alan Hale) complaining to a soldier in uniform (Tom D'Andrea) (Warner Bros./Courtesy Photofest).

Bosley Crowther's enthusiastic review demonstrates the film's importance for contemporary audiences:

> *This is the Army* is still the freshest, the most endearing, the most rousing musical tribute to the American fighting man that has come out of World War II . . . buoyant, captivating, as American as hot dogs or the Bill of Rights . . . a warmly reassuring document on the state of the nation; it should frighten our enemies more than dire threat or epithet. It is, from beginning to end, a great show. It is great because somewhere amid its hurly-burly humor, its sentimentality, its riotous shenanigans, it has caught the American pulse. It is as explosively spontaneous as a soldier's leave. It should be intimate to any American who knows another American in uniform—and who doesn't? Somehow one doesn't remember individual performers in the show's enormous cast; but one does remember that every soldier in the show seems to resemble all the American soldiers one has known in this war. It has the lighthearted confidence, the homely yearnings, the screwball gags of the kind of boys who went into the Army and now are helping to win it far from home.[14]

This commentary is reminiscent of Jonathan Auerbach's description of how the first war films served the needs of audiences in 1898: "Whether the projection on the screen was the actual battleship *Maine* or another ship posing as the *Maine*, the phantom image was immediate, vivid, and powerful, capable of invoking immense patriotic responses from cheering vaudeville audiences."[15] What links the audiences separated by over fifty years is their joint enthusiasm and support for the war efforts. Moreover, in the case of *This is the Army*, the viewing audiences in 1943 could identify with the audiences shown watching the performances of the servicemen in the theaters.

## War Films and "History"

Burgoyne's interest in the American historical film invites consideration of its potential as a source of information. War films are always about a particular war or battle, whether these are identified indirectly or directly. Even the apparent exception proves the rule. For example, Thomas Ince's *Civilization* (1916) deals with inhabitants of the nonexistent country of Wredpyrd. Set during a conflict in which submarines sink ships carrying innocent women and children, it is immediately recognizable as a film that is "really" about World War I and the sinking of the *Lusitania*.

As we saw, particular conflicts or war in general can generate anti- or pro-war films, or both: World War I films made in the 1920s (many of them anti), World War II films made during the conflict (uniformly pro), and Vietnam films made during and after (pro and anti). The situation is made even more complicated when we distinguish war films made during or very soon after a conflict is occurring from those that deal with one *retroactively*. Under these circumstances, it is possible that in the same year one film sympathetic to involvement in a past/present war may appear while another is critical of a past/present war. For example, in 2005, *The Great Raid* offered a supportive view of the liberation of prisoners of war who survived the Bataan death march during World War II, while *Jarhead* presented a stinging critique of US involvement in the Gulf War.

Another issue is accuracy, the extent to which the fictionalized narrative restages or reworks aspects of a war. For example, historian Anton Kaes suggests that the Vietnam War films *The Deer Hunter* (1978) and *Apocalypse Now* (1979) do not show isolated pictures of accidental, contingent events, but rather select, narrativize, and thereby give shape to the random material of history. . . . Cinematic images have created a technological bank that is shared by everyone and offers little escape. It increasingly shapes and legitimizes our perception of the past. Memory in the age of electronic reproducibility and dissemination has become public; memory has become socialized by technology.[16]

One of the most notorious cinematic images that entered into the "technological bank" was that of the Russian roulette game American prisoners of the Viet Cong are forced to play in *The Deer Hunter*, an event having no basis in fact, but which attained a sense of reality by virtue of its sensational qualities. The game connected to an indelible image from the Vietnam War, one already part of Americans' memory bank: Eddie Adams' photograph of a Vietnamese police officer shooting a Viet Cong soldier through the head. Here's a case where an image from the war is appropriated and narrativized in a film, becoming part of our communal bank of images. Another aspect of historical accuracy can relate to something as important as the composition of platoons. For example, even though historically inaccurate, African American soldiers are shown serving in white fighting units in the World War II films *Bataan*, *Guadalcanal Diary* (1943), and *Home of the Brave* (1949).

An even more complicated aspect of the relationship between history and a war film arises when a film about one war can be read as being really about another. Examples of this are increasingly numerous. In addition to Robert Altman's *M*A*S*H*, noted earlier as a commentary on Vietnam, Zack Snyder's *300* (2006), which depicts the Spartans' defense of Thermopylae against the Persians, has been interpreted in terms of the involvement of the United States in Iraq. Here, the heroic King Leonidas and his band of 300 soldiers are read as George W. Bush and US forces fighting a war on principle, even though outnumbered and criticized by their countrymen.[17]

A variation of this situation has been explained by historian Robert Brent Toplin: "Often the creators of motion pictures address the concerns of the present when they fashion stories about the past." He cites *Patton* (1970) as an example. Because of the controversy about Vietnam in the late 1960s, "the filmmakers shaped their story and advertising in ways that suggested a complex and sometimes critical portrait of their subject's militarism."[18] Ironically, Richard M. Nixon took the cinematic Patton as a model of behavior for himself and justification for his handling of the war.[19]

In a commentary on historical considerations, Burgoyne draws on Mikhail Bakhtin's concept of "genre memory": "Genres function, Bakhtin writes, as 'organs of memory' for particular cultures, providing crystallized forms of social and cultural perception that embody the world views of the periods in which they originated, while carrying with them 'the layered record of their changing use.' Genres 'remember the past [and] redefine present experience.' "[20] Burgoyne thinks the "concept of genre memory provides a way of approaching one of the most remarkable aspects of . . . films [westerns, war films, melodramas]: the fact that their appeal to new forms of social coherence is to a large extent shaped by the rhetoric, imagery, and genre patterning of what might be called the war myths of the national past." He notes the impact of various forms of communication such as the "novel, the newspaper, and film" on a nation's sense of itself, but notes that "many of these influential approaches overlook . . . one of the most significant and obvious forms of national mythology: the war stories of the nation-state."[21]

Others have explored the issue of memory in relation to genre and the war film. Rick Altman observes:

> Whether or not genres derive from specific cultural rituals they clearly serve a memorial function, commemorating key aspects of collective history. . . . All genres serve to share the epic function of recalling the origins and justifying the existence of current practices. . . . However much genre texts may recollect events, locations, or relationships, they must also recall previous texts or they will fail to assure the genre's continued existence.[22]

In fact, he argues, contemporary producers of films use genre films as a way to create a kind of memorial bond: "When trying to bring together spectators who actually share less and less, what better meeting place than the common past provided by the genre itself?"[23]

Marita Sturken's discussion of Vietnam War films and cultural memory relates to constitutive aspects of genre in general. She defines "cultural memory" as "a field of contested meanings in which Americans interact with cultural elements to produce concepts of the nation, particularly in event of trauma. . . . [This memory] is shared outside the avenues of formal historical discourse and yet is entangled with cultural products and imbued with cultural meanings."[24] Our awareness of what "war" is and of what any specific war was in previous centuries is closely linked to records that were made then.

Each new war enters into two distinct but related regimes, the history of war films and the history of war, because for contemporary viewers since the silent era, the history of war is to a great extent the history of its representation. Stephen Ambrose tells about one of his students who asked: "World War II? Isn't that the one fought in black and white?"[25] There is a great deal of significance to this anecdote because, for the student, the actual war is known only as something experienced on a screen, not as something from immediate experience. Even though Lewis Milestone, who directed *All Quiet on the Western Front* (1930), had been in the Signal Corps in World War I, he did not engage in actual combat. Although not the same as the student mentioned above, since he lived through the war, he experienced it at one remove, through the medium of film. John Whitclay Chambers explains:

> As Milestone recalled in an interview . . . "having examined thousands of feet of actual war footage while stationed at the Washington, DC War College during the war, I knew precisely what it was supposed to look like." A decade later he drew on that background. . . . What he did was to draw on his experience with documentary photographic representation of the battlefront to create the "reality" for his dramatic representation of battle and the battlefront.[26]

Very few people who see a war film today have ever experienced "real" war. Indeed, for most people today, the genre provides the only way to experience war, short of newsreels and documentaries like Ken Burns' *The War* (2006), which mixes documentary footage with occasional clips from war films. But to draw on language the film theorist Peter Wollen introduced some years ago, following C. S. Peirce, films bear both an iconic and indexical relationship to what they represent. An iconic sign is one that is motivated by a resemblance between the object and the image, like a photograph. An indexical sign is one "by virtue of an existential bond between itself and its object" such as a sailor's "rolling gait," the appearance of a jockey, "a bowlegged man in corduroys, gaiters, and a jacket," and the action of a weathercock, "a sign of the direction of the wind which physically moves it." In these indexical examples the thing itself, the signifier, is bound up existentially with the thing signified, the meaning to which it points.[27]

Without being aware of Peirce, film theorist André Bazin suggested that photography bears an indexical relationship to its objects:

> The photographic image is the object itself . . . freed from the conditions of time and space that govern it. . . . The image . . . shares, by virtue

of the very process of its becoming, the being of the model of which it is the reproduction; it *is* the model. . . . The cinema is objectivity in time. . . . Now, for the first time, the image of things is likewise the image of their duration, change mummified as it were.[28]

In *War and Photography* Caroline Brothers draws on suggestions from Allan Sekula and Rosalind Krauss to make a similar point: "As 'the effect of radiations from the object,' [Allan Sekula] photographs are thus also indexical signs where paintings and drawings remain iconic; it is their indexical quality that seems to set photographs apart as having 'special status with regard to the real' [Krauss]."[29]

Certainly, viewers today are sufficiently aware of the ways photographs can be altered and computer graphics used to "create" realities that never existed. Nonetheless, documentary footage of battles, which sometimes gets inserted into fictional war narratives, shows the real thing. It's not a reenactment, although both can appear in a narrative film. Even if battles are reenactments, though, what distinguishes war films from any other genre is that their images blend iconic and indexical signs. Viewers perceive combat in this way because of the ongoing historical presence of war, whether conveyed by newsreels, as occurred during World War II, or by televised images of war, as happened in the "living room war" of Vietnam (to use Michael Arlen's famous phrase), or the night vision records of attack in the Gulf War, or the newspaper and magazine photographs of video images from the Iraq War.[30] That is, the images of war we experience in film have a built-in inflected valence of reality because of the indexical quality of the historical recorded images.

I mean by this something different from Paul Virilio's startling assertion that "*War is cinema and cinema is war*."[31] As Bernd Hüppauf has explained, Virilio's point is that "war and cinema are linked by a structural homology which results in the 'complete destruction of traditional fields of perception.'"[32] That is, in contrast to earlier warfare, waging war today involves utilizing powers over vision (aviation, special cameras, surveillance) that are similar to the staples of cinema itself. Brian DePalma's *Redacted* (2007) offers a relevant example from the Iraq War, since the soldiers make extensive use of camera phones to capture the records of the events. As J. David Slocum has observed, "To speak of war as a way of seeing . . . is to recognize the emergence of perceptual and discursive fields that has coincided with the increasing social priority of militarization."[33] Even if we are not at war in a given period, war's presence is felt through films which reinforce historical memory with our genre memory. These two memory banks not only support one another; the one has the effect of validating the sense of reality of the other. War films seem real, in part because they actually use material taken from battlefields, but also because the reality of the actualities bleeds into the reenactments. The authenticity of the one generates an ontological authority for the other.

## War Films and "Realism"

To add more to this commentary on the theoretical framework for thinking about the war film, we can connect the iconic and indexical nature of photography, described above, to spectators' experience of war. Those first viewers of actualities and reenactments saw works that presented the content specified in the titles. The language used in the production companies' catalogs is an unlikely but still viable source of the earliest theory and criticism of the war film. First, the Edison catalog says of *9th Infantry Morning Boys' Wash* (1898):

> Imagine forty or fifty soldiers each with a pail of water on the ground before him, sousing and spattering and scrubbing away for dear life. Soap and towels, too. Every man jack of them looks as if he were enjoying the wash immensely, and also the novelty of having his picture taken. The big fellow in the center of the picture is laughing heartily. All the figures are clearly outlined, and the whole group is true to life.

A much more serious tone appears in the second example, a Biograph summary of *Wounded Soldiers Embarking in Row Boats* (1898):

> This picture was taken after the battle of Las Guaymas, and shows a large number of wounded soldiers embarking in a rowboat from an extemporized dock, on their way to the hospital ship "Olivette." A high sea was rolling in at the time, which made embarkation exceedingly difficult, and the pitiful condition of the wounded soldiers under conditions can readily be imagined. This picture is remarkably fine photographically, and has made a marked sensation wherever it has been shown.[34]

The descriptions can be read as proto-critical/theoretical commentary. Part of the pleasure in seeing the happy boys in *Morning Wash* derives from their awareness of the photographic process capturing them, and also the link forged with the spectators who realize they are "true to life." Sympathetic support for the wounded is underscored because the picture, which is "remarkably fine photographically," puts spectators in touch with the difficulties of the embarkation and, even more, with the "pitiful condition," thus making it possible to imagine what they are experiencing. The life-like accuracy of the films provides the opportunities for experiencing the full range of the soldiers' lives, from horseplay to pain.

In addition to the Edison catalogs, contemporary advertisements in the *Yankee Clipper*, an early trade newspaper, give a sense of what "realism" meant at the time to audiences. Advertising the film of the funeral of the *Maine* victims on April 30, 1898, the F. Z. Maguire Company appealed to the realism of the images and to their effects on audiences: "This is one of the most impressive scenes ever taken. It will produce a thrill of sympathy in every American heart. . . . The whole scene passes before the spectator just as it occurred, and its effect is pathetically realistic."[35] An advertisement by Lubin on April 22, 1899 about the *Battleship Oregon in Action*, stated: "The entire picture is full of action and is very exciting. The smoke from the cannon and guns give a most realistic view of a battleship in action. You imagine you can hear the cannon firing their deadly missiles and the exploding shells add realism to the scene."[36]

Clearly, the advertisers use the terms "realism" and "realistic" to appeal to the patriotic and imaginative spectators supporting the war. Watching these films will permit them to experience it as if they were actually there. When we look at the films available at the Library of Congress website, some of the obviously staged scenes in reenactments hardly seem "realistic." But it's not just that what is "realistic" in war films is relative to the times in which films were made. Rather, it's that for those early viewers, there was virtually no disconnection between the images and their referents. We should understand the term "realism" as a function of the degree to which iconicity and indexicality are operating for particular spectators at a specific historical moment. For those early viewers, "realism" did indeed seem to be a radiation or emanation from the object. Films became alternative and rival sources of information about war for audiences in 1898–1899. The emphasis on accuracy in the film's advertisements highlights the competition for claiming value as sources of information. The film's images are more real for them because they are taken as an event unfolds in time. This is not a single photograph, like shots of the dead such as emerged from Civil War photography, but a series of images that move. *The recording of the event is itself part of a historical process.* That is, the language of those early advertisements and descriptions shows how important both the process as well as the product were to contemporary viewers.

The praise of realism continues to appear in reviews of some of the silent masterpieces about World War I. King Vidor's *The Big Parade* (1925) prompts the *New York Times* critic to note how it exceeds what spectators can conceive of in regard to war: "It is a subject so compelling and realistic that one feels impelled to approach a review of it with all the respect it deserves, for as a motion picture it is something beyond the fondest dreams of most people." Moreover, it exceeds expectations in regard to the use of genre conventions: "There are incidents . . . which obviously come from experience, as they are totally different from the usual jumble of war scenes in films. It is because of the realism that the details ring true."[37] Notice, the standard of realism is being used not only in terms of the events but also in terms of the genre. The review in *Variety* displays a corresponding awareness of genre history as it approaches the film from two perspectives: "Everything one can expect from real war is in this picture . . . the various branches of artillery in action, plenty of hand grenades and machine-gun warfare." The reviewer realizes that some of the film consists of documentary material drawn from history: "It was obvious that a good portion of the long shots and battles . . . were stock material. . . . Whether or not this stuff comes from the Signal Corps' large stock of film, the picture as put together is sure-fire entertainment."[38]

Reviewers praised documentaries made during World War II for their immediacy and the actual risk involved in capturing the information. John Ford's *The Battle of Midway* (1942) gives "actual combat, pictures of the young, tense, grinning, lean, clean, fine-drawn faces of American boys before, during, and after a great and horrible battle. The impact is as quick as a wound and deep as loneliness."[39] John Huston's *The Battle of San Pietro* (1944) was "daringly shot by Signal Corps front-line photographers" who succeeded in "getting pictures of the fighting men in tight-lipped close-ups. As a consequence, most of the picture—most of the combat scenes, that is—has the taut, nervous 'feel' of the actual battle as sensed by the individual man."[40]

*Objective, Burma!* (1945), one of the most violent narrative war films to emerge at the end of the conflict, drew praise for using realism for functional purposes, among them giving the spectators a sense of what the men experienced. Describing the 150-mile march taken by the soldiers, the *Time* reviewer observed: "From here on, things are really —and realistically—tough. This story is used not as an excuse for histrionic detail, but as a basis for a good deal of dogged, specific detail about men at war."[41] The *New York Times* reviewer spoke about "the startling degree of realism," noting "there are no phony heroics . . . these boys conduct themselves like real soldiers. . . . Many of the scenes are the real thing, and the shots of the boys jumping out of the planes look as though they were borrowed from the Army's film archives. In fact, the whole picture has a strong documentary quality."[42] These reviews of films about World Wars I and II indicate the extent to which the desire for and praise of realism established in response to films about the Spanish-American War continued to function.

Reviews of war films made after World War II treat the issues of "realism" and "reality" in a somewhat different way. This may be a function of a number of complex forces. The revelations of Nazi atrocities in the Holocaust exposed viewers of newsreels and photographs to unimaginable horrors, made even more loathsome because they were, indeed, inescapably real. Examination of Production Code Administration files indicates that concerns continued to be raised about violence in films made during the Korean War, but not to the extent apparent during World War II when Joseph I. Breen and others with the PCA were constantly warning filmmakers about scenes that were too "gruesome." The Vietnam War and the revelations about the various atrocities associated with it, combined with the graphic photographs in magazines and the explicitness of the details on television coverage, obviously generated a level of awareness about war's effects. But, as noted, practically no commercial films about the war were made when it was being waged. By the time of the Vietnam War, the PCA's strictures had been replaced with the Motion Picture Association of America's ratings system, instituted in 1968, which assigned categories to films on the basis of their presentations of sexuality and violence. The "real" images of the Viet Cong soldier's murder and the little girl burned by napalm running naked on the road, widely available on television and in Peter Davis' *Hearts and Minds* (1974), exceeded in explicitness anything ever seen before. When Vietnam War films finally do appear under the new ratings system, the issue of realism as such has shifted from praise of documentary and fictional films that show what is happening to concerns about the historical reality of the narrative, as noted in the concern about the Russian roulette in *The Deer Hunter*, and even more to the way the films' representations of violence serve a moral purpose in exposing the horrors of war.

For many viewers, the ultimate in war violence occurred when Steven Spielberg devoted over twenty minutes to recreating the Omaha Beach landing on D-Day in *Saving Private Ryan*. A common theme in reviews of the widely revered film was the extent of violence in this sequence. But I find no one praising it the way earlier reviewers lauded such moments in films like *Objective, Burma!* Rather, the violence of *Saving Private Ryan* in some ways became an issue in regard to the genre itself. For example, Roger Ebert says:

> The movie's opening sequence is as graphic as any war footage I've ever seen. In fierce dread and energy it's on a par with . . . *Platoon*, and in scope surpasses it—because in the bloody early stages the landing forces and the enemy never meet eye to eye, but are simply faceless masses of men who have been ordered to shoot at one another until one side is destroyed. Spielberg's camera makes no sense of the action.[43]

Owen Gliberman observes:

> For nearly half an hour, Spielberg uses his unparalleled kinetic genius to create an excruciatingly sustained cataclysm of carnage, nausea, and death. Everywhere, there are men with their limbs blown off, their insides hanging out, and the lapping tides run dark with blood, yet, like the soldiers, we seem to register each atrocity out of the corner of our eye. Working with the cinematographer Janusz Kaminski, Spielberg overexposes images, skips frames, and speeds up the action almost subliminally to create a heightened, leaping newsreel effect. It's as if we

**PLATE 7** *Saving Private Ryan* (Steven Spielberg, 1998). Captain Miller (Tom Hanks), the respected leader (Amblin Entertainment/Courtesy Photofest).

were experiencing the battle as a documentary hallucination – a cinema verité nightmare. Spielberg is making a perceptual statement about World War II: He's saying that it was every bit as merciless and agonizing, as "insane," as Vietnam.[44]

## Guidelines for Considering Individual Films in the Genre

The reference to critical responses to the issue of realism in *Saving Private Ryan* can serve as an introduction to the guidelines in play for looking at war films and the genre in Chapters 3 to 8. First, ideally we should try to contextualize any war film of interest to us within its period and determine its relationship to the culture in which it appears. Second, we should investigate the response of its contemporary public. Third, we should ask if there other films being made about the same war and/or other wars at that time. Fourth, we want to think about whether a film addresses a current war immediately or an earlier war retrospectively. This can be a significant issue, particularly when we look at current films dealing with an ongoing war at the same time multiple earlier conflicts are being treated retrospectively. Even if the film focuses on an earlier war, we want to think about how it speaks to the period in which it is produced and released. Fifth, we need to examine what use the film makes of conventions from the genre to see how it relies on or varies those in earlier war films. Sixth, we need to see how it connects to films from other genres. While it will not be feasible to provide detailed information for all the works considered here, attempting to do so can enrich our understanding of the films and the genre.

For example, recall the sharply defined focus of the earliest films about the Spanish-American War discussed in the Introduction and the interest and enthusiasm of those films' audiences for reports. Using some of the criteria mentioned above, contrast these early films and their audiences with what we know about the contemporary situation at the time of the release of *Saving Private Ryan* made one hundred years later. After an introductory section at a French cemetery in Normandy, the film presents a bloody and graphic account of the landing on Omaha Beach on D-Day, June 6, 1944. The story concerns a platoon led by Capt. Miller (Tom Hanks) seeking a soldier (Matt Damon) so that he can be sent home; his brothers have been killed, and the War Department has determined there should be no more losses for his family. *Ryan* displays many of the conventions associated with combat films of World War II mentioned in the Introduction and articulated by Basinger: the representative melting pot of ethnicities and character types in the troop (Jewish, intellectual, Italian, New Yorker, Southern boy, etc.); the heroic leader (Miller); conflicts within the group (whether or not to kill a German POW); absence of women; typical war iconography; questioning values; death.[45] It premiered in August to generally ecstatic reviews, was the biggest domestic money-maker for the year ($216,119,491), and the most successful war film financially ever made in the United States.

The next major American war film of the year would appear in December, *The Thin Red Line* (Terrence Malick), an adaptation of the James Jones novel about operations in the Pacific. A foreign film about World War II, Roberto Begnini's *Life is Beautiful*, opened in October. This film about a father (Begnini) trying to protect his son in a concentration camp began as a limited release and did well financially for a foreign film, eventually earning over $57 million domestically by October 1999. Begnini won the Best Actor award at the Oscars for 1998. *Saving Private Ryan* received five Oscars, including Best Director for Spielberg.

While not a significant year for the genre in terms of the number of films released, all the war-related films joined two other films that dealt with Americans encountering a deadly force that has to be eliminated: the disaster films *Deep Impact* (eighth highest box office) released early in May, and *Armageddon* (second highest), which opened in time for the July 4 weekend trade. The first deals with the efforts of astronauts to divert/destroy a comet headed toward earth, the second the attempt of astronauts assisted by oil drillers to destroy/disable an asteroid headed toward earth. Disasters occur in both (New York is overtaken by a tidal wave; meteors damage New York and Paris), but America survives.

Both films evoke the memory of *Independence Day* (1996), released two years earlier on the July 4 weekend. This film, ranked number one in box office for the year, concerns the only partially successful efforts of the US armed forces and president to fight off an alien invasion of the world—an attack that destroys a lot of property in the US and elsewhere, including the White House. The president himself (Bill Pullman) takes to the air in a jet to attack the invaders.

Significantly, in 1998, war films and two disaster films all deal with the United States at risk. The popularity of such works, which obviously play to anxieties, says something about our culture. Even though the country was not at war and the dot-com boom was generating billions economically, the year 1998 still had more than its share of international tensions. These included bombings of American embassies in Kenya and Tanzania by Al-Qaeda, resulting in 224 deaths and 4,500 injured, followed by US retaliatory air attacks on Al-Qaeda in Afghanistan. There was continued frustration caused by Iraq's refusal to respond to the United Nations' call for information on its disarmament actions. Domestically, the nation had been watching the Clinton-Lewinsky scandal unfold, a saga that would eventually result in the president's impeachment by the House in 1999.

While these varied pieces of information may not explain everything, they provide an example of the kind of contextualization I have in mind in regard to *Saving Private Ryan*. The credentials of the major artists involved with the film were exemplary. Spielberg's *Schindler's List* (1993), which was about the Holocaust, had won seven Oscars, including Best Picture and Best Director. The star of *Saving Private Ryan*, Tom Hanks, who won back-to-back Oscars in 1993 and 1994 for *Philadelphia* and *Forrest Gump*, had become one of the most popular and revered actors in American film. Matt Damon, who plays James Ryan, the object of the search, had shared an Oscar with Ben Affleck for co-writing *Good Will Hunting* the previous year. The advance word on the film about a war we had won decisively was positive. This contrasted with the seemingly lingering inconclusiveness of our victory in the Gulf War and the embarrassment of the American debacle at Mogadishu in 1995, as Albert Auster and others have suggested.[46] The film appeared at a time when the leader of the free world was himself an embarrassment, in a year when disaster films about threats to the country were making lots of money. In fact the combined domestic gross of *Ryan* and the two disaster films amounted to over $600 million.

Of immense significance was the appearance of Tom Brokaw's book *The Greatest Generation* in November 1998. In it he pays tribute to his parents' generation, those who fought in World War II, by following the lives of veterans and their spouses. As was clear from the national statistics, that generation, mostly born in the 1920s, had begun to die off, taking with them the memories and values of those who fought in and survived World War II. Thus at a time of national uncertainty we have a war film that champions the heroic values associated with World War II, using one of American's most popular actors playing a strong, unambiguously moral leader whose sacrifice guarantees the continuity of American values. We see the film in two related frameworks: the genre itself and the way it conforms to its conventions and confirms its values; and to the time and place of its appearance, the United States of 1998, and the way the film offers both a corrective to current leadership by reviving a model of exemplary morality from what Studs Terkel had earlier called "the good war."[47]

# CHAPTER 3

## ALL QUIET ON THE WESTERN FRONT (1930)

*All Quiet on the Western Front*, based on Erich Maria Remarque's novel of the same name, is generally regarded as one of the greatest anti-war films ever made.[1] It won two Academy Awards, for Best Picture and Best Director, Lewis Milestone (1895–1980). *All Quiet* was his second Academy Award winning film about World War I, the first being *Two Arabian Knights* (1927), a comedy with a happy ending about two soldiers who escape from a German prison camp. Milestone, who was in the Photographic Signal Corps during World War I, would go on to make several more films about World War II. These included a documentary, *Our Russian Front* (1942), made with Joris Ivens; *Edge of Darkness* (1943), about the Norwegian resistance to the Nazi occupation; *The Purple Heart* (1944), which presents the mock trial of fliers captured by the Japanese after the bombing raid of Tokyo in 1942; *A Walk in the Sun* (1945), a chronicle of the adventures of a patrol in Italy showing how different soldiers respond to the psychological pressures of battle; *Arch of Triumph* (1948), primarily a love story set in France around the time of its entrance into the war (also based on a novel by Remarque); and *Halls of Montezuma* (1950), about an excellent but physically afflicted leader of Marines. His last war film, *Pork Chop Hill* (1959), concerns an event that actually occurred near the end of the Korean War during truce talks when US forces had to persevere in a hopeless campaign for a tactically worthless hill, at a cost of many lives. *All Quiet* made a star of Lew Ayres, then a young actor (born in 1908), who credits the film as a contributing factor in his decision to be a conscientious objector during World War II.[2]

## Background

Production of the film began shortly after the Wall Street Crash in October 1929, an event that led to the Great Depression. The effects of that economic cataclysm on Hollywood production budgets would soon be felt, but the $1 million Universal Studios put into the film was well spent, since it became the fourth highest grossing film in 1930 ($1.5 million).[3] When it premiered in April, it entered into a discourse in which spectators were experiencing lingering disillusionment regarding World War I and a new destabilizing force in their lives, as the Depression resulted in bank failures, the loss of jobs, and the often hostile and even violent moves toward unionization.

In addition, 1930 is an interesting year to consider along the lines of what was suggested in Chapter 2 about 1998, when *Saving Private Ryan* was released. *All Quiet* premiered as a "road show" in Los Angeles and New York at the end of April 1930 before opening nationally in August. Films exhibited in this manner were shown only twice a day during the week, and usually three times a day on weekends, rather than being available to patrons on a continuous admission basis. The varying price structure for performances was higher than that in theaters showing films on a continuous basis. They were accompanied by souvenir programs containing information about the production and stars.[4] The kind of release signaled the prestige and importance of the film. James Whale's *Journey's End*, an anti-war film, had opened as a road show in April. This focuses on the day-to-day desperation of soldiers in a war zone.[5] This film and *All Quiet* were joined in November by another road show, Howard Hughes' anti-war epic *Hell's Angels*. The heroes of this film are English brothers (played by Americans) who are pilots. The climax of the film involves one killing the other in order to keep him from divulging information that could be used by their German captors against the British soldiers.

It is important to realize that a number of prestige anti-war films from the 1920s receiving road show exhibition had preceded *All Quiet* and these other 1930 films. *The Four Horsemen of the Apocalypse* (1921), the second highest grossing film of the decade, stars Rudolph Valentino.

It depicts the devastating effects of war on families from different countries torn by divided loyalties to their homelands. King Vidor's *The Big Parade* (1925), the fifth biggest money maker of the decade, follows three men of different social classes and shows how they become friends during basic training. A central focus is the love affair between one of them and a French woman he meets at the front. His friends die, and although he survives, one of his legs has to be amputated. He returns to France after the war and succeeds in finding his love. Raoul Walsh's *What Price Glory?* (1926), based on a popular play, mixes humor, a romantic triangle, and harrowing battle scenes in a powerful condemnation of war. *Wings* (1927), the first film to win an Academy Award for Best Picture, clearly delineates the awful costs of the war on human relationships. Two friends, fliers in love with the same woman, engage in successful dogfights with the Germans, but one ends up mistakenly shooting down the other's plane, causing his death.[6] These successful films helped prepare a climate of reception for works like *Journey's End*, *All Quiet*, and *Angels*, The number of anti-war films released in this manner suggests that the studios and exhibitors assumed that the public was heavily invested in supporting a negative view of war and was willing to pay extra.[7]

## The Film and Conventions

Milestone begins by photographing soldiers marching in the street seen from various perspectives: first a home, then a store, and finally a school-room. The soldiers proceed in the same direction, thus connecting the disparate places and establishing one of the film's central themes: the pervasiveness of war and its effects on all aspects of life—home, business, and school. When we reach the last site, Milestone, using what will be a characteristic camera movement throughout the film, pulls back his camera as the parade of soldiers ends and the diegetic music accom-panying them fades. He has now established a signature shot: showing military activities photographed from the relative safety of an interior space. But the safety of the interiors will increasingly be threatened by what's outside. This is particularly true once the young soldiers find themselves inside the makeshift facilities in the trenches.

In the classroom, a militaristic classics teacher encourages his students to fight in the war. In a succession of quick subjective shots, we see they are imagining to themselves how they will look as soldiers and how their families and women will respond to their uniforms. Stirred by the teacher's urging to fight for the fatherland, Paul Bäumer (Ayres) and his friends decide in a body to enlist, throw their school books and papers in the air, and leave the schoolroom exultantly. We see them through the windows of the now-empty schoolroom, moving in the same direction followed by the soldiers, thus underscoring their changed status and entrance into the dangerous outside world.

Their enthusiasm for military life quickly cools once they begin their training and encounter Himmelstoss, formerly their postman with whom they had friendly relations. Now their sergeant, he makes their lives miserable and bullies them maliciously. Elevated from his job as a minor civic functionary and given power, he enjoys terrorizing the boys and forcing them to endure excessive and demanding physical activities, including crawling through the mud. The training camp scenes present him as a tyrannical squad leader, a conventional character that recurs in war films. One example of the playfulness of the recruits evokes the blanket tossing seen in the early Spanish-American War film. Unified in their disdain of Himmelstoss, they get their revenge one night when they capture the drunken sergeant returning from the tavern, wrap

PLATE 8 *All Quiet on the Western Front* (Lewis Milestone, 1930). The recruits forced to crawl through mud (Universal Pictures/Courtesy Photofest).

him up in a sheet, and throw him in the water. When he reappears later in the film and joins the boys at the front, he displays cowardice, and tries unsuccessfully to escape battle on the basis of a minor wound.

In contrast to Himmelstoss is the kind and caring Kat Katczinsky (Lewis Wolheim), the seasoned older leader who takes care of them and helps them adjust to army life and the horrors of war. We first see him as he forages for food and uses a clever ploy to steal a pig that he brings back to his famished men. This gesture typifies the loving and maternal care he extends to them all, such as encouraging them during battle (down-playing the embarrassment of a young soldier who wets his pants), fighting for food later when the camp cook refuses to give the boys the portions to which they are entitled, and serving as the force of stability as the fighting and war become increasingly horrendous. He sees the absurdity of war and suggests that instead of armies fighting one another, the leaders of the warring countries should fight each other in their underpants, thus saving the soldiers in the armies.

The film contains a number of conventional scenes and situations that will recur in later war films. Some sequences contrast the oppressive scenes of killing. One occurs as the men, who have been deprived of anything like adequate provisions for a long time, enjoy a large meal and sit around, in a pleasantly lazy manner, simply enjoying being alive. Another happens in a beer garden as Paul and a friend look at a poster of a young girl and imagine what it would be like to be with her. This introduces the issue of sexual initiation as the clearly virginal Paul looks longingly at the girl whose appearance is so far removed from the grime and misery of their current lives.

The film develops this aspect of Paul's life when one afternoon he and his friends go swimming. In this bathing scene, the men, who are nude, see French women who live on the other side of the river that separates the Germans from their enemy; they arrange for a visit later at night. The most extended sequence of relief from the killing occurs when Paul and two others swim across the river that separates them from the French and spend the night with three French farm girls to whom they bring food. While it is clear that the men have sex with the women, they are not prostitutes, the film implies, but, rather, desperate, hungry victims of the same war as Paul and his friends. The advertising and promotional material for the film as well as the souvenir program foregrounded the women, suggesting that they played a more significant part in the film. Even though this was not the case, the decision to do this indicates how the producers were counting on audience expectation about liaisons on leaves as a plot element. The

**PLATE 9** *All Quiet on the Western Front* (Lewis Milestone, 1930). Paul (Lew Ayres) and a buddy display longing for women and a world separate from the war (Universal Pictures/Courtesy Photofest).

men's bathing scene in the first encounter with the women and the assignation scene at night did not pass censorship restrictions at the time in certain states, and upon the reissue of the film for the next several decades, these scenes were cut in various ways to play down the sensuality. In its original form, now restored, there is a long take in which the camera shows only the interior of a room. Although we do not see Paul and the woman he's with, we hear their halting conversation as they try to converse in different languages. Paul says he knows they will never meet again, a poignant reminder of war's effects.

After surviving a near-fatal wound, Paul is sent to a hospital. His stay there anticipates other terrifying experiences encountered in later war films. He gradually becomes aware that patients who are taken out to the "bandaging room" are in fact being taken to a holding area to die, since they are beyond help. But he survives, and after recuperating, returns home on leave and encounters utter ignorance in the older men who have no idea what's involved for the soldiers. He visits his school and criticizes his former teacher who is trying to get his much younger students to enlist. His mother, who is ill, tries to warn him about prostitutes. When Paul returns to the front, hardly any members of his troop remain. But Kat, the person he most wants to see, has survived. Paul brings food back from home for the men, and in a scene that parallels his first encounter with Kat, he becomes the motherly dispenser of needed food for the starving soldiers, who are boys rather than adult men.

He and Kat have a happy reunion, but a plane hovers ominously over them. As they walk, it drops a bomb that injures Kat's leg, and Paul carries him on his back. Another attack by the plane proves fatal to Kat, but Paul is unaware of his friend's injury and continues talking to him. When he gets back to camp, the doctor tells him Kat is dead. In one of the most pathetic moments in the film, Paul tries to give water to the dead man. Totally devastated, Paul returns to the trenches. In the only scene in the film with non-diegetic music, a mournful harmonica is heard as he reaches for a butterfly seen through an opening. A sniper kills him, a fact made known to us by Milestone's close-up of Paul's now-unmoving hand. The film ends with a ghostly parade of dead soldiers superimposed over a shot of a cemetery. They turn and look back, in a visual echo of the same glances backward we saw earlier as they went into their first battle. The film is utterly bleak and offers no hope, only the relentless succession of deaths of men fighting in a hopeless cause.

*All Quiet* displays a number of characters who illustrate the conventions associated with the war film. The camp/platoon clown is Tjaden (Slim Summerville), a character/actor who would reappear seven years later in James Whale's *The Road Back* (1937), another film based on a novel by Remarque, a contributor to the screenplay. Tjaden is the humorous counterpart to Kat, offering sly comments on the war. Paul's mother is loving and sustaining, but she doesn't have the slightest clue about what life is really like for him at the front. Paul's younger sister adores him and plays an important part in introducing the theme of tenderness and vulnerability. When home on leave, Paul talks with her about his butterfly collection, thus setting up his death scene in which he is shot by a sniper as he reaches for a butterfly from his foxhole.

The green and inexperienced recruits quickly realize what war involves, especially in the battles made all the more excruciating for us by the sights and sounds of warfare. Milestone uses a variety of cinematic techniques to convey the horror. One comes in his use of the long take. His immobile camera focuses on a shelter in the trenches, creating a claustrophobic sense because all the soldiers, cramped into a small space, are terrified as parts of the makeshift roof fall on them and as the shelling continues without ceasing. Using rapid editing, he shows the men's revulsion as they fight the rats that have overrun their space in search of food. The film powerfully renders their fear during the first battles and their ensuing despair as comrades die, forcing them to confront their own vulnerability. One of the most famous sequences in the film occurs with the death of a friend whose leg was amputated. He had been very proud of the special boots he owned and leaves them to his surviving friends. Milestone uses a montage sequence that shows the vulnerability of the young men by following the deadly trajectory in the ownership of the boots as each new recipient dies, one while marching, another while firing in the trenches.[8]

The scenes of war are still outstanding. The night attacks and the hand-to-hand combats that extend to the trenches are harrowing. Of particular note is the way Milestone cuts between panning shots of the attacking forces and static shots of a firing machine gun. Robert Baird suggests: "Milestone joins the clackety mechanization of cinema (camera/projector) to the mechanization of the machine gun, the success of the mechanical camera panning/projecting ironically critiquing the ease of machine-gun panning—a horrible harmony of form with content."[9] Equally impressive are the moving crane shots of the men in the trenches intercut with shots of the approaching enemy on land. Milestone used a huge crane to traverse the battlefield as he tracked with the moving soldiers. A picture of this equipment was featured prominently in the souvenir program, in which one reads: "a giant crane, weighing 280 tons, carrying cameras and sound equipment, was used to give absolute realism in sight and sound to the making of the great scenes." While the weight stated for the crane seems highly improbable, the reference to "realism" is reminiscent of the interest in this topic mentioned in Chapter 2. In the first major attack, he shortens the length of each shot and accelerates the rhythm of the editing. An indelible image of battle, which never fails to unsettle first-time viewers, is a brief shot of two hands clinging to barbed wire, detached from their dead owner.

Another notable sequence in the film involves the aftermath of hand-to-hand combat after Paul stabs a French soldier who has entered his foxhole. The man takes many hours to die, and Paul experiences the horror of having to watch the man he attacked expire before his eyes. He realizes how they both have been victimized by the war.

As can occur in war films, he has a moment of enlightenment in which he realizes that he and the dying man might even have been friends in a different environment. Milestone shoots this protracted sequence in a way that forces us to observe the face of the dying and then dead man. We cannot turn away, much as we would like to, just as Paul is trapped in the trench with his victim and silent accuser. At times the dying/dead man's face appears to have a smile, thus accentuating the horror and absurdity of war. A similar disturbing image occurs in Abel Gance's anti-war film *J'Accuse* (1919) when we see a dead soldier buried in dirt with a smiling expression on his face.

## Reception

The laudatory reviews indicate how audiences responded to the film's message. The reviewer for *Variety* praised this "harrowing, gruesome, morbid tale of war." He quotes Paul's diatribe against his school-master's urging young boys to join the army: "'war is dirty, it is death,' and the glory—to hell with the glory of country,'" and suggests that "no one in the audience could help but endorse that sentiment, for those before the screen had endured with the German soldiers all of their horrors, frights, amputations, privations and deaths." The reviewer acknowledges the film's technical achievements in an impassioned description, almost as if he were at the front: "And the shells come hurtling over, the incessant noise, louder and hotter now and again, but always there; always war, and that running explosion of a ground set of torpedoes that blew everybody and everything to bits as it progressed. It's all here and it's all war."[10] Mordaunt Hall of the *New York Times* also praised the sound in a way that should remind us how new this total experience of war on film was for viewers in 1930. Although sound effects were added to the New York showing of *Wings* at the Criterion Theater three years before, it was only the spectators at such road show venues who had the privilege of experiencing sounds accompanying the images of war. Hall connects the realism of *All Quiet*'s scenes to the filming of real war:

> Often the scenes are of such excellence that if they were not audible one might believe that they were actual motion pictures of activities behind the lines, in the trenches and No Man's Land. . . . In looking at a dugout one readily imagines a long line of such earthly abodes. When shells demol-ish these underground quarters, the shrieks of fear, coupled with the

rat-tat-tat of machine guns, the bang-ziz of the trench mortars, and the whining of shells, it tells the terrors of fighting better than anything else so far has done in animated photography coupled with the microphone.[11]

Given Milestone's experiences with the Photographic Division of the Signal Corps during the war, Hall's praise indicates the success of the director in transferring his knowledge from one venue to another. It also speaks to the skillfulness of Arthur Edeson, the noted German photographer.

Interestingly, while the film focused entirely on the devastating effects of war on German soldiers, its message was clearly interpretable in human terms in regard to all soldiers and the universality of the suffering it causes. Obviously, its successful box office results indicated that American audiences responded to the agonies faced by everyone in war. Even though its treatment of the Germans is sympathetic, and various scenes were cut or trimmed to be less critical of aspects of the German military, the film was eventually banned there.[12] In contrast, a German anti-war film, *Westfront 1918*, was shown in the United States without incident. Released in June 1930, it focuses on a number of young men whose lives are disrupted and ultimately destroyed by the war. A young student dies soon after his sexual initiation; a soldier on leave discovers his wife has been unfaithful; a lieutenant unable to withstand the pressures of war loses his mind.

## All Quiet *and Remakes of War Films*

*All Quiet* is the only film receiving detailed attention in a separate chapter in this book to have been remade.[13] The film was redone in 1979 as a made-for-television movie starring Richard Thomas as Paul and Ernest Borgnine as Kat. Thomas at the time was famous for having played the youthful John Boy on *The Waltons* from 1972 to 1978. Choosing a star who embodies an innocence similar to that evinced by Lew Ayres has the effect of underscoring the awful effects of war. It premiered on November 14, shortly after Armistice Day, and was given a theatrical release in England but not in the United States. Directed by Delbert Mann, the film won both a Golden Globe for best motion picture made for television and two Emmy awards for editing.

The film reworks many of the original's elements, although the Himmelstoss character (Ian Holm) is not the former postman. Paul's death is caused by paying attention to a bird, rather than a butterfly.

The film presents him as a potential artist, who is seen earlier sketching a bird he sees out the window from his classroom rather than paying attention to the lesson. While it received a minimum amount of attention in the press, one comment from an English reviewer in the magazine *Time Out* is relevant. He criticizes the substitution of the bird, seeing it as part of an attempt to make the film more relevant to its current time:

> A horrible instance of international packaging . . . that has all the excitement of a financial balance sheet. Remarque's classic novel resists the attempts, signposted by the American presence of Thomas and Borgnine in the World War I German trenches, to make it "relevant" to post-Vietnam. The desperate substitution of a twittering bird for the famous butterfly at the climax marks the extent to which the 1930 version remains a Milestone around director Delbert Mann's neck.[14]

Released one year after the major Vietnam films mentioned in chapter 1, the film thus becomes for that reviewer a sign of Americans' lingering negative reaction to that war. One could add to the objection to the bird the suggestion by Thomas Schatz that the film "traces a harrowing descent . . . into the depths of Paul's own psyche. . . . His disillusion deepens until the film's final moment, when Paul reaches out to touch a butterfly and is killed by a sniper's bullet." That is, in effect the scene provides evidence about what Schatz earlier observes regarding "Paul's own character as he comes to appreciate the value and beauty of life, even among the carnage of trench warfare."[15] In fairness to the remake, though, one could add that in both cases, Paul's interest in a living creature suggests how desperately he is trying to escape the carnage of death.

Only four other major films about World War I have been remade. The first is *The Four Horsemen of the Apocalypse*, redone by Vincente Minnelli in 1962 as a film updated to cover World War II. John Ford, already famous for his films about World War II such as *The Battle of Midway* (1942) and *They Were Expendable* (1945), kept the World War I setting of Walsh's *What Price Glory?* in his 1952 remake. Howard Hawks' *The Dawn Patrol* (1930) was remade by Edmund Goulding in 1938, with a script by its original writer, John Monk Saunders, the author of *Wings*. While they retained the basic plot of the original, an examination of the pressures faced by air squadron commanders during World War I forced to send out pilots to certain death, the foreword added to the remake is significant:

Today, when ominous rumblings of war echo throughout the world again, this story of the last great war is especially significant. On the Western front in 1915, Britain's Royal Flying Corps found itself engaged in a desperate struggle for existence against an enemy of superior size, strength and experience. At that time, the Royal Flying Corps had little except magnificent courage and a grim determination to do its job.[16]

Certainly, Warner Bros.' decision to remake a film to which it already owned the rights was understandable financially. In addition, more money was saved in the production itself. As noted in the entry on the film in the American Film Institute Catalog: "Extensive aerial footage and exterior shots from the Hawks film were used in the 1938 remake. According to memos in the Warner Bros. files on the film, scenes were planned around the 1930 footage to minimize production expenses." More important than the economic aspects, though, is the shift in the film's message. Given Warner Bros.' early opposition to Germany and the studio heads' well-founded concerns about the rise of Nazism, it is important to see how the remake deals with Von Richter, the German ace who is the chief antagonist. In the original, he survives and is given a somewhat ennobling gesture at the end of the film; having shot down the hero, he nonetheless displays some humanity in acknowledging the power of his opponent. But in the remake, Von Richter himself is shot down. Thus the remake serves as a way to draw on the earlier film's scenes but also to reiterate negative images of the German military. Therefore, the remake is relevant, given our continuing interest in seeing how films about the past speak to the present.[17]

The following year, Warner Bros. would release the first film from a major studio warning about the rise of German power, *Confessions of a Nazi Spy* (1939). Edward G. Robinson plays Edward Renard, who successfully leads an FBI investigation that results in the exposure and conviction of a number of Nazi agents in the United States. Germany's protests against the decision to make and release the film included direct appeals to the Production Code Administration. According to Michael E. Birdwell, having failed to stop its release, "Nazi authorities banned the film throughout their occupied territories and tried to suppress its release elsewhere, including Latin America."[18] Germany's banning of the film on this scale served as a grim reminder of its earlier suppression of *All Quiet on the Western Front*.

The other important remake of a World War I film is the 1957 version of *A Farewell to Arms*, which revisits the 1932 version by Frank Borzage of Ernest Hemingway's novel. The remake was given a lavish production by David O. Selznick, who starred his wife Jennifer Jones and the immensely popular star Rock Hudson in the roles originally played by Helen Hayes and Gary Cooper. Here, though, there seems to be no ideological agenda at work. Rather, the film served as yet another vehicle for Selznick to promote Jones, even to the point of having the script rework the novel's treatment of the love story.[19]

Remakes of World War II films include Fred Zinnemann's *From Here to Eternity* (1953), which became a 360-minute television miniseries in 1979 with Natalie Wood and William Devane. *The Thin Red Line* (1964), Andrew Marton's film of another James Jones novel, was remade in 1998 by Terrence Malick, but the latter is more a new adaptation rather than a return to the original film.

# CHAPTER 4

## *DESTINATION TOKYO* (1943) AND RETALIATION FILMS

The deadly attack on the United States by Al Qaeda on September 11, 2001 offers us a grim perspective for trying to empathize with the sense of violation and outrage Americans experienced when the Japanese bombed Pearl Harbor on December 7, 1941, killing over 2,400 sailors, Marines, and civilians. Declarations of war against Japan, Germany, and Italy followed the attack on Pearl Harbor, plunging the United States into World War II. The Japanese quickly scored other victories in the Pacific at Wake Island, Bataan, and Corregidor. While an American bombing attack on Tokyo in April 1942 did not harm Japan militarily, it provided enormous psychological encouragement to beleaguered Americans. A more substantive boost to morale occurred when the victory at the Battle of Midway in June 1942 proved clearly that America had successfully begun to reclaim the Pacific. As discussed in Chapter 1's historical overview, Hollywood's response to World War II included several kinds of war films: combat, home front, service comedies, and musicals. The emphasis of this chapter is on how Hollywood's treatment of the attack on Pearl Harbor and its aftermath led to a cycle or sub-genre of retaliation films. These works deal with the short- and long-range effects of Pearl Harbor on men and women in various branches of the armed forces in the Pacific theater.

While some of the directors of the retaliation films such as Edward Dmytryk, Howard Hawks, and Lewis Milestone had previously made war films, several were more associated with other genres such as gangster films (Mervyn LeRoy), musicals (Mark Sandrich), and westerns (Richard Thorpe). *Destination Tokyo*, the primary focus of this chapter, was the first film of any kind directed by Delmer Daves (1904–1977), by that time a noted writer. He would go on to make several war films: *Hollywood Canteen* (1944), a musical review about the USO; *The Very Thought of You* (1944), about wartime romances; *Pride of the Marines* (1945), based on the true story of Al Schmidt, a Marine blinded in battle; *Task Force* (1949), about a naval commander advancing the role of aircraft carriers; and *Kings Go Forth* (1958), about a romantic triangle set in wartime France. *Destination Tokyo* was one of the most important films made during World War II, given its position in the retaliation cycle of films about Pearl Harbor. The actions of the men on the submarine the *USS Copperfin* make possible the first air strike by the United States against Japan, the bombing of Tokyo on April 18, 1942. Some of the actions depicted in the film, even if not historically accurate, extend and complement the narrative and propagandistic aims of a number of important war films made between 1942 and 1945.

## Plot and Conventions

The film begins by showing the United States Capitol and then a shot of the typing of a top secret coded message with information about the submarine *USS Copperfin*'s orders. Then the film switches to shots of equipment and weapons being loaded on the ship in San Francisco, the introduction of some of the crew, and most importantly, of Captain Cassidy (Cary Grant). Daves cuts from the captain delivering a short speech to shots of various attentive and enthusiastic auditors whose expressions indicate their respect for him. Early scenes give a sense of shipboard life and the camaraderie among the men: joking, singing Christmas carols, and talking about religion, life back home, family, and girls. The men play a trick on Wolf (John Garfield), the boastful womanizer on board, by sending a false report over the intercom about him being wanted for his behavior in the last port. Cookie (Alan Hale), dressed up as Santa Claus, delivers presents. The men give him a set of new knives. Other principal characters include a young boy, Tommy (Robert Hutton), the pharmacist's mate, Pills (William Prince), and the machinist, Tin Can (Dane Clark).

Scenes of increasing tension occur, often in connection with the display of various genre conventions. Early, the inexperienced Tommy sights what he thinks is an enemy aircraft. While this turns out to be a false alarm (it was only a bird), the scene nonetheless allows Daves to show how the captain responds to external threats by submerging, one of the staples in submarine films. Key events early in the film include the men learning their destination and orders, and picking up a meteorologist who will be conducting a survey of the Tokyo Bay. When the ship is attacked by Japanese planes, the crew experiences its first casualty when Mike, a kindly older sailor, is brutally murdered by a downed Japanese pilot whom he was trying to help out of the water. His death is followed by a mournful funeral and burial at sea as his flag-draped coffin is put in the water.

Then the men have to deal with the aftermath of the attack: defusing a bomb lodged in the ship. Because he is so thin, Tommy is able to crawl under the deck and remove the firing pin. Increasing tension comes when the ship enters Tokyo Bay by following underneath a Japanese ship through the aquatic mine fields. The meteorologist, radio man,

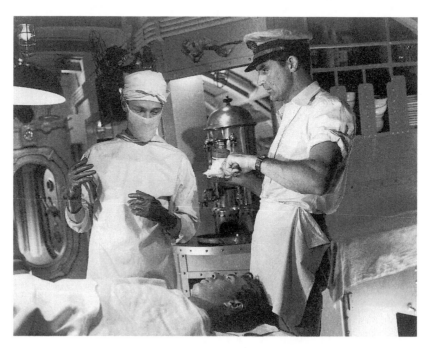

**PLATE 10** *Destination Tokyo* (Delmer Daves, 1943). Pills (William Prince) about to operate on Tommy (Robert Hutton) as Captain Cassidy (Cary Grant) looks on (Warner Bros./Courtesy Larry Edmunds Bookshop).

and Wolf go ashore and gather information needed for the eventual bombing raid. Tommy develops acute appendicitis and needs surgery. Although not a doctor, Pills successfully performs the operation (using Cookie's gift knives). He not only saves Tommy's life, but he also experiences a conversion from his former skepticism about religion. The last part of the film shows the sub leaving Tokyo Bay, wracked by the numerous depth charges that cause dangerous leaks and threaten the sub. It survives the attacks and successfully launches a torpedo that destroys the enemy ship pursuing it. This section also includes brief scenes of the bombing raid on Tokyo. The men happily return to San Francisco and contemplate what they will do on leave. The film ends as the captain sees his wife and children at the dock.

The film goes beyond presenting a conventional seasoned, older, kindly figure by actually sharing this function with two characters. Cookie, like Kat in *All Quiet*, is a matronly source of food and good humor. Before receiving his Christmas gift, he asks: "Who practically mothers all the guys on this ship?" Mike, who is killed, offers fatherly support. The latter has the bunk below Tommy, who feels particularly guilty at not having done enough to save him. Earlier, they talk about religion, a key concept that will figure in the film's tense operation scene. This begins with Tommy praying before going under the anesthetic and concludes with him waking up saying the last part of the Lord's Prayer.

Tommy is more than just an inexperienced youth. His naivety appears obvious in his lack of knowledge about women, his immature appearance (he only needs to shave twice a week), and his boyishness (the captain constantly refers to him as "son"). Because he is so slender (one of his other names is Slim), he can slide into the area where the bomb has fallen and save the crew from an explosion. The scene in which the crew members wait to hear if Tommy has successfully defused the bomb is matched later on with a rhyming sequence when Tommy undergoes emergency surgery. There is another period of anxious waiting, registered by numerous close-ups, and questions on how long it has been. The second scene plays like a birth scene from a different film, as if the men were waiting to hear about the delivery of a baby, which, in a way, Tommy still is.

In contrast, Wolf, the womanizing ladies' man, is appropriately named. He constantly boasts about his sexual exploits, emphasized by the female doll he has brought on board, the long story about visiting a woman whose name he gets at random from the phone book, and his recounting of a successful pickup of a woman outside a lingerie shop. But the latter event, shown as a flashback while he narrates, seems to be more a figment of his imagination, since the height of the woman we see does not square with his description of her to the men.[1]

Women and children play a role, even if hardly visible. There are photographs of loved ones, the fantasy figure in Wolf's story, a scene imagined by the captain of what his wife and children are doing back home as he writes them a letter, and their appearance at the film's end. One of the film's poignant moments occurs when grieving crew members listen to a record that Mike has been playing. On it his wife's voice is heard talking about how she and the children want him home. Cassidy explains to the men that the biggest event in his life the previous year was taking his son to the barber for his first haircut and the boy's telling those in the shop that Cassidy was his daddy. The scene appears later as a momentary flashback in the captain's mind during the incessant attacks of the depth charges. But ideologically, the role of children is important here, for their innocence contrasts with what Cassidy identifies as the pattern of development in Japanese youth. He says they learn how to use weapons early in their lives; some of the girls are turned into prostitutes.

This utterly negative conception of the Japanese is consistent with the demonization of them throughout the film, conveyed most vividly in the treachery of the pilot who stabs the kindly Mike literally in the back. Some of the language is surprisingly strong. As Cookie fishes for salmon in the Aleutian waters while the crew awaits a plane, he says he'd like to hook a fish with a "Jap" in it, and then have "fried Jap with tartar sauce." His companion says he'd rather have his "boiled in oil." Such uncompromisingly negative comments on the enemy in war films would be tempered as the conflict drew to a close, but only to an extent, since the same kind of hostile terminology appears in *Objective, Burma!* and *God Is My Co-Pilot*, which both appeared in the last months of the war in 1945.

Submarine films have a unique mise-en-scène, and *Destination Tokyo* is no exception. The interior spaces are uniformly cramped and produce a claustrophobic sense. Stairways lead somewhere up or down; we are never exactly sure where. Corridors are narrow. There are more shots of ceiling structures here than in *Citizen Kane*, given the way Daves constantly makes us aware of how vulnerable the men are to leaks from above them in the cabins. The appearance of the sleeping quarters clearly delineates the differences in rank: even though private, the captain's are small; the crew members share a large public space with bunks. Eating areas are always crowded with men packed tightly at the tables. Daves frames his shots for the maximum effect in giving a sense of claustrophobic

**PLATE 11** *Destination Tokyo* (Delmer Daves, 1943). The cramped mise-en-scène of the submarine. Wolf (John Garfield) and Tin Can (Dane Clark) are in front (Warner Bros./Courtesy Photofest).

space by using a number of close-ups and close shots that cramp the men together, thus underscoring not only the limited space but their close bonding and brotherhood.

Various mechanical activities are routinely presented in this film. Following directions from the captain or second in command, the sub can surface or submerge, the latter usually punctuated with shots of the depth dial. At the point of submerging, men outside the ship scramble down the hatch, which is then closed. Attacks by ships take two forms: torpedoes, which are shown being launched and heading in the direction of the sub; or depth charges that are dropped from the attacking ship. As these near the sub, there is always an ominous "ping" from the sonar, indicating the sub's vulnerability. Shots through the periscope of what's up or out there are routine. *Destination Tokyo*'s oscilloscope shots actually generated concern with the military because they appeared to demonstrate too much knowledge on the part of the filmmakers about detecting devices used on the ships. Attacks that partially succeed produce leaks that must be plugged quickly, and flooding, dealt with by bailing. At some points subs sometimes cut their engines, and are in a state of "silent running." At others, they may rest on the bottom of the ocean, as occurs during Tommy's surgery.

## Reception

The film received a warm welcome at the box office, earning $3.2 million, ranking twelfth for 1944.[2] The strong earnings were matched by enthusiastic reviews, such as appeared in *Newsweek*: "Even moviegoers who have developed a severe allergy for service pictures should find [this film] . . . high among the superior pictures of the war. Certainly in technical exposition and sheer, harrowing melodrama, the Warner Brothers' newest tribute to the armed forces rates very near the top of the list."[3] The *Variety* reviewer also puts the film ahead of others: "In a season replete with many war dramas, [the film] is a standout addition. For sheer intensity of melodrama it certainly takes its place with any film to come out of this war." The reviewer treats the cast as if it were a unified fighting unit, rather than merely actors: "Here is a film whose hero is the Stars and Stripes; the performers are merely symbols of that heroism. . . . Cary Grant and John Garfield . . . are no less the stars than the comparatively insignificant character one may find at the bottom of the casting credits. Here is a film fully representative of a wartime Lady Liberty."[4]

The reviewer spoke somewhat cautiously on how much of the film's details were in fact accurate, a view echoed in Bosley Crowther's comments in the *New York Times*: "Mind you, we don't say it's authentic. . . . Mind you, we don't say it's credible; we don't even suggest that it makes sense. But it does make a pippin of a picture, purely from a melodramatic point of view."[5] The issue of authenticity arose because of various aspects of the plot. Though none of these reviews mentioned this specifically, anyone who does the temporal math discovers the glaring narrative-historical disconnect in the plot. The *Copperfin* is leaving San Francisco Bay in December 1942 to gather information to be used in the Doolittle raid on Tokyo. But the raid had *already* occurred in April of that year. There had been newspaper reports of emergency appendectomies on board submarines, but none on a ship that gets into Tokyo Bay. That reconnaissance mission itself is fabricated.[6]

Trade journals joined in the praise. The *Hollywood Reporter* lauded the actors and predicted: "The box office course of 'Destination Tokyo' is truly charted as a dead-center smash."[7] *Motion Picture Daily* noted:

"Tokyo was its destination on celluloid. Box-office business of impressive size is the unquestioned destination of this new package of excitement and wallop from Warners."[8] Both the use of nautical language and the play on the idea of "destination" connect with the studio's plans on how to exploit the film. A lobby card with photographs of Grant and Garfield described the film as "Warner Bros.' explosive story . . . big as the broad Pacific!" The film appeared at a propitious time when scrap metal drives were occurring throughout the nation. One photograph of the drive in a version of the advertising press book for the film contains the motto: "Pitch it! Salvage more in '44—Destination Tokyo."[9] A memorandum in the *Destination Tokyo* file at the Academy of Motion Pictures Arts and Sciences Library advised "a salvage truck tie-in. Every salvage truck that carries scrap metal should be bannered for the month of December with: 'Destination Tokyo.' "[10] Thus the film's announced goal and the patriotic activities of devoted citizens are united.

## Retaliation Films

Some of the actions depicted in the film, even if not historically accurate, extend and complement the narrative and propagandistic aims of a number of important films made between 1942 and 1945, all inflected thematically and narratively by the attack on Pearl Harbor and the need for revenge.[11] The air raid on Tokyo led by Lieutenant Colonel Jimmy Doolittle in April 1942 served as the first successful act of retaliation to which Americans could point since the war had begun. Even if, as appears, it achieved little of significance in inflicting major or devastating damage on Japan, it was nonetheless important for American morale. *Destination Tokyo*, the first film to address the raid, appeared over twenty months later. It would be followed by Lewis Milestone's *The Purple Heart* (March 1944), a drama in which eight surviving members of a bombing crew captured after the Tokyo raid are put through an unfair mock trial in a Japanese courtroom. Though they defend themselves eloquently and demonstrate courage, the film ends with our knowledge that they all will be put to death. The first extended treatment of the preparation for and execution of the raid appeared in late December 1944, in Mervyn LeRoy's *Thirty Seconds Over Tokyo*, based on Ted Lawson's autobiographical account. Spencer Tracy plays Doolittle, and Van Johnson plays Lawson.

A number of war films in the retaliation cycle that appeared after the April 1942 attack on Tokyo do not acknowledge the raid, and, in

**PLATE 12** *The Purple Heart* (Lewis Milestone, 1944). The heroic fliers, now prisoners of war, led by Captain Ross (Dana Andrews) subjected to a mock trial by their Japanese captors (Twentieth Century-Fox Film Corporation).

fact, stress the devastating effects of Pearl Harbor. John Farrow's *Wake Island* (September 1942) showed the annihilation of a force of doomed soldiers and civilians who could not withstand the assault on the island launched by the Japanese immediately following Pearl Harbor. Its opening foreword connects the men with earlier victims of obliterating attacks in American history:

> In this picture the action at Wake Island has been recorded as accurately and factually as possible. However, the names of the characters are fictional and any similarity to the personal characteristics of the officers and men of the detachment is not intended. America and Americans have long been used to victory but the great names of her military history—Valley Forge, Custer's Last Stand, The Lost Battalion—represent the dark hours. There, small groups of men fought savagely to the death because in dying they gave eternal life to the ideas for which they died. Such a group was Marine Fighting Squadron 211 of Marine Aircraft Group 21 and the Wake Detachment of the First Defense Battalion, United States Marine Corps, the units which comprised the garrison at Wake Island.

The characters include two soldiers who are friendly rivals, Joe Doyle (Robert Preston) and Smacksie Randall (William Bendix); men who are at odds with one another because of disagreements about how to secure the island, Major Caton (Brian Donleavy) and a civilian, Shad McClosky (Albert Dekker); and various others who all display courage in the face of certain defeat. There is also a company dog, who has puppies. One of the most poignant scenes in the film is a simple burial of a fallen pilot. Except for a few soldiers who manage to fly to safety, everyone else dies trying to defend the island, the last a radio operator who is gunned down as he tries to signal. The film received Academy Award nominations for Best Picture, Best Director, Best Supporting Actor (Bendix), and script. According to the American Film Institute catalog, at one of the theaters in which the films premiered in Los Angeles, "forty marine recruits were sworn into service onstage." It had the eighth highest box-office gross in 1942, earning $3.5 million.[12]

One of the greatest World War II films, Howard Hawks' *Air Force* (March 1943), follows the crew of a B-17 bomber, the *Mary Ann*, as it flies from San Francisco to Pearl Harbor on December 6, 1941. The pilot, Irish Quincannon (John Ridgely), has earlier tangled with the gunner, Joe Winocki (John Garfield), but they put their differences aside in the course of their flights. Unable to land at Pearl Harbor, they go to Maui, and then to Wake Island. There they take on a dog that belonged to the remaining Marines, and proceed to Manila, where they arm themselves in order to fly to Australia. Even though they have been witnesses to one scene of defeat after another, and are distraught because of the death of their captain, nonetheless their reports are instrumental in leading to an attack on Japanese ships. Here again, the printed matter that supplements the film is worth noting. It begins by quoting Abraham Lincoln speaking about the Civil War as a means to praise the heroes of the present war:

> It is for us the living . . . to be dedicated here to the unfinished work which they who fought here have thus far so nobly advanced. . . . It is . . . for us to be here dedicated to the great task remaining before us . . . that this nation, under God, shall have a new birth of freedom and that government of the people, by the people, for the people, shall not perish from the earth.

The film's narrative ending is followed by a promise of victory: "This story has a conclusion but not an end—for its real end will be the victory for which Americans—on land, on sea and in the air—have fought, are fighting now and will continue to fight until peace has been won."

MGM's *Bataan* (June 1943) goes even farther than *Wake Island* in showing the defeat and eradication of a group of overmatched soldiers. Jeanine Basinger's discussion of its conventions and generic integrity is essential reading. She uses it as a model of the genre in regard to its "democratic ethnic mix," as appears in Plate 13, which shows the men listening to a radio that's playing music from home, a common convention of war films. She also connects it with the generic pattern present in *The Lost Patrol* (1934), which follows the near-total destruction of a group of soldiers.[13] What is particularly important to grasp is how this film deals with defeat by promising victory. At the end, after all the men in the totally representative squad have been killed (Polish, African American, Jew, Filipino, Hispanic, old man, kid, WASPs), the doomed sole survivor, Sergeant Bill Dane (Robert Taylor), shoots a machine gun at the Japanese from within his foxhole, which is also going to be his grave. But the negativity of the narrative

**PLATE 13** *Bataan* (Tay Garnett, 1943). The doomed men listen to the radio. Sergeant Bill Dane (Robert Taylor) is third from the right (MGM/Courtesy Photofest).

ending is counteracted by both the foreword and the concluding titles. The film begins with a dedication:

> When Japan struck, our desperate need was time—time to marshal our new armies. Ninety-six priceless days were bought for us—with their lives—by the defenders of Bataan, the Philippine army which formed the bulk of MacArthur's infantry fighting shoulder to shoulder with Americans. To those immortal dead, who heroically stayed the wave of barbaric conquest, this picture is reverently dedicated.

It ends by praising the dead: "So fought the heroes of Bataan. Their sacrifice made possible our victories in the Coral and Bismarck Seas, at Midway, on New Guinea and Guadalcanal. Their spirit will lead us back to Bataan!"

These important references to the later victories foreground the issue I'm working with here. Even though Bataan had been the site of a terrible loss, it still contributed to a legacy of victories that had occurred by the time of the film's release. The present successes enumerated in the closing words provide a historical rationale and justification for seeing what appears to be a defeat as an enabling step in permitting documentable victories. That is, the film plays with time in a complex manner. It shows a negative past that has made a positive present possible, one that can be appreciated by contemporary viewers.[14]

Made shortly after at MGM, Richard Thorpe's Cry "Havoc" (November 1943) deals with Bataan from the perspective of nurses (actual and volunteer) working at the hospital, which is twice bombed by the Japanese. An egregious atrocity is inflicted on them when a Japanese plane strafes and kills Connie (Ella Raines) as she swims in a pond. As the nurses lament her loss, one says dispiritedly, "We can't win." But Pat (Ann Southern) responds, "We can't lose" and pulls out a map she has been given by an officer. She spreads it on the table, and Thorpe uses two close-ups of her hand on the map as she explains the course of the Japanese attack thus far. It began in Luzon, and she says they intended to take Bataan quickly as they proceeded to the Philippines. Once that fell, they would take New Guinea, the Solomons, Wake, Midway, and then the next step, California. But instead of overwhelming Bataan in two weeks, as they had planned, the battle has taken them two months and the resistance they encountered has forced them to use 200,000 soldiers, significantly affecting their original timetable. "We just didn't like the idea of them marching through so easily. . . . Our boys stopped them." Then she asserts: "We're winning the war." She admits that the nurses probably won't survive, and then repeats: "We're winning the war, that's all." The claim made in the concluding written scroll of *Bataan* is here presented dramatically by having a character boast of how their courage has delayed the Japanese plans. But those in the audience watching the women go out at the end with their hands up, following the orders of their Japanese captors, know that, except for Wake Island, the sites mentioned by Pat did not in fact fall. All contributed in 1942 to the establishment of American supremacy in the Pacific. Even though there is personal defeat for them—"We don't have a chance"— they know they have helped contribute to the country's victory.

Mark Sandrich's *So Proudly We Hail!* (September 1943) was another high-grossing film, earning $3 million.[15] It also depicts the harrowing trials faced by nurses displaced by the attack. Presented as a flashback, it begins before Pearl Harbor on a ship carrying nurses to Hawaii. Like the crew of the *Mary Ann*, they too have to go to different locations than they were intending. After the attack, they are taken to Bataan, and from there to Corregidor, from which place the survivors eventually are able to get to Australia. They suffer grievous personal losses, and one, Olivia D'Arcy (Veronica Lake), blows herself up with a grenade in order to kill Japanese and save her companions. Like *Bataan* and *Cry "Havoc"*, it opened after key victories in the Pacific. Thus, once more, audiences were watching a *fictional* film about loss and heroism from a *historical* vantage point that establishes the improved condition of the United States. In fact, the narrative structure of *So Proudly* confirms this ideological purpose. The unusual flashback is initiated when a nurse explains what has happened to their group and to Janet Davidson (Claudette Colbert), the heroine who is now unable to speak or function, having been so traumatized by the war and the fear that she has lost her husband. Once the flashback is concluded, she learns that he is alive, and can begin to speak again. This positive ending supports the pattern of films in the retaliation cycle wherein the negative effects of Pearl Harbor are in a way actually contained by the present, in this case positive word about her husband.

Combat films that follow *Bataan* and *So Proudly* display the effects of the successful fighting made possible by the earlier sacrifices. *Guadalcanal Diary* (November 1943) and *Gung Ho!* (December 1943), one fictional and one factual, both focus on the American victories achieved starting in August 1942. The first is about Marines who succeed in taking the island. It has the conventional melting-pot assemblage of heroic men: the kid, Chicken Anderson (Richard Jaeckel); the Catholic, in this case a priest, Father Donnelly (Preston Foster); the

Hispanic, Soose Alverez (Anthony Quinn); the Brooklynite, Taxi Potts (William Bendix); and the Jew, Sammy Klein (Robert Rose). After initial success in landing, they encounter various setbacks and the deaths of some men.[16] The second concerns Evan Carlson (Randolph Scott), the actual leader of the attack on Makin Island. Here again, the printed material in the foreword helps us see how audiences were being encouraged by positive news: "This is the factual record of the Second Marine Raider Battalion, from its inception seven weeks after Pearl Harbor, through its first brilliant victory." That is, the date of the birth of this immensely successful company is positioned in relation to Pearl Harbor. According to the American Film Institute Catalog, the "group of 210 Marines, later known as 'Carlson's Raiders,' killed 348 of the 350 Japanese soldiers stationed on the island, while suffering only thirty casualties. These raiders further distinguished themselves in various battles during World War II, particularly those at Guadalcanal."[17]

John Ford's Oscar-winning documentary *The Battle of Midway* was released in September 1942, the same month as *Wake Island*. In Technicolor, it presented the victory at Midway Island when the United States reclaimed the site in June 1942, the first major success for the United States since the attack. The first narrative film to treat the victory was *A Wing and a Prayer* (August 1944). But this film about the war in the Pacific and restoring American pride after the attack on Pearl Harbor appeared in a different chronological framework. The war in Europe had taken a definite turn for the better, given the successful D-Day invasion on June 6, 1944.

*Thirty Seconds Over Tokyo* (released November 1944 in New York and December in Los Angeles before wide national distribution) had been in production for several months before and after D-Day. It appeared at a time when American ascendancy in both the Pacific and in Europe had been confirmed in both historical terms and in narrative films. It opened to positive reviews and eventually earned well over $4 million. About one half of the film shows the arduous training the men have to undergo. Their primary challenge is learning how to take off their B-25 bombers from an aircraft carrier that is designed for the launching of smaller fighter planes. In addition, it introduces us to Lawson, his pregnant wife, and their friends. The second part of the film shows the raid, the plane's crash landing, and the rescue of the crew. General Doolittle (Spencer Tracy) is a stern but kind leader. Van Johnson plays Lawson, the real character whose book describing the event appeared in 1943, and was serialized in May and June in *Colliers Magazine*. When their plane crashes in China after the raid, he and his men are rescued by some Chinese. Although all survive, Lawson's leg has to be amputated. The film's national release and distribution coincided roughly with what would be the last major land battle in Europe, the Battle of the Bulge, which lasted from December 16, 1944 into the last week of January 1945. Contemporary viewers would have been aware from newspaper coverage of the progress and eventual victory of the American forces in the battle.

Here's a case where a genre film celebrating retaliation actually becomes the matrix of a number of elements: representing a historical triumph while another transpires in the present, thus extending the narrative work begun a year earlier by *Destination Tokyo*, and compensating for the surface defeat of the pilots captured and tried in *The Purple Heart*. That is, *Thirty Seconds*, the last cinematic word on the raid on Tokyo, is the most positive and supersedes the fates of those caught up in something that hasn't happened yet to the pilots in the temporal reality of the film. Even though some men died in the raid and Lawson lost his leg, audiences were given assurances of victory by the film that in its way corrects and compensates for the deaths of the victims in *The Purple Heart*. It's important to appreciate how genre films provide a fluid continuum in which the historical present and narrative time are capable of permutations, transcending the inevitability of chronology. A film celebrating what was not a tactical victory serves as a vehicle for its audiences who are watching from the vantage point of those who have seen victories in both factual and fictional accounts of the war.

The impact of Pearl Harbor was felt in two more films in 1945. Edward Dmytryk's *Back to Bataan* presents John Wayne as Joe Madden, a courageous soldier involved in restoring the island to the Philippines and in freeing the prisoners of war who survived the notorious death march that transpired after Bataan fell in 1942. General Douglas MacArthur's imminent return thus fulfills his promise to the Philippine people when he left in early 1942. After the war was over, a film that had been in various stages of production since 1942 opened in December, John Ford's *They Were Expendable*. Ironically, six months after the other film in which John Wayne helps reclaim Bataan, here he plays Rusty Ryan, the commander of a torpedo boat caught up in the events immediately preceding and then following Pearl Harbor. The film ends after MacArthur's departure from the Philippines, as Ryan and others leave the area. We realize that the men who remain are surely doomed to imprisonment or death. Thus there's an extraordinary coming full circle. The last major war film of 1945 is about defeat and loss, and stars someone who a few months earlier was leading a successful reversal of the defeat. My only explanation for this treatment by Ford, who had made the important record of the triumph at Midway, is that by this point in the history of the war he wanted to celebrate the heroism of those who survived and continued working for the victory that was ultimately achieved. There's a mournful quality to the ending as the plane carrying Wayne takes off, and the men remaining on the island watch it helplessly. It may seem as if the retaliation cycle has been undermined, strangely after the war is over, by a film that ends with defeat. But possibly one way of processing the meaning of the film is to see it as itself equivalent to the last words of *Bataan*, cited above: "Their sacrifice made possible our victories in the Coral and Bismarck Seas, at Midway, on New Guinea and Guadalcanal. Their spirit will lead us back to Bataan!" Spectators at this point in December 1945 knew in fact that we did go back and win.

So, two trends are apparent in how the retaliatory genre films work with historical reality. On the one hand, we see a withholding of the full treatment of the Tokyo raid until there have already been a number of military victories that confirm the thrust of the raid. On the other, we have the subject matter of Pearl Harbor and its aftermath refusing to go away in *They Were Expendable*, possibly a somber reminder of the inevitability of war. Thomas Schatz's view of genres functioning like myths, cited in the Introduction, seems particularly relevant in this case. They arise as a way of letting a society deal with contradictions, and show us "a society collectively speaking to itself, developing a network of stories and images designed to animate and resolve the conflicts of daily life." "Genre films, much like the folk tales of primitive cultures, serve to defuse threats to the social order and thereby to provide some logical coherence to that order."[18]

Films in this special cycle or sub-genre share certain features. Not all elements appear in every film, but the following are common: a focus on doomed men and women who lose their lives or freedom because of Japanese treachery; various scenes of hopeless last-ditch efforts by individuals who know their efforts may be futile; evidence that those who have died have in fact contributed to the current progress that is known to have occurred historically; particular military actions that signal the possibility of a long-range victory.[19] In this regard, generically the films are distinguishable from later films about Pearl Harbor such as *Tora! Tora! Tora!* (1970) and *Pearl Harbor* (2001). Of course, the last two were made many years after the attack and thus lack the immediacy of those in the cycle. But there's something else. Films in the cycle participate in an interesting movement towards closure and resolution. Those that show the most discouraging defeats, as occurs in *Wake Island* and *Bataan*, position their characters as human beings whose fates call for present action *now*, given the iniquity of the attackers and the unfairness of innocent deaths. The individuals in the fictional narratives represent thousands who died horribly but whose deaths have been or are being revenged in the present historical reality of the viewer. In a curious way, the promise of retaliation for doomed characters comes from the historical conditions of those who are alive to watch the films. And the steady progress in battles mentioned in forewords and conclusions is confirmed by the newspaper and newsreel reports of increasing victories.

As such, the Pearl Harbor retaliation cycle contrasts with what has occurred after 9/11. In a thoughtful assessment of Paul Greengrass' *United 93* (2006) and Oliver Stone's *World Trade Center* (2006), Robert Burgoyne suggests that "both films perform a certain kind of cultural work, reframing trauma as a narrative of heroic agency."[20] But in contrast to 1942–1945, spectators today have experienced no closure at all, no historical reality such as Midway and Guadalcanal to prove that there has been an answer to the attack on 9/11. This may be part of the reason for the lack of interest in films about the Iraq War, since unlike those in the earlier period, the fictional films are not complemented by a historical reality that suggests victory. Ali Jaafar offers a useful suggestion on this issue:

> Today's Iraq films . . . are writing the script as they go along—and with the long-term outcomes as yet unknown, there's no opportunity for a dramatically satisfying epiphany. This may be one of the reasons why most of the Iraq themed films have failed at the US box office. For the fact is that there are no heroes in Iraq, and what these films tend to show is simply that war is hell.[21]

Imagine someone watching *Bataan* in 1943. Even though Bill Dane is about to die, the viewers had the comforting reassurance that other soldiers were still fighting because of Bill Dane's sacrifice and had won some strategic victories. Our situation as of 2009 is like someone watching *Bataan* as if there had been no victories at all. The title of Charles Ferguson's 2007 documentary about the Iraq War is unsettling and accurate: *No End in Sight*. It's interesting to speculate that one reason there were practically no films made about the Vietnam War when it occurred is that it also seemed to have no end in sight. Films in the retaliation cycle could be made because there was evidence that the war would eventually end.

# CHAPTER 5

# PLATOON (1986) AND FULL METAL JACKET (1987)

Changes in narrative patterns and conventions reflect the enormous effect of the Vietnam War on the American public and, in turn, the war film genre. These appear in several stages: (1) the first wave of Vietnam films in the 1970s; (2) the revisionist extraction films of the 1980s; and (3) Oliver Stone's *Platoon* and Stanley Kubrick's *Full Metal Jacket*. These two films reveal the most complex alterations of genre, at times by undermining the conventions of the war film. Going beyond the first wave of Vietnam films of 1978 that demonstrated the inadequacy of the sustaining myths emerging from films about World War II, Stone and Kubrick show uncompromisingly how the Vietnam War made it increasingly impossible to draw on the earlier myths and genre conventions.

## Vietnam and the War Film Genre

As noted, except for *The Green Berets* (1968), no significant films about the Vietnam War appeared during the actual conflict. Those made soon after its conclusion were uniformly critical of it and/or of war itself, as is evident in the documentary *Hearts and Minds* (1974), and four narrative films that were released in 1978: *Go Tell the Spartans, Coming*

*Home*, *The Deer Hunter*, and *The Boys in Company C*. Watching them through the perspective of the narratives, conventions, and values of earlier war films, one sees that the Vietnam films are in a dialectical tension with their generic predecessors. For example, the annihilation of all the Americans at the end of *Wake Island* (1942) and *Bataan* (1943) was bearable because contemporary audiences knew that some progress had been made in winning the war. No such comfort was possible at the end of *Go Tell the Spartans*, since audiences watching in 1978 knew that the human waste achieved nothing. Only one of the American "advisers" in this film about 1964 survives the devastating attack on the base camp. The rest of the advisers, including Major Barker (Burt Lancaster), lie bloodied and naked on the sand. Instead of the positive rehabilitation of physically and emotionally wounded soldiers by family and friends in *The Best Years of Our Lives* (1946) and *Bright Victory* (1951), there is an adulterous affair, a suicidal veteran, and anti-war activism in *Coming Home*. Japanese captives in a mock trail standing up to their captors and asserting principles of freedom in *The Purple Heart* (1944) are replaced by desperate prisoners of war engaged in a murderous game of Russian roulette in *The Deer Hunter*. With few exceptions, the respect we see for officers in *Destination Tokyo* (1943) is missing from *The Boys in Company C*. As indicated in Chapter 1's historical overview, *Apocalypse Now* (1979), released the following year, assails the war by having a madman in charge of military operations.

"Extraction films" like *Missing in Action* (1984) and *Rambo: First Blood, Part II* (1985) show veterans of the conflict returning to reclaim missing prisoners of war. In the first, Chuck Norris's James Braddock, haunted by his own experiences as a POW, rescues those still held by the Vietnamese, even though they deny having any. In the second, Sylvester Stallone's Rambo, a returning veteran imprisoned for his civil crimes in *First Blood* (1982), is released so that he can help the government prove there are no prisoners of war left from the war. He too discovers the opposite and rescues the men. Rambo's famous question, "Do we get to win this time?" can be seen as a kind of tagline for both films since the heroes reclaim the men and the values for which they fought. Generically, these men bear noting as more than just embodiments of right-wing revisionism. As if to signal the effects of the war on the genre, these heroes evoke characters from very different kinds of narrative: the lone courageous cop and the hard-bitten private eye. Clint Eastwood's Harry Callahan in *Dirty Harry* (1971) and *Magnum Force* (1973) has to go around the power structure of authority to solve crimes because those in command are either incompetent or corrupt. The only way Harry can achieve justice is to buck the system. Humphrey Bogart's Sam Spade in *The Maltese Falcon* (1941) and Philip Marlowe in *The Big Sleep* (1946) are similarly hamstrung by having to function in a world of deception, finally succeeding when they penetrate appearances and expose the full nature of the corruption operating in their worlds. Braddock and Rambo are generic brothers of such characters, even without the presence of the duplicitous femmes fatale, because they are constantly being blindsided by powerful figures who want to keep hidden the truth about American prisoners of war. The links to resourceful heroes whose skills are more mental than physical, at least compared to Braddock and Rambo, make these men something more than action figures and, in effect, connect them to the mythic values of their generic brethren.

Such a phenomenon invites consideration of the question of how and why genres are modified over time. Focusing on 1970s films, John G. Cawelti offers a theory of generic transformation in "the western, the detective story, the musical, the domestic comedy." Without including war films, he identifies various kinds of generic transformations that signal "the feeling that not only the traditional genres but the cultural myths they once embodied are no longer adequate to the imaginative needs of our time."[1] His analysis of Roman Polanski's *Chinatown* (1974) focuses on "demythologization," one of the four generic transformations that can occur. The others include "humorous burlesque, evocation of nostalgia . . . and the reaffirmation of myth as myth."[2] Cawelti speaks of "the tendency of genres to exhaust themselves . . . and . . . to the decline of the underlying mythology on which traditional genres have been based since the late nineteenth century."[3] But missing from his analysis is any suggestion about specific external historical causes that might account for the generic transformations that occur when particular myths can no longer be sustained by the genres that previously served them.[4]

Even more surprisingly, he doesn't mention the Vietnam War in his commentary on *Chinatown*. Its genre and complicated plot make it seem about as far removed as possible from the war, which finally concluded in 1973. Yet the murky lack of stability and utter confusion between appearance and reality in *Chinatown* replicates the United States' experience in Vietnam, where you could not tell your enemy from your ally. Some critics suggest that the film can be viewed as an allegory about the war.[5] Even if taken as a metaphorical treatment rather than as a partial allegory about the United States' failure in Vietnam, *Chinatown* still fits into a cultural context inflected by other relevant contemporary events, specifically Watergate and the disruption of the American government, climaxing in the resignation of Richard Nixon. Films respond to and reflect the particular historical pressures occurring when they are created. It is not that genres get exhausted so much as that historical events make it increasingly difficult and problematic for a genre to continue offering the kinds of expected narratives and conventions that previously sustained audiences.

Thomas Doherty has suggested the war itself was perceived in largely cinematic terms. Initial reluctance to film it occurred because "it was a lousy narrative with a vague beginning, an ungainly middle, and no end in sight."[6] When films do begin to get made about it, "Assuming the motion picture past as shared background and prime mover, the Vietnam film set about defacing the classical Hollywood picture. It found no larger purpose in war, ripped apart the union of the combat squad, and turned within to confront the true enemy. The Warner Bros. platoon killed the Nazis; Oliver Stone's *Platoon* killed each other."[7] Vietnam changed the nature of the war film genre. The Korean War may have been inconclusive, but filmmakers could still present characters, no matter how hardened, who connected to their forebears in World War II films. Treatments of that conflict during and after Vietnam show some of its effects on the genre, as occurs for example, in choosing to make a film about a complex hero like Patton, whose own moral ambiguities connect with Vietnam, or one about a disastrous Allied failure in Holland. As noted, the one major exception to this is *The Big Red One* (1980), an uncompromisingly positive revisiting of World War II by a veteran of that conflict. Sam Fuller, who presents a highly autobiographical account of heroism and sacrifice based on his own experiences, wanted to make a Vietnam War film that would unambiguously expose its mistakes and awful failures.

## Platoon

The first film ever made by Oliver Stone (b. 1946) was a short, *Last Year in Vietnam* (1971), in which he plays an isolated, disillusioned veteran living in New York. Scenes alternate between examples of his brooding despair and shots of a jungle. It concludes as he throws his medals and framed commendation into the river. A Vietnam veteran and recipient of the Bronze Star and Purple Heart, Stone revisited the war in *Platoon*, the third highest grossing film in 1986, which won four Oscars, including Best Picture and Best Director.[8]

*Platoon* tells the story of Chris Taylor (Charlie Sheen), like Stone, a young man who left college to join the army as an infantryman. The film opens as the inexperienced youth arrives in a combat zone, disgorged with other soldiers from an immense transport plane. The platoon's first night patrol constitutes Taylor's initiation into war and establishes the structural pattern for the rest of the film. Each patrol will provide him increased opportunities to learn about the war, and, ultimately, himself. The first serves as a lesson in not carrying too much gear and introduces him to Staff Sgt. Barnes (Tom Berenger) and Sgt. Elias (Willem Dafoe), who will become his symbolic guides to manhood. Earlier war films have accustomed us to tough sergeants like Sgt. Zack in *The Steel Helmet* (1951). Such men combine con- tradictory qualities of warmth and flintiness. Stone's sergeants are polar opposites, and represent a splitting of the generic figure in two, although he does this in a complex manner. Both are excellent strategists. Although Barnes feels for his men, he is ruthless, uncom- promising, and capable of the cold-blooded murder of innocents. Elias, who also cares about the platoon, has ceased to believe in the war, and knows it will be lost. It is as if Stone's practice here illustrates Cawelti's concept of demythologization by saying that this war makes it practically impossible to have the kind of sergeant we are used to from earlier war films. Hence, he splits the characteristics of warmth and toughness.

The night patrol is followed by a daytime helicopter landing in a new combat area and our introduction to a number of men in the platoon, many of them African Americans. On the next night patrol, Stone intensifies the dangers. Taylor is wounded, a soldier he has just met is killed, and Barnes' rough nature is displayed more pointedly, especially as he tells the dying soldier to "Take the pain" and advises the sur- vivors to "take a good look at this lump of shit," the corpse. In this he is reminiscent of Sgt. Zack, whose response to the death of a soldier from a booby trap is similar: "A dead man's nothing but a corpse." But there is a major difference, in that Zack has another, more humane side, evidenced in his growing affection for Short Round. On his return from the hospital, Chris is introduced to another dimension of the platoon when he visits Elias's compound, and enters a virtual lair with red, lurid colors and warm bonding among the men who sing and dance with each other, play Motown music, and smoke pot. Stone moves from this site of sensuality to that associated with Barnes, where his supporters play poker, drink beer, and listen to country music. By crosscutt- ing between the camps, Stone underscores the differences between the leaders and the inevitability of the tensions that will develop between them and their respective supporters.

The next patrol intensifies the violence. One soldier loses his arms when a booby trap explodes, and another is viciously murdered and nailed to a tree. In a vengeful mood, the platoon enters a village thought to be inhabited by VC sympathizers, and, violently angry because of the murder, terrorizes the people. Bunny, one of Barnes' men, murders a retarded youth by dashing his brains out with a rifle. The massacre extends to a woman whom Barnes shoots in cold blood when she won't stop talking. As Barnes threatens to shoot a little girl unless her father provides information about the VC, Elias breaks up the awful scene and fights with Barnes, thus initiating the inevitable conflict that will lead to Barnes' murder of Elias. This sequence evokes the infamous My-Lai massacre in which over 300 Vietnamese villagers were murdered by an infantry division led by Lt. William Calley. Thus far in the film, Stone gives us voice-over commentary by Taylor as we hear what he has been writing his grandmother. The last such utterance occurs after the massacre, when he tells her about the "civil war in the platoon" and says, "I can't believe we're fighting each other when we should be fighting them."

**PLATE 14** *Platoon* (Oliver Stone, 1986). Sergeant Barnes (Tom Berenger) about to shoot an unarmed woman (Cinema 86 Hemdale Corp./ Courtesy Photofest).

The next patrol is the most deadly so far, a tactical disaster because of the inept leadership of the lieutenant whose stupidity leads the platoon into the middle of a crossfire. Here as before in the patrols, Stone makes it difficult to make out what is happening narratively in terms of the opposition and defense, and spatially in terms of where we are at any given point. This is an important technical variation in how the genre has presented battles. Roger Ebert explains this brilliant strategy by suggesting Stone

> abandoned the choreography that is standard in almost all war movies. He abandoned any attempt to make it clear where the various forces were in relation to each other, so that we never know where "our" side stands and where "they" are. Instead of battle scenes in which lines are clearly drawn, his combat scenes involve 360 degrees: Any shot might be aimed at friend or enemy, and in the desperate rush of combat, many of his soldiers never have a clear idea of exactly who they are shooting at, or why.[9]

Having provided the most disorienting battle photography thus far along the lines identified by Ebert, Stone then reverts to the most traditional kind of cutting pattern to build to the climax of Elias' confrontation with Barnes. Stone tracks from left to right, rapidly following Elias through the densely overgrown trees, and then cuts to Barnes and tracks from right to left with him as he works his way ahead. The crosscutting intensifies, building to increasingly tight close-ups of the faces of both men before Barnes murders Elias in cold blood, just as he had shot the woman earlier. This traditional pattern of cutting and tracking not only departs from the operative mode of the film's battle choreography, to use Ebert's term. It also recalls the editing pattern associated with the western genre and the final showdown between the good guy and the bad guy, except in the fractured world of this film, the bad guy triumphs.

Barnes lies to Taylor, telling him that Elias is dead because of the VC, but his complicity in the murder becomes apparent when they spot the still-alive Elias from a helicopter taking them back to base. As many have suggested, the image of his death with outstretched hands evokes images of Christ's crucifixion. A tense confrontation occurs that night between Barnes, Taylor, and Elias' supporters. Just as Bunny had earlier suggested murdering Elias by fragging him using a grenade to kill, Taylor voices the same idea about Barnes, who overhears this. He fights with Taylor and cuts his face. The mounting tensions erupt in the final battle of the film, in which chaos dominates. Many of the platoon are

**PLATE 15** *Platoon* (Oliver Stone, 1986). Chris Taylor (Charlie Sheen) before he finds and shoots Barnes (Cinema 86 Hemdale Corp./Courtesy Photofest).

killed, and fire power called in by the US commander blasts the forest where the battle occurs just as Barnes is about to murder Taylor. He in turn kills Barnes the next morning, after the latter says, "Do it." Wounded once more, Taylor can now leave Vietnam forever. As the helicopter carries him away, he reflects on how they had not been fighting the enemy since the enemy was in them. In the moral economy of the film, Elias and Barnes have been fighting with each other as well as for Taylor's soul.

Here Stone reworks another convention of the war film genre by taking to a different level and register the usual trajectory that follows an inexperienced youth who becomes tough and wise. Taylor absorbs both the positive and negative elements of his mentors: the nobility of Elias and the murderousness of Barnes. As Susan Jeffords has observed:

> By killing Barnes, Taylor ends the film, not in the position of the masculine *or* the feminine, but in both . . . while Taylor incorporates Elias's femininity and attitude toward the war into his final character, he uses Barnes's methods to do so. . . . He must become Barnes—the masculine—in order to successfully create a space in which he can be "born" as the masculine/feminine child.[10]

Taylor's unrelieved weeping at the end suggests what a torturous effect this assimilation of contradictory personalities has had on him.

The pressure of the Vietnam War on the genre appears in other aspects of the film as well. We have seen innocent children die before: Short Round who is killed off screen in *The Steel Helmet*, and the Holocaust victim who dies before our eyes as the sergeant carries him in *The Big Red One*. But we have never watched a youth getting his brains beat out. Thankfully, Stone refrains from an actual shot of the impact of the rifle on the retarded boy's head, but he does show the blood that splatters up as it hits the faces of Bunny, the killer, and Taylor. Others before Stone had pushed the limits in showing violence in Vietnam War films, most notably Michael Cimino in the bloody Russian roulette game imposed on prisoners of war who are forced to play it. But Stone goes farther than anyone in demonstrating the full extent of the evil results of war by focusing on the helpless and innocent youth. After the shots of the blood on the faces of the soldiers, Stone cuts to a pathetic older woman (his mother?) who is immobile, paralyzed with horror.[11]

Rape is another issue treated uncompromisingly that had not received such foregrounding in this way in the genre. Scenes of rape had appeared in Vittorio DeSica's *Two Women* (1960), for which Sophia Loren won an Oscar as Best Actress, and the lesser known *Town Without Pity* (1961). In the first, Moroccan soldiers rape a mother and her 13-year-old daughter who are caught in the chaos of the occupation of Italy in World War II. In the second, Kirk Douglas plays a lawyer defending four GIs charged with raping a teenager in post-war Germany. But neither has the same ignominious associations with what occurred in Vietnam. As Mark Baker and Susan Brownmiller have shown, rape during the Vietnam War was a common and insidious practice.[12] *Platoon* is the first Vietnam film to confront it squarely. After the murder of the retarded youth and the fight between Elias and Barnes, the men torch the village and prepare to leave, carrying some children with them and leading the villagers. But before he leaves, Taylor sees Bunny, another white soldier, and the African-American Junior—all Barnes' men—raping young Vietnam girls. Taylor breaks up the rape and leads the girls to safety. Stone breaks new generic ground in acknowledging the rape and showing a different kind of violation of innocence and helplessness, a bi-racial gang rape against children.

As we saw, Fuller thematizes issues of discrimination in *The Steel Helmet*. Drawing in part on his own experience as an upper-middle-class white soldier serving with African Americans, Stone brings a sociological level of accuracy to his depiction of the traditional ethnic melting pot in the infantry. As Brian J. Woodman has shown, Stone is the first filmmaker to introduce the hitherto unexamined issue of class itself. Many of those who escaped the draft during the Vietnam eras were able to do so because of student deferments, an option not so easily available to many in the lower classes, particularly African Americans: "Stone connects the film's racial tensions to issues of class, particularly the fact that many blacks who fought in Vietnam were poor draftees." Specifically, he cites the scene in which King (Keith David) discusses Taylor's presence in Vietnam:

> Stone is able to make a sly maneuver. He connects race and class in a way that suggests black soldiers were sent to Vietnam in disproportionate numbers, and he also demonstrates how such poor blacks . . . are given the worst jobs. . . . He reveals through Chris, who represents the young Stone in the film, the classist assumptions of many whites toward blacks in Vietnam.[13]

*Platoon* draws on many of Stone's experiences as a soldier. He would subsequently make two more biographical films about the Vietnam War that are accounts of other participants whose lives were affected by the war. *Born on the Fourth of July* (1989), for which he won Best Director Oscar, stars Tom Cruise as Ron Kovic, a Marine who supports and fights in the war but is severely wounded in a battle that leaves him a paraplegic. The film follows the hellish process of Kovic's partial rehabilitation in a filthy Veterans Hospital, his change in view about the value of the war, and his eventual role as a spokesman for Vietnam Veterans against the War. The film's climax occurs as Kovic prepares to address the 1972 Democratic Convention. *Heaven and Earth* (1993) is based on the life of Le Ly Hayslip (Hiep Thi Le), a young Vietnamese woman whose life and family were torn apart by the war. Relief and escape from a life of prostitution appear possible with marriage to an American soldier, Steve Butler (Tommy Lee Jones), but life with the troubled veteran in the United States proves a disaster, climaxed by his suicide. These two films add to Stone's achievements in *Platoon* and make striking contributions to the war film genre not seen before: an honest and often disgusting exposé of medical treatment during rehabilitation; uncompromising exploration of impotency and mental illness; and exposure from the inside out of how American intervention disrupts family life in Vietnam, with particular emphasis on a woman's feelings and experience.

# Full Metal Jacket

*Full Metal Jacket*, directed by Stanley Kubrick (1929–1999), also reflects the pressure of the war on generic conventions. Kubrick's war-related works prior to his Vietnam film deal respectively with World War I, *Paths of Glory* (1957); the Cold War, *Dr. Strangelove or: How I Learned to Stop Worrying and Love the Bomb* (1964); and the Seven Years War, *Barry Lyndon* (1975).[14] *Paths of Glory* is based on a true story about French soldiers who were wrongfully court-martialed and executed during World War I. Defended by Colonel Dax (Kirk Douglas), they die in order to satisfy the venal and corrupt ambitions of their commanders. The black and white film displays some of the most brilliant camerawork seen thus far in any war film, particularly the tracking shots on the battlefield and within the trenches. In its searing exposure of the cynicism of the leaders and depiction of the helplessness of infantrymen who must obey suicidal orders, it evokes *All Quiet on the Western Front* (1930). *Dr. Strangelove* is a satirical projection of the nuclear war we hope never occurs. The film has a number of hilarious scenes, especially those in which Peter Sellers demonstrates his acting genius portraying three distinct roles (president, military man, creepy atomic scientist). But the overall tone is set by the maniacal General Jack D. Ripper (Sterling Hayden), who illegally initiates a nuclear war with Russia. Attempts to stop the attack on Russia prove futile, and the film ends with hydrogen bombs exploding, as we hear Vera Lynn singing "We'll Meet Again." *Barry Lyndon* uses the war, shown in the first part, as a backdrop for the complicated adventures and deterioration of its titular hero, who actually fights on both sides of the warring parties. While the films demonstrate Kubrick's disdain for corrupt and inept military leaders, none can be said to reflect the kind of significant changes to the war film genre visible in *Full Metal Jacket*. The pressures on the genre's traditional elements appear throughout the film, most graphically in the overall structure, characterization, and self-reflexivity.[15]

Based on Gustav Hasford's novel *The Short-Timers*, the film's script was written by Kubrick, Hasford, and correspondent Michael Herr, whose book *Dispatches* chronicled the war in 1967–1968. One notable element in this film involves a major change from the novel, which devotes the first one-sixth to the training of young Marines at Parris Island. In contrast, the film spends almost one-third of its running time on this section, creating a striking structural imbalance. The only war film made before this that put so much emphasis on training, *Winged Victory* (1944), did so in very different ways by following a group of idealistic young men who aspire to be pilots from home, through to induction, training, and, finally, action in the South Pacific. Narrative continuity was maintained by keeping the focus on the same group of men and their wives. In contrast, while *Full Metal Jacket* keeps its hero, Private Joker (Matthew Modine), and his friend Cowboy in both parts, the film has two very distinct sections, each with its own characters, narrative trajectory, and climax.

In the first section, we meet Joker, Cowboy, and other recruits, including Leonard, dubbed Gomer Pyle (Vincent D'Onofrio) by Gunnery Sergeant Hartman (R. Lee Ermey). Hartman is ironically named, since he shows absolutely no warmth or indications of humanity. Rather, he brutalizes the recruits, lacerating them verbally and assaulting them physically, in order to make them into killing machines. The generic tough sergeant with some element of warmth is gone; even Sgt. Barnes in *Platoon* demonstrates feeling when one of his men is killed. Kubrick presents numerous scenes showing Hartman toughening up the men with marches, runs, and maneuvers through obstacle courses. His power is underscored by several sequences within the barracks in which the recruits, in their underwear, are subject to diatribes from the clothed

**PLATE 16** *Full Metal Jacket* (Stanley Kubrick, 1987). Sergeant Hartman (R. Lee Ermey) engaged in a verbal tirade in the barracks (Warner Bros./Courtesy Photofest).

Hartman, presented as he walks by their bunks, tracked relentlessly by Kubrick's camera. One of the best-known scenes occurs when he has the men, who are carrying rifles, grab their genitals to demonstrate they know the correct term to use for their weapons, as they chant: "This is my rifle, this is my gun; this is for fighting, this is for fun."

The narrative conflict in the first part involves dealing with Pyle's incompetence and inability to perform, for which Hartman punishes all the men. In contrast to the revenge taken by the frustrated recruits in *All Quiet* against Himmelstoss whom they wrap in a blanket and dump in the water, they punish Pyle in a "blanket party" during which they beat him in bed at night using bars of soap wrapped in towels. Certainly, the war film has come a great distance from the innocent camaraderie of the recruits in the 1898 Spanish-American War film who tossed the new recruit in a blanket. Pyle begins to improve, and his developing skill with his rifle (which he names Charlene) earns him favor and respect from Hartman. But Pyle has been losing his mind, and after graduation, he goes completely insane, shoots Hartman (who, at that point, is not in uniform except for this hat), and then commits suicide.

The form this event takes represents a first for the war film. The Vietnam War became known for incidents of fragging. Such widespread occurrences of events indicated the breakdown of order and the destabilization of the chain of command. Willard's murder of Kurtz in *Apocalypse Now*, done with a machete, represents a kind of fragging, but one authorized by the madman's superiors in Washington.[16] *Full Metal Jacket* is the first war film in which a soldier driven insane during the training process murders a sergeant. The event demonstrates how successful Hartman has been: Pyle has in fact become the ultimate killing machine, one who has lost his reason. More, though, it suggests a corruption of the generic conventions. Instead of a young inexperienced recruit learning how to be a good soldier under the stern but compassionate tutelage of a tough but really kind sergeant, we have Pyle joining the ranks of two men whose shooting skills are clearly respected and praised by Hartman: Lee Harvey Oswald, who assassinated President John F. Kennedy in 1963, and Charles Whitman, a sniper who shot and killed 32 people and wounded many more from his perch on a tower on the University of Texas campus in 1966. In a grim kind of military catechism, Hartman asks the recruits if anyone can identify Whitman and Oswald (some recruits do) and then where they learned to shoot. Joker correctly answers, "Sir, in the Marines, sir!" Hartman's response is chilling: "In the *Marines*! Outstanding!

Those individuals showed what one motivated Marine and his rifle can do! And before you ladies leave my island, you will be able to do the same thing!"

Immediately after Pyle's graphic death, the screen goes black and we then move to Vietnam and find Joker with Rafterman (Kevyn Major Howard), another Marine working for *Stars and Stripes*, a military newspaper, as they bargain with a prostitute. Besides Joker, the only character to reappear from the training section in the second part is Cowboy (Arliss Howard), whom he encounters shortly after the Tet offensive on January 1, 1968. The rest of the film depicts the military response to the offensive, combat on the route to Hue City, another encounter with a prostitute, and the prolonged battle to secure Hue, the key to which involves successfully getting rid of a sniper who is picking off members of the patrol. The killer turns out to be a young VC woman whom Joker kills to put her out of her misery after she has been shot by Rafterman.

**PLATE 17** *Full Metal Jacket* (Stanley Kubrick, 1987). Joker (Matthew Modine) on the way to Hue City. "Is that you, John Wayne, is this me?" (Warner Bros./Courtesy Photofest).

Structurally, these two parts invite the question of why Kubrick devotes so much time to training. Cynthia Fuchs, Susan White, and I explore parallels between the treatment of Pyle and the sniper.[17] Another issue to consider is that the final confrontation, when Joker kills the now unarmed and helpless woman, links him inescapably with Pyle, who shoots the unarmed Hartman. The long opening section, which departs from the ordinary amount of time devoted to basic training, is such because it helps account for Joker's internal development, not just Leonard's deterioration. The first physical action Joker has to perform for Hartman is to make a war face, after he tells Hartman he joined "to kill, sir!" He is the only character to address the insanity of war, with a peace button and a "Born to Kill" insignia on his helmet, "that Jungian thing," he explains to an officer. The first section is as much about Joker as it is about Pyle and Hartman in that it shows how the moral Joker is trained to become a killer, which will occur when he shoots the sniper. Certainly, his action is necessitated directly and immediately by the dying sniper's call to "shoot me." This is an uncanny echo of Barnes' statement to Taylor to kill him, "Do it," and points to the effect of the war on the young heroes. The insanity of this war brings decent human beings to positions where the only logical action open to them is killing an unarmed person. If, as Jeffords suggests, Taylor is a divided person, torn apart by dealing with the internal warring forces of Barnes and Elias, so too is Joker, but in a different way.

Kubrick develops Joker's complicated nature, using the film's references to John Wayne to present an indirect critique of the very genre he's making. Herr's *Dispatches* contains a number of mentions of the star, known in particular for his work in war films such as *Sands of Iwo Jima* (1949).[18] And Hasford's novel has a scene on New Year's Eve, 1968, just before the Tet offensive begins, in which Joker, the narrator, describes watching *The Green Berets*: "We go into a movie theater that looks like a warehouse and we watch John Wayne in *The Green Berets*, a Hollywood soap opera about the love of guns. . . . I prop my boots on the seats and we watch John Wayne leading the Green Beanies. John Wayne is a beautiful soldier, clean-shaven, wearing boots that shine like black glass." Men in the audience laugh when Wayne's character speaks to an actor they recognize from *Star Trek*, and are even more convulsed at the film's end when Wayne watches a sunset, impossibly in the east, given his geographical location at that point: "The grunts laugh and whistle and threaten to pee all over themselves. The sun is setting in the South China Sea—in the East—which makes the end of the movie as accurate as the rest of it."[19] Although such a scene was in the shooting script, Kubrick wisely eliminated it since it would have continued to maintain the major temporal error in Hasford's novel.[20] The Marines *cannot* be watching *The Green Berets* "on the Chinese New Year's Eve" just before the Tet offensive since it was not released until July 1968, seven months after the offensive began.

Kubrick, Hasford, and Herr foreground Wayne in a different manner. There are four specific references, all effected by Joker doing an imitation. When we first meet Hartman and the recruits, Joker responds to a racist comment by Hartman to Private Snowball by saying, in a John Wayne voice: "Is that you, John Wayne? Is this me?" After determining who said this, Hartman punches him in the stomach. The second reference occurs in the barracks, just before the Tet offensive. In Wayne's voice, Joker tells the character Payback: "Listen up, pilgrim. A day without blood is like a day without sunshine." Then he observes: "Don't listen to any of Payback's bullshit. Sometimes he thinks he's John Wayne." The third imitation comes after Joker meets the tough Animal Mother, who threatens to "tear him a new asshole": "Well, pilgrim, only after you eat the peanuts out of my shit." The last imitation occurs as we track with a crew of cameramen who are filming Joker and the squad, and at this moment, Joker asks: "Is that you John Wayne? Is this me?" Cowboy: "Start the cameras. This is Vietnam, the Movie!" Eight Ball: "If Joker can be John Wayne, then I'll be the horse." "Animal Mother can be the rapid buffalo." "I'll be General Custer." "The Gooks can play the Indians."

These inscribe John Wayne as a palpable presence, both as hero of war films and of westerns, but in a way that offers a critique of everything he had come to stand for by 1987.[21] As Michael Anderegg observes: "It may in part be a vague awareness of Wayne's ambivalent status as an icon of martial heroism that lends such ambiguity to the Wayne allusions that inform so many Vietnam texts. 'John Wayne' seems simultaneously a potent symbol of toughness and bravery and a grim joke."[22] By not referencing *The Green Berets* specifically, Kubrick avoids the temporal inconsistency of the novel, yet he manages to allude to the film and its retrograde message as well as the whole cult of tough heroism associated with the actor who, in fact, never served in the military. Even more, Joker's first imitation and question define him as a divided being. The "Jungian thing" extends to more than just love and hate. Joker's questions, "Is that you, John Wayne? Is this me?" actually define a more complex identity: am I a killer, a creation of Hollywood, or my self? What am I as a human being in this insane war? By the end he has come to an acceptance that he is all of these: "I am so happy that I am alive, in one piece and short. I'm in a world of shit . . . yes. But I am alive. And I am not afraid."

Before the encounter with the sniper, the camera crew interviews members of the squad about their perceptions of how the war is going. One contemptuously imitates Lyndon Baines Johnson's famous speech that he would not send American boys halfway around the world to fight unnecessarily. Animal Mother is all for winning. Cowboy points out the cowardice of the South Vietnamese they're defending. The comments add up to a stinging condemnation of the war. And they also foreground the presence of the media in bringing the "living-room war" home, since television reports increasingly exposed the failures of American intervention.[23] Moreover, the scene obliquely points to a visit to Vietnam that Walter Cronkite made shortly after the Tet offensive, after which he made clear he did not think the US could win. Since Cronkite was at that time the most trusted news commentator in the nation, his negative evaluation of the war was devastating. One character earlier says he hears Cronkite will be coming out against the war.

Thus Kubrick's use of John Wayne and of the media coverage look backward to the history of the genre and forward to the way television becomes a source of documentary evidence about it. His is the first film to infuse the narrative and the genre with a full recognition of the extent to which the Vietnam War is an overdetermined site in terms of film and media. That is, the war film genre now comments on its own historical past, in regard to one of its leading heroes, John Wayne, and acknowledges its status as an object of media attention in the present.

# CHAPTER 6

# *GLORY* (1989)

Edward Zwick (b. 1952), the director of *Glory*, has treated conflicts from various periods: *Courage Under Fire* (1996), the Gulf War; *The Siege* (1998), a political action film about Arab terrorists who attack New York City, prompting a complex standoff between the FBI and a rebel US military unit; *The Last Samurai* (2003), a former Civil War soldier serving as a military adviser for opposing sides in nineteenth-century Japan; and *Defiance* (2008), about three brothers during World War II trying to save their fellow Jews from the Nazis. This chapter explores the relation of his first war film to the genre by (1) paying particular attention to the role of African-American soldiers in relation to conventions and to their appearance in earlier war films, especially those about Vietnam; and (2) by positioning it in relation to war films in what can be called the "reenactive mode."

## *African Americans in War Films*

Civil War films first appeared in the silent era in works by Thomas Ince and, most importantly, by D. W. Griffith, with *The Birth of a Nation*

(1915). The home front plays an important part in that film since during the war the southern Cameron family is threatened by a militia, and after it ends, by the effects of Reconstruction and newly empowered African Americans. In terms of this chapter's focus on *Glory*, the attack on the Camerons' home during the war is notable since the militia is comprised of African Americans led by a white Union officer, identified as a "scalawag" in the intertitle. Significantly in terms of the genre, the first appearance of African-American soldiers in a major narrative film is utterly negative and demonstrates the overall demonization of blacks that informs Griffith's racist agenda.[1]

In contrast to this are the appearances of African-American soldiers in other war films. They were first seen in an actuality made early during the Spanish-American War, *Colored Troops Disembarking* (May 1898). Lasting 47 seconds, the film shows a number of African-American soldiers descending a gangplank at a port in Tampa, Florida. The first film to record and document the contribution of a racial minority to war, it also demonstrates that the troops were segregated.[2] As far as I know, only two films about World War I acknowledge the presence of African Americans. The first, *Anybody's War* (1930), is a comedy in which two white actors in blackface portray Amos and Willie, two African-American characters.[3] In contrast to the offensive casting of whites in blackface, the second film, *Stormy Weather* (1943), acknowledges the contributions of African Americans. Set during World War II, it includes a scene in which the hero remembers marching with others in his black regiment in New York in 1918 after returning from World War I. Close to the conclusion of the film, we meet a young African-American soldier who is on his way overseas.

The most concentrated focus on their contributions to American wars came the next year with Stuart Heisler's documentary *The Negro Soldier* (1944), the first film systematically to trace and praise their role as soldiers in American history.[4] HBO produced *The Tuskegee Airmen* (1995), a made-for-cable film that concentrated specifically on the contributions of African Americans during World War II. The film was not released in theaters. The first film given commercial distribution focusing specifically on African-American soldiers during World War II is Spike Lee's *Miracle at St. Anna* (2008), set in Italy.

African-American soldiers appear serving with white troops, inaccurately, in World War II films such as *Bataan* (1943), *Guadalcanal Diary* (1943), and *Home of the Brave* (1949). After President Harry S. Truman's order to integrate the armed services in 1948, they are seen, accurately, in Korean War and Vietnam War films, such as *The Steel Helmet* (1951) and *Platoon* (1986). No Civil War film had ever foregrounded their importance. They were not acknowledged at all in *The General* (1927), *Gone with the Wind* (1939), and *The Red Badge of Courage* (1951). *Gone With the Wind*, in particular, perpetuated negative stereotypical images of blacks. Other major films about the ante-bellum South, such as William Wyler's *Jezebel* (1938), or those with Civil War themes and background preceding *Glory*, simply maintained stereotypical images of African Americans. Brian Henderson has suggested that John Ford's *The Searchers* (1956), which concerns the attempt by former Confederate soldier Ethan Edwards (John Wayne) to reclaim his niece who has been kidnapped by Native Americans, is really about racism and fears of miscegenation, given the film's appearance shortly after the *Brown vs Board of Education* decision by the Supreme Court in 1954.[5] But no African Americans appear in or are mentioned in that film.

Two films need referencing since they are relevant to a consideration of *Glory*. In the first, John Ford's *Horse Soldiers* (1959), Lukey, an African-American maid played by the world-famous Althea Gibson, who broke the color barrier in professional athletics, cooperates with her mistress Hannah Hunter (Constance Towers), a southern woman who conspires against Union soldiers. Eventually, though, Hunter and Lukey become friendlier to the Union men, led by John Marlowe (John Wayne) and Hank Kendall (William Holden). When Lukey is shot and dies, the sympathies and concerns of the characters are evident.

Sam Peckinpah gave African-Americans an even more prominent role in *Major Dundee* (1965). Brock Peters plays Mr. Aesop, a Union soldier who volunteers himself and five other "coloreds" (his use of the term) to ride with Dundee (Charlton Heston) on a raid against a notorious Native American who has kidnapped children. When Dundee asks why he's volunteering, Aesop says: "We've been standing guard and cleaning stables for nearly two years." Dundee accepts them. Shortly after, though, tensions develop, since the group of raiders assembled by Dundee includes, as the narrator notes, "civilians, criminals [Confederate prisoners], southerners, and Negroes." One of the southerners calls Aesop "boy" and uses the "N" word to him as he demands he take off his boots. A minister who is part of the group beats the man, and Captain Tyreen (Richard Harris), the leader of the Confederate unit pressed into service, makes a point of complimenting Aesop, calling him "Mister," for his work on the river crossing earlier that day. This is the first Civil War film to explore the presence of black Union soldiers and to thematize the issue of racial bias within the ranks.

## Conventions

*Glory* opens in 1862 with scenes of white soldiers relaxing and playing baseball in a Union camp before the Battle of Antietam. We hear the voice-over of Colonel Robert Gould Shaw (Matthew Broderick), a Boston aristocrat speaking what he has written about African Americans in a letter sent to his home. Historian Robert Rosenstone comments on the generic nature of these opening moments of the film in terms of Civil War histories:

> All these images, which set the stage for what is to come by evoking the mood and feeling of the war before the Battle of Antietam, represent no more than the cobbling together of familiar (to Americans) elements from the Civil War. They certainly do not comprise a literal construction of the past, but a kind of generic construction. The film suggests that this is more or less the way a camp looked, those are the sorts of activities that went on between battles, these are the sorts of sentiments some northerners had.[6]

Rosenstone's comment on a kind of generic representation is relevant because so much of what follows has to be understood in relation to generic patterns in films about the Civil War in particular and the war film in general.

The conflict at Antietam is conducted in a manner familiar to viewers who have witnessed war films depicting battles before the advent of trench warfare. Here, as occurs in films such as *The Patriot* (2000), a major form of combat involves opposing armies marching in line formation towards each other and then commencing to fire. Shaw is wounded and falls. Fortunately, Rawlins (Morgan Freeman), a grave digger who is gathering up bodies, observes that the wounded Shaw is still alive. After being treated, he returns to Boston where, at a reception with his family, Frederick Douglass, and leaders of the white Abolitionists, the governor invites him to command the 54th Regiment of Massachusetts. His friend Cabot Forbes (Cary Elwes) joins him, as does Thomas (Andre Braugher), an educated African American and another close friend. The film presents other volunteers in the regiment, including Rawlins, Trip (Denzel Washington, winner of the Oscar for Best Supporting Actor), an escaped slave, and Sharts (Jihmi Kennedy). In contrast to the presentation of anonymous and threatening black soldiers commanded by a repellant officer in *Birth of a Nation*, or the positive rendering of Mr. Aesop in *Major Dundee*, *Glory* foregrounds and gives narrative prominence to a significant number of men who are humanized and individualized.[7]

*Glory* displays some but not all of the conventions of war films. The recruits receive instruction from a ferocious drill instructor, Sgt. Mulcahy (John Finn), an Irishman whose verbal and racist attacks recall Sgt. Hartman's in *Full Metal Jacket*. The film covers basic training in detail as the men learn about marching, bayoneting techniques, and how to load and reload rifles rapidly. Thomas shares a tent with Rawlins, Sharts, and Trip. The latter treats him with contempt and hostility because of his higher intellectual status.[8] This kind of tension based on background and intellectual qualities had appeared in *The Young Lions* (1958), a film about World War II. There, Montgomery Clift plays a Jew who is discriminated against in the barracks because of his religion but also because of his intellectual qualities, signaled by the fact that he is reading James Joyce's *Ulysses.*

*Glory* differs in the training section from other war films in its treatment of punishment. Instead of gut punches and grueling exercises and workouts, the film shows how infractions are punished with whipping. Because basic clothing supplies, especially shoes, are at a minimum, Trip leaves the training camp to try to find some even though that is forbidden. Caught, he is returned in disgrace and has to endure a whipping administered by Mulcahy but supervised by Shaw, who does not know at that time the reason for Trip being awol. Zwick shoots this disturbing scene, which seems to last endlessly, in a way that cuts between close shots of Shaw and Trip, as they stare at each other. Towards the end, we see that Trip has shed one tear. Once Shaw discovers Trip's reason for leaving, he makes sure that medical care is given to his already whip-lacerated back, and arranges for the men to get shoes and socks. Leading a revolt against the bureaucracy that wants to pay blacks less than whites for fighting, Shaw joins with his men who are ripping up their paychecks as a sign of protest.

Several military actions occur. In the first, the troop gets a chance for active fighting and turns back a southern regiment in a fierce battle. Thomas is wounded but wins the respect of Trip by saving his life. Second, Shaw is forced by an unscrupulous general to burn a small town inhabited only by defenseless citizens. Shaw later gets back at him by threatening to expose the way the general is illegally sending home loot gained by fighting. The climax of the film occurs when the 54th engages in a doomed attack on Fort Wagner in Charleston, South Carolina, Shaw having volunteered to lead the assault. Shaw has tried earlier to get Trip to be the standard bearer and carry the colors, but the latter refuses. As the battle continues, Trip eventually does assume that role after the actual bearer falls. But the men are hopelessly out-numbered, and their progress towards the fort is made impossible because of their visibility and exposure on the beach. In one of the bloodiest and most violent battle scenes of any war film, most of the soldiers in the 54th are killed, including Shaw, Thomas, and Trip. The morning after the battle, Shaw's body lies with hundreds of others in a massive grave into which Trip's body is thrown, rolling on to Shaw's in a manner that brings them together in death.[9]

In evaluating *Glory*, many critics speak about the way it conforms to the generic convention of having a varied composition of the men who share the tent. They are seen in stereotypical terms in regard to their race and as black equivalents of the melting-pot pattern used in representing white soldiers. For example, Gary Giddens points to the conventional aspects: "as usual in army movies, the regiment is decon-structed into one tentful of representative blacks: Trip, the escaped slave . . . ; Rawlins, the wise middle-aged volunteer; Thomas, the educated free black . . . ; and Sharts, a field hand who stutters for comic relief."[10]

Jude Davies and Carol R. Smith approach this generic element in a different way, arguing that "the representations of the black soldiers relate to two sets of Hollywood stereotypes." The first, "derived from classic war movies," includes "the headstrong youth . . . the father-figure . . . the backwoods recruit . . . and the bookish, middle-class recruit." The second appears when these are "brought up against Hollywood stereo-types of African-American masculinity." While the depiction of "Trip's talk patterns, his youth and his highly developed physique flirt with the Hollywood stereotype of the buck," the treatment of him and the revelation about his motivation for leaving camp to find shoes, along with the film's critique of Sgt. Mulcahy's racism, help to undermine "the 'buck' stereotype," which "is demonstrated to constitute a mis-perception in the minds of the white protagonists."[11] In addition, the treatments of both Rawlins, which "recalls that of the Tom stereotype," and the "rites of passage observed in Thomas and Sharts," "imply a rethinking of notions of positive images."[12] Even so, they see the film as dominated by Shaw and white values, as reinforced by the letters Shaw writes to this mother and to the visual treatment of him, signaled by the way "Hollywood conventions (voice-over, point of view, camera-work) have been organized along lines of white dominance."[13]

John Pym offers a significant exception to these views about stereo-types: "The black players, notably Morgan Freeman . . . and Denzel Washington . . . perform with a notable reined-in dignity. These are repressed, disenfranchised men on the verge of a kind of equality with their white officers; and there is nothing in them of that old demeaning stereotype, the dignified slave."[14]

But in explaining this generic aspect of the film, none of theses critics goes far enough. They position the stereotypes in two frames of reference: the war film in general (age, youth) and perceptions of blacks in particular (Uncle Tom, buck). But no one examines the soldiers in terms of prior representations of African Americans in earlier war films.

The significant representation of African-American soldiers in war films really begins after 1948. The issue of prejudice figures prominently in *Home of the Brave, The Steel Helmet,* and also *Bright Victory* (1951). In each, an African American (played in all cases by James Edwards) is singled out because of his race. In *Home* he is bullied by a racist corporal and brought to a nervous collapse when his best friend dies, after almost using the "N" word to him. In *Helmet* he fends off the taunts of a North Korean prisoner of war who ridicules him for fighting for America. And in *Victory* he is crushed when his white friend, like him physically blinded by the war, uses the dreaded epithet since he is unaware that his buddy at the rehabilitation hospital is black. But in each of them, the character is more than simply a representative of an oppressed race, there as a way of making a social commentary. Each character has a life as a feeling and thoughtful human being capable of reflecting on the inequalities of racial prejudice and rising above it with a display of integrity. These characters are all men, not just tokens in a racial tract.

The treatment of African-American soldiers becomes even more impressive during and after the Vietnam era. Repellent as the film may be, *The Green Berets* (1968) nonetheless has Raymond St. Jacques, an African American, playing Doc McGee, a medic of sorts.[15] James Edwards plays a sergeant who attends to the often difficult needs of General George Patton in the 1970 film of that name. David Alan Grier has the important responsibility of providing strength and stability in the troubled barracks depicted in *Streamers* (1983), in which another African American and white soldiers are locked in complex psycho-sexual tensions as they are preparing to go to Vietnam. Howard Rollins, Jr. plays a captain who is a lawyer brought in to investigate the murder of another African American on an Army base in Alabama during World War II in *A Soldier's Story* (1984). Brian J. Woodman talks at length about examples of Vietnam combat films in which African Americans are foregrounded significantly: the leadership of Stan Shaw in *The Boys in Company C* (1978); the positive characters of King (Keith David) and of Harold (Forrest Whitaker) in *Platoon*; and Doc (Courtney Vance), Motown (Michael Patrick Boatman), McDaniel (Don James), and Washburn (Don Cheadle) in *Hamburger Hill* (1987).[16]

The last film is particularly relevant, coming as it does only two years before *Glory*. One common expression used by both white and black soldiers in the film is: "It don't mean nothin'"—an appropriate sentiment given the Sisyphean task that forms the factual subject of the film, which shows how a band of soldiers eventually succeeds in taking a hill after ten agonizing days. The refrain sustains the men as they deal with the absurdity of their lives, but it also becomes a bonding element, nowhere more prominently than in a scene when Doc, Motown, and Washburn attempt to come to terms with their grief over McDaniel's death. The repetition of the line sustains them in a manner that anticipates what occurs in the scene in *Glory* the night before the final battle. There Rawlins, Sharts, and Trip, accompanied by singing and clapping from their brothers, speak to the collective assembly about their lives, their faith, and, in Trip's case, how the men constitute family. The scene recalls the chant in *Hamburger Hill*, for in both cases bonding and mutual support result as an adjunct benefit of language and ritual.

**PLATE 18** *Glory* (Edward Zwick, 1989). Rawlins (Morgan Freeman), now Sergeant Major Rawlins, no longer a grave digger (TriStar Pictures/Courtesy Photofest).

Doc's character is of particular importance. He speaks more than any of the African Americans about prejudice, and underscores how difficult it is to maintain a sense of self-worth in a white man's world, observing that the powers that rule "won't be happy until they get all my people killed." He tells his sergeant that the men, both black and white, are "all niggers." In a scene reminiscent of one in *Platoon* in which Chris's college education is mentioned, Doc criticizes all the white men going to college, and points out that the brothers aren't going there. For the whites who are here, the war began when they fought. In contrast, he says, "I was born into this shit." But this prompts a rebuttal from Beletsky (Tim Quill), a white man who reminds him that he is there too, not at a country club. Doc acknowledges the truth of this.

*Glory* owes more to Vietnam war films than to conventions of World War II films (the melting pot) or to stereotypes of blacks (bucks, Uncle Toms). Films about Vietnam continue and solidify the progress started after the integration of the troops in 1948 in regard to registering African Americans as human beings, not as ancillary fixtures. The chief black characters in *Glory* can be more fully appreciated in relation to their positive cinematic forebears in war films, especially those about Vietnam. That is, in a curious example of retroactivity, films made in the 1980s, twenty years after the conflict, create a new standard for showing blacks

**PLATE 19** *Glory* (Edward Zwick, 1989). Trip (Denzel Washington) leading the hopeless charge (TriStar Pictures/Courtesy Photofest).

by offering a perspective based on the historical reality of black participation in the war, particularly their uneven numbers. In a way the devastating attack on the 54th that concludes the film underscores the disparate number of black casualties in Vietnam. Drafted because they had much less ability to get deferments, and serving in a disproportionate ratio in Vietnam, they become a shadowy mirror of the black regiment that was mowed down by whites at Fort Wagner as the white Colonel Shaw and Major Forbes lead the doomed charge of hundreds of African Americans.

There appears to be a connection between the conversation in *Hamburger Hill* about blacks serving in Vietnam and an important scene in *Glory* in which Shaw asks Trip to be the standard bearer for the battle. Shaw compliments him on his fighting, notes he's going to receive a commendation, and asks him to fill this important role. Trip refuses: "I'm not fighting in this war for you sir. . . . I mean, what's the point? Ain't nobody going to win. It's just going to go on and on." Shaw says: "It can't go on forever." Trip: "But ain't nobody going to win." Shaw: "Somebody has to." Trip: "Who? I mean, you'll get to go back to Boston to a big house and all that. What about us? What do we get? . . . It stinks." Shaw admits: "Yes it stinks bad." Trip: "And we all covered up in it. Ain't nobody clean." Like the scene in *Hamburger Hill*, this one foregrounds the social and class inequalities in the composition of the soldiers, acknowledging a racial imbalance that will not go away. For one thing, the line "We're all covered up in it" recalls the ending of *Full Metal Jacket* and Joker's comment that he lives "in a world of shit." Equally important, for a 1989 audience it connects with other films from that year that also deal with the quagmire of Vietnam: "ain't nobody going to win." Brian DePalma's *Casualties of War*, which opened in August 1989, concerns the rape and murder of a Vietnamese girl by an American patrol. Oliver Stone's *Born on the Fourth of July*, which premiered just twelve days after *Glory*, is about Ron Kovic, whose wounding and rehabilitation are eventually followed by him becoming a protestor against the war. Gary Giddens finds the scene "distressing . . . a centrally placed conversation between Shaw and Trip, who, expounding 1989 politics, argues that the war is pointless."[17] But, as we have seen elsewhere, war films about an earlier period often comment on the period of their creation. Thus *Glory* joined two fact-based Vietnam films that opened in 1989, another reminder of a war we did indeed lose.[18]

One instance in which *Glory* does evoke a World War II film, but not in any manner that involves racial stereotyping, occurs in the chanting scene, referred to as "the shout," the night before the doomed battle. Robert Burgoyne suggests: "The shout in many ways functions as a kind of nerve center of the text, bringing the issues of race and national identity from below and identity from above, into a vivid conjunction."[19] When Rawlins takes his turn, he buoyantly proclaims:

> Lord, we stand before you this evening to say thank you for your grace and your many blessings. . . . I ask your blessings on all of us so that if tomorrow is our great gettin' up morning, if tomorrow we come to meet the Judgment Day, we are fighting amongst those who are fighting our oppression. Oh Heavenly Father we want you let our folks know that we died facing the enemy, that we went down standing up, we want them to know that we died fighting for freedom.

Rawlins' joyful utterance thus connects with what might seem at first to be the opposite of the famous "I'm just a guy" speech delivered by an anxious Taxi Potts (William Bendix) in *Guadalcanal Diary* (1943). He says this as their camp is being bombarded by the Japanese. Huddled in a make-shift shelter with his fellow soldiers, one of them Jewish, and the company chaplain, a Catholic priest, Taxi talks about faith, his sins, and their chances of surviving. He concludes with a powerful affirmation of a belief in God, to which all assembled say "Amen." That is, in this moment, *Glory* joins another film in which the unity of the potentially doomed men in prayer transcends individual differences. In addition, its focus on the sustaining power of religion recalls the importance of prayer and faith in *Destination Tokyo* (1943), in which the skeptical character Pills finds religion during the crisis occasioned by performing an emergency appendectomy.

### Reenactments

Another important aspect to consider about *Glory* generically is its relation to reenactments, which first appeared in films about the Spanish-American War. Obviously, all war films use these in the depiction of battles. But certain Civil War films are highly inflected by what can be called a "reenactive mode," in which the creators strive for an accuracy that will give the film a historical validity over and above simple "realism."[20] One element contributing to this in *Glory* was Zwick's use of a group of "reenactors." According to Bruce Chadwick, "Reenactors—men and women history buffs who dress in period costumes to help reenact historical events—began to appear in the early 1960s. They helped museum and battlefield curators stage Civil War battles."[21] He indicates that *Glory* used "some 6,000 white amateur soldiers and more than two hundred blacks."[22] Even more reenactors were used in the next major Civil War film, Ronald F. Maxwell's *Gettysburg* (1993), and again in the prequel, *Gods and Generals* (2003).

Their presence raises pertinent questions to think about in regard to realism. At one level it's not the same as Sam Fuller and Oliver Stone playing the parts of soldiers in their own war films *The Big Red One* (1980) and *Platoon*, since both men actually fought in the wars they're filming. The reenactors are indistinguishable from professional actors dressed in the same costumes; all are following the same directorial commands and none ever fought in the Civil War. And yet, especially in the large battle sequences, their presence lends a historical validity to the films that is absent from war films that rely on computer generated imagery to "create" soldiers. To return to the point I made in Chapter 2, given that the indexical aspect of war films affords them a kind of ontological reality, images of war we experience in film have a built-in inflected valence of reality because of the indexical quality of the historical recorded images. Even though there were never any films of Civil War battles, we are still watching "real" people who in some cases are not just professional actors, but, rather, people who have been reenacting the battles being photographed. They occupy a liminal space, between real soldiers (impossible, given this particular war) and real actors and, as such, lend a certain kind of authority to the depiction of the battles. It's not the same, but nonetheless somewhat close to what occurs in war films when actual combat footage is inserted during battle sequences, as occurs in a number of films.[23]

CHAPTER 7

# THE IRAQ WARS
# ON FILM

Films about the war with Iraq present complex challenges in thinking about the genre. For one, there are two separate but related conflicts. The Gulf War began in August 1990 and ended six months later, after the United Nations coalition succeeded in pushing Iraq out of Kuwait as a result of Operation Desert Shield and Operation Desert Storm. An uneasy peace followed for twelve years, marked by tensions caused by violation of no-fly zones. Al Qaeda's attack on the World Trace Center on September 11, 2001 energized the Bush administration to find ways to justify an attack on Iraq in order to eliminate Saddam Hussein permanently. Although Osama bin Laden engineered the 9/11 attack, the Bush administration suggested that Hussein was complicit, and argued that intelligence reports proved Iraq harbored weapons of mass destruction (WMDs). This was the key ploy used to justify the allied attack on Iraq that began on March 23, 2003. Hussein was captured the next month and executed in 2006; no viable evidence was ever produced that there were really WMDs in Iraq.

This chapter looks at generic developments in three films about the Gulf War: two made before the Iraq War began, Edward Zwick's *Courage Under Fire* (1996) and David O. Russell's *Three Kings* (1999); and one made during it, Sam Mendes' *Jarhead* (2005). None presents a traditional treatment of war. Instead of focusing on and celebrating how the war was "won," all three destabilize generic expectations in ways that constitute a critique of United States policy and conduct in the conflict. *Courage Under Fire* exposes various lies about individual scenes of combat in which Iraqi soldiers are defeated. *Three Kings* examines the aftermath of the war in order to suggest how the United States betrayed the citizens who supported it in the conflict. And *Jarhead* shows how soldiers respond when they cannot wage war they have been trained to fight. The chapter concludes with commentary on the generic features of films about the Iraq War that began in 2003.

## Courage Under Fire

*Courage Under Fire*, the first narrative film about the Iraq conflict, stars Denzel Washington as Lieutenant Col. Nate Serling, a tank commander who mistakenly kills some of his own men, including his friend, with friendly fire during the confusing night battle with which the film begins. He's awarded the Medal of Honor for his actions during the tank battle. Once at home, he's tortured by his guilt for the deaths and drinks excessively. Then he's assigned to investigate whether Capt. Karen Walden (Meg Ryan) should receive the Medal of Honor. She was the commander of a Medevac helicopter that attacked Iraqis who were assaulting Americans. Before being driven off, though, the Iraqis shot down her helicopter. Ironically, she died on the same day of Serling's fatal error. His investigation involves interviewing the men whose lives were saved by Walden's rescue and the crew of her helicopter to determine the precise nature of the events. Among these are Monfriez (Lou Diamond Phillips), Ilario (Matt Damon), and Altameyer (Seth Gilliam). During his investigation, Serling interacts uneasily with Tony Gartner (Scott Glenn), a reporter who is trying to determine what happened with the friendly fire incident.

Each of Serling's interviews with various eyewitnesses to the events produces a flashback. The first occurs when he questions Lieutenant Chelli (Ned Vaughn) and other soldiers saved by Walden's attack on the Iraqi soldiers. Next, Serling talks to Rady (Tim Guinee), her co-pilot who was unconscious during most of the conflict. His account confirms Chelli's report. Then he interviews Ilario, who describes events not known to the first two interviewees and who appears nervous and uncertain as he explains what happened during the night after their helicopter was shot down. His claim to have sent a letter from Walden to her parents proves false. In addition, Ilario's account doesn't square with the report from Chelli about hearing an M-16 rifle. Serling then talks to Monfriez, who at first treats the investigation somewhat contemptuously and Serling threateningly, before stating that Walden was a coward not a hero. Serling's efforts to get information from Altamayer are useless since the latter is dying of cancer and is unable to speak. Confronted with inconsistencies about his account, Monfriez commits suicide. Ilario goes awol, but is found by Serling, who hears his tearful confession as we see the "true" flashback about what really happened: Monfriez led a mutiny against Walden, accidentally shot her, and then left her to die when the rescue helicopter arrived. Thus we get five flashbacks: two accurate ones from Chelli and Rady, and two false ones, from Ilario and Monfriez, before we finally get the truth.

As virtually every commentator on the film observes, the film's basic structure and design draw on Akira Kurosawa's *Rashomon* (1950). In that film, told in several flashbacks, various characters provide contradictory stories about a murder: a wife presents it as an incident of rape and

**PLATE 20** *Courage Under Fire* (Edward Zwick, 1996). Serling (Denzel Washington) elicits the truth from Ilario (Matt Damon) (Fox 2000 Pictures/Courtesy Photofest).

assault followed by the robber-rapist killing her husband; the robber says the wife instigated the events; and the husband's ghost condemns them both. The film is commonly cited as an example of the elusiveness and relativity of truth, as well as an example of the medium's power to make events appear real, even when contradictory. The inescapable connection to *Courage Under Fire* foregrounds these issues, although in the later film we do, in fact, gain a full understanding of what really happened.

The structure of *Courage* departs significantly from that of war films. As noted, although unusual, some war films use flashbacks. *Passage to Marseille* (1944) even has a flashback within a flashback. But the kind of complex and/or conflicting multiple flashback structure in *Courage Under Fire* is to my knowledge unheard of in the war film. It appears in other kinds of narrative dramas, though, most notably in Orson Welles' *Citizen Kane* (1941). What has been dubbed the false or lying flashback, which presents as really having happened an event shown later to be false, appears in Alfred Hitchcock's *Stage Fright* (1948) and John Ford's *The Man Who Shot Liberty Valance* (1962). The traditional generic narrative of the war film follows a linear pattern, wherein achieving the goal—taking a city or a beachhead—has a clearly marked beginning, middle, and end, often with various obstacles serving as temporary impediments.

A linear pattern appears with a major variation in the first war film written and directed by Patrick Sheene Duncan, author of *Courage Under Fire*. His Vietnam War film *84C MoPic* (1989) demonstrates one way the genre responds to an erosion of any sustaining myth about the positive aspects of war. Even though he uses a traditional linear narrative trajectory there in terms of temporal progression, he presents it in a highly unusual way: told with a first-person point of view technique by a cameraman attached to a squad. As the group makes its way through various checkpoints, engaging in skirmishes, and interacting with each other, the cameraman records all the events in a cinéma verité style, keeping out of the action except to comment occasionally. The film ends as he is killed. By choosing the first-person narrative technique, and using a subjective camera throughout, Duncan achieves a remarkably pressing and inescapable immediacy to the action he records. But the linear narrative pattern ultimately underscores the hopelessness of the war itself. One event follows another, leading ultimately to no victory, only the death of the person recording the events. It's possible to see his film as complementing *Platoon* (1986), another transgressive Vietnam War film. Like Stone, an infantryman in the war, Duncan insists on showing us relentlessly what the war is like from the inside out.[1]

Such an emphasis on using the camera to capture the truth of war explains, in part, his decision to vary the generic structure so radically in *Courage Under Fire*. Duncan and Zwick are saying something about the elusiveness of truth regarding the Iraq conflict itself. Some of the "evidence" we receive in the form of flashbacks turns out to be incomplete or downright false. Serling's initial error that results in the deaths of others in friendly fire initiates the pattern of acting on information that turns out to be wrong. In other words, the narrative form, unlike that of any other war film made before it, is itself related to the uncertain conflict it presents. That is, both plot lines demonstrate that one cannot believe initial reports about the battles; something else has occurred. Such uncertainties speak to the dubious status of belief in regard to the validity of war itself and the United States' involvement in it.

Serling's superior officer takes him off the investigation when it appears his quest to find out whether Walden deserves the medal will result in an embarrassing outcome. He tells him that he wants Walden to get the medal, "one shiny piece of something for people to believe in."

**PLATE 21** *Courage Under Fire* (Edward Zwick, 1996). Captain Karen Walden (Meg Ryan) defending her men (Fox 2000 Pictures/Courtesy Photofest).

Serling himself is haunted by the fact he has received a medal even though he inadvertently killed his own men, a distortion of the truth. As it turns out, Walden does indeed deserve her medal. But ideologically the film is asserting that, even though truths may be elusive, hard to ascertain and troubling, one must try to determine them. The character's quest for truth becomes a way of commenting on the need for those in the audience to confront the actual and dirty truths about the Iraq War.

In addition to offering a radically different structural form for a war film, another major generic innovation comes with the role of Karen Walden. Films about women fliers during wartime are rare but not unheard of. In one notable example from World War II, *A Guy Named Joe* (1944), Irene Dunne plays a female cargo plane pilot who substitutes herself for her boyfriend (Van Johnson) and flies a dangerous mission (aided by the ghost of her dead fiancée Spencer Tracy) on which she successfully bombs a munitions dump. In *Ladies Courageous* (1944) Loretta Young is a member of the Women's Air Force Ferrying Squadron with the important responsibility of flying planes to bases where they are needed. But *Courage Under Fire* is the first film in which a woman is in command of an aerial vehicle, in this case a helicopter, and in which her being an officer directing men becomes a narrative issue—both genre-bending elements.[2]

In terms of genre conventions, the melting pot array of ethnic and racial combatants in a squad is both maintained and critiqued. Rady and Ilario are white, with no identifiable ethnicity; Altamayer is an African American; and Monfriez vaguely Latin or Mediterranean. In place of an ethnic or racial outsider, Walden represents a gendered "other." Her status as a woman is foregrounded when she cries because of her frustration and pain and Monfriez accusingly points out her weakness, prompting her to remind him she knows all about pain, having delivered a nine-pound baby. Monfriez's baleful influence on Ilario and Altamayer causes them to remain silent when he tells their rescuers that Walden is dead, even though all three know she is still alive. So here the discriminated-against "other" of the squad, who earlier had been represented by an African American in a film like *Home of the Brave* (1949), is now a woman.

The distinctive aspects of *Courage Under Fire*—its conflicting flashback structure, focus on the moral issues involved with friendly fire, and foregrounding of gender—underscore its uniqueness as the first film to treat the Gulf War. Interestingly, these features also make us aware how atypical the work is generically as a war film. Its thematic emphasis on finding the truth about the actions of individuals is at the center of the film's moral stance, which is to expose the truth about the war itself. Even though the usual concerns of war films are present—bravery, winning victories, dealing with the deaths of comrades—they are secondary to other narrative emphases.[3]

## Three Kings

Directed by David O. Russell (b. 1958), *Three Kings* presents a different generic challenge. It begins as the war ends, when Troy Barlow (Mark Wahlberg) asks if the war is still on and then shoots an Iraqi soldier, whose graphic death throes upset him. Other soldiers are buoyant since they have had so little opportunity to engage in killing. In fact, as occurs in *The Big Red One* (1980), the death that begins the film occurs after the truce. The wild celebration of that in the American camp serves as an introduction to the principal characters in addition to Troy: Archie Gates (George Clooney), Chief Elgin (Ice Cube), and Conrad Vig (Spike Jonze). As a result of stripping Iraqi prisoners, the main protagonists discover a map hidden in a man's anus and learn

**PLATE 22** *Three Kings* (David O. Russell, 1999). The bullion hunters on guard (George Clooney, Mark Wahlberg, Ice Cube, Spike Jonze) (Warner Bros./Courtesy Photofest).

that it can lead them to a bunker with millions of dollars of bullion and goods taken from Kuwait by Saddam Hussein. They divert attention from Adriana Cruz (Nora Dunn), a television correspondent, and proceed to the site. While they find the bullion, they also encounter helpless Iraqi citizens who, having been encouraged to reject Hussein by President George H. W. Bush, are now being tortured and oppressed by remnants of the army still loyal to Hussein who know that Americans cannot intervene to protect the rebels. Doing so would be a violation of the truce.

Fighting erupts after a mother is shot in the head in front of her child. Accompanied by many of the citizens, the heroes try to escape but encounter many problems: a gas attack, Troy's capture, Conrad's wounding, and loss of vehicles. Making their way to another town, they bargain for luxury cars to be used in rescuing Troy and bringing the Iraqi citizens to the Iranian border, where they can cross over to safety. Although rescued, Troy is severely wounded, and Conrad killed. The film's climax occurs when the US Army tries to stop the theft of bullion and illegal assistance to the citizens. But the conclusion is positive: the citizens cross over, and the remaining heroes escape a court martial.

In terms of traditional generic features, obviously the main characters illustrate the melting pot: the Chief is African American; Troy and Archie are white; Conrad is a redneck southerner, given to racist remarks. The Arab enemy is demonized in a manner familiar from war films in which Americans fight an ethnic or racial other. But Russell, who wrote the film, constantly reworks some of the generic features. Conrad apologizes for his racism and ironically ends up being given a traditional Muslim burial. An Iraqi Arab is one of the heroic citizens defying Hussein. Even though Troy's chief captor, another Arab, tortures him mercilessly, and forces him to drink oil—of course, the real cause of the war—he's presented as a counterpart to him, another young father caught in a horrible conflict that endangers wives and children. It is he who raises the question to a somewhat baffled Troy about why Michael Jackson has changed the pigmentation of his skin.

Russell shoots the film in an unsettling manner: distorting the color, overexposing film to emphasize the bleak desert, using wide-angle lenses and night-vision goggle shots that trouble vision. Roger Ebert suggests: "We've seen desert warfare before, but usually it looks scenic. Russell's cameraman . . . uses a grainy, bleached style that makes the movie look like it was left out in a sandstorm."[4] Todd McCarthy says Russell felt compelled, or liberated, to fashion a new-look war film, appropriate to an era in which the public's images of warfare are defined by inelegant CNN pictures of nocturnal explosions and the resultant destruction. Certainly nothing else explains the deliberately grainy, bleached-out almost digital look of this widescreen adventure, in which any sense of heroism is canceled, military grandeur is neutered and desert beauty not allowed.[5]

On the DVD commentary Russell indicates he was aiming for a look that conveyed "the moral blankness that attended the war." Possibly the most arresting visual innovation in the film involves demonstrating what happens when a bullet enters vital organs. As Archie explains this to the men, Russell shows a graphic image of how parts of the body are destroyed. The image recurs when Troy is shot, a hard-to-watch reminder of the lethal realities of warfare.

But the most notable aspects of the film have to do with genre. In the DVD commentary Russell himself acknowledges that the basic goal of the heroes—getting the gold bullion—makes this something of a heist movie, although one consistent with his goal of making an anti-war statement even as it displays aspects of the action film. He sees the film as "shattering the genre." I cannot think of another war film before this that elicits such a range of critical comments on its genre. The fact that so many designations are used demonstrates how much the war has destabilized traditional generic patterns. It has been called a "screw-loose war picture" (Roger Ebert); "less a war movie than a classic western" (Gene Seymour); a "bloodthirsty . . . Hollywood service comedy" (J. Hoberman); and "a classically structured mercenary adventure story . . . paced and shot with the jacked-up frenzy of an existential war-is-hell epic" (Owen Gliberman).[6]

The range of terms used to describe the film's genre says a great deal about its innovativeness, but even more about the Iraq war film emerging at the end of the twentieth century. Russell's transgressive work exemplifies how the conventions and visual appearance of the earlier war films won't work for the new kinds of war we find ourselves fighting. Particularly coming as it does after the opening the previous year of *Saving Private Ryan* and *The Thin Red Line*—films that evoke the classic Hollywood World War II film's values and heroism—*Three Kings'* subject matter, a "heist film"—to use Russell's phrase—about stealing millions in gold bullion, serves as a commentary on the real issue underlying the war—getting control of oil by discrediting and neutralizing Hussein as a force in the Middle East. So there is, in fact, no myth that can be sustained by the ordinary genre conventions. We must understand the transformation of genre conventions as a reflection of Russell's desire to ground events in history and expose the actual truths about our involvement in the war.[7]

## Jarhead

*Jarhead*, directed by Sam Mendes (b. 1965), provides another example of destabilizing the genre. It is based on Anthony Swofford's immensely popular account of training as a sharpshooter in the Marines and his experiences in Iraq. He wrote the film script with William Broyles, Jr., a Vietnam veteran who earlier had published a highly regarded memoir of his experiences, *Brothers in Arms: A Journey from War to Peace* (1986), thus making this the first war film written by veterans (both Marines) of two different wars.

The film follows jarhead Swofford (Jake Gyllenhaal) (so called because of the extreme haircut given the Marines) from basic training, where he is first terrorized by a crazed drill instructor and then put under the guidance of the admirable Staff Sergeant Sykes (Jamie Foxx), to a base for specialized instruction in being a sharpshooter. There he befriends Troy (Peter Sarsgaard). After being flown to Saudi Arabia in anticipation of a war, the men train endlessly in the desert, awaiting orders for battles that do not occur. We see them bonding, exulting in a fight between scorpions, lamenting the loss of cheating girlfriends and wives (their pictures posted for public viewing on a "wall of shame"), and trying to cope with months of inaction. When a team of media personnel visits the base, the men, encased in their uniforms in the blistering heat, start playing footfall, which quickly turns into a "field fuck." This highly sexualized and aggressive game designed to unsettle the media involves taking off their uniforms and simulating sexual interactions. Like other events in the film it signals the sexual frustration felt by the men. At one point, for example, Swofford is seen trying unsuccessfully to masturbate. The sense of impotency is connected to the emphasis on guns they can't use.

Possibly the most erotically charged scene in the film occurs when Swofford stages a bacchanalian Christmas party. Wearing only a thong and a Santa Claus hat, with another covering his genitals, he oversees a riotous booze-filled celebration that is ruined when the camp loser Fergus (Brian Geraghty) causes a fire that leads to an explosion of ammunition. Instead of the shooting war the men have hoped to see,

**PLATE 23** *Jarhead* (Sam Mendes, 2005). Swofford (Jake Gyllenhaal) and Troy (Peter Sarsgaard) at the Christmas party (Universal Pictures/ Courtesy Photofest).

they have instead a spectacular display of rockets exploding uselessly. This scene takes us well beyond the obvious connection between rifles and male genitalia familiar from the chant, "This is my rifle, this is my gun; this is for fighting, this is for fun." In effect it provides a symbolic rendering of the collective sense of failed sexuality: all explosions with no satisfaction or pleasure.

The men finally become actively involved in the war when they enter Kuwait in February. Even though they still are not shooting, they experience friendly fire, and are made aware of the effects of the war, most graphically when they discover dozens of blackened automobiles and corpses.[8] In one particularly striking scene, an addition by Broyles and stunningly photographed by Roger Deakins, Swofford encounters a solitary horse drenched in the oil that rains down on them all because the oil wells have been ignited by the Iraqis. Finally, the sharpshooters are given orders to kill two Iraqi officers. When the order is rescinded, Swofford and Troy protest vehemently, to no avail. The war ends for them without having had a chance to fire a rifle in battle. They return to a camp scene of celebration for the end of the four-day shooting war. In a scene whose release of frenzy evokes the opening moments of *Three Kings*, the frustrated men shoot their rifles into the air. In a coda to the film, we learn that Troy, who was drummed out of the Corps for previous criminal acts, has died, and that Swofford appears to have a lonely existence.

In terms of the genre, even though it concerns a war we won, *Jarhead* often calls up films about the Vietnam War we lost. While Sgt. Sykes evokes the tough but understanding good leaders of earlier films, the brutalizing drill instructor is a twisted descendent of Sgt. Hartman in *Full Metal Jacket*. Also reminiscent of that film is the repeated emphasis on the importance of the Marines' rifles and the reiteration of the "Rifleman's Prayer," which Joker and others have to recite as they lie in their bunks holding their rifles.[9] Possibly the most direct allusion to the genre occurs in an incident originally in Swofford's memoir in which we see the recruits exulting in the helicopter scene from *Apocalypse Now*; to the accompaniment of Wagner's "Ride of the Valkerie," deadly napalm is dropped on Vietnam. Of course, their cheering is at odds with the intentions of Francis Ford Coppola's original presentation of the scene, here used with ironic bite by Mendes and Broyles. A complex allusion occurs in another scene when the Marines watch a war film. They gather before a television set and VCR to look at a tape of Michael Cimino's *The Deer Hunter* (1978) sent by a Marine's wife. But the tape contains a home video recording of the wife having sex with their neighbor and a shot of her giving her husband the finger. Owen Gliberman suggests how the film puts a particularly savage twist on the convention of the "Dear John" letter, seen earlier in the film when Swofford is dumped by his girlfriend: "In past war films, even the psychedelic spectacles of Nam, a girl back home was a comfort, but *Jarhead* presents us with strutting bruiser kings for whom wives and girlfriends are matters of anxiety—an ongoing reminder of the possibilities of adultery and betrayal."[10]

While *Three Kings* prompted critical disagreement about its generic status, *Jarhead* has led critics to comment on its uniqueness as a (non) war film. Remarking on a question asked by a Marine, "Are we ever going to get to kill anyone?" A. O. Scott calls it "a strange question to hear in a war movie, but *Jarhead* about an unusual war, the first gulf war, is a curious example of the genre."[11] J. Hoberman notes: "Mendes has contrived a combat film almost entirely without combat."[12] Similarly, its uniqueness prompts Todd McCarthy to call it "a war film without the war. Part absurdist drama, part personal observational commentary and part hormonal explosion, all seen through the filter of previous war pics."[13] Jim Emerson notes similar generic affinities: "*Jarhead* plays like a dry, post-modern essay on the idea of The War Movie, a picaresque series of ironic references to other combat pictures, lacking any animating spark of its own."[14] Again, we see how expectations about traditional uses of genre conventions are challenged because of transformations accounted for by history and the changed perception of a war's legitimacy. As David Denby observes, "The old war-story narrative may have run aground in the Gulf War."[15]

## The Iraq War

Films made about and during the second Iraq War present their own generic features. As noted earlier, these films have fared poorly at the box office. Some have not received a wide release, others none at all. This is the first time a number of narrative and documentary films have been made about an ongoing unpopular war. Some characteristic aspects can be identified. In contrast to films about the Gulf War, which make extensive use of wide-angle shots conveying the bleak and endless desert landscape in which fighting occurs, these have a distinctive mise-en-scène that immerses us in cramped doorways and narrow, almost impassable streets. The soldiers either cannot tell whether they are seeing an enemy (the endless checkpoint confrontations) or are incapable of seeing them until it's too late (the suicide bombers' cars that explode, the gunfire that rains down from snipers above). Atrocities appear with frightening regularity, as in *The Situation* (2006), *In the Valley of Elah* (2007), and *Redacted* (2007). Of special interest is the way new technology is used in presenting the imagery of the war. Images on cell phones proliferate, and in *The Valley of Elah* and *Redacted* provide crucial information about atrocities. The general tone of the films is despairing, totally the reverse of the loyal and enthusiastic support we see in films made during and about World War II.

Veterans and their families and survivors find little if any solace, as in *Home of the Brave* (2006) and *Grace is Gone* (2007). In *Home*, Dr. Will Marsh (Samuel L. Jackson) returns with a drinking problem and needs rehabilitation in order to continue functioning as an effective physician. Vanessa Price (Jessica Biel) has to learn to live with a prosthetic arm. And Tommy Yates (Brian Presley), who finds it impossible to adjust to life as a civilian, returns to Iraq as the only way to find any meaning in his now shattered existence. In *Grace is Gone*, Stanley Phillips (John Cusack) takes his daughters on an aimless road trip as he tries to escape the burden of telling them their mother has been killed in combat.

In a way that revives memories of films about Vietnam, protests against the war and conscription now appear. In *Day Zero* (2007), set in the near future, three friends react negatively to being drafted to go to war in the continuing battle with Iraq and Iran. One kills himself rather than serve. *Stop-Loss* (2008) is a searing condemnation of the Bush administration's policy of forcing veterans who have served one year in Iraq to return for yet another. Directed by Kimberly Peirce, this film follows Sergeant Brandon King (Ryan Phillippe) who is just completing his tour of duty in Iraq. After his triumphant return and warm welcome home by his parents and girl in Texas, he discovers he must return because of the stop-loss policy. Rather than comply, King goes awol. He takes Michelle (Amy Cornish), the former girlfriend of his buddy Shriver (Channing Tatum), with him on a desperate attempt to flee the country to Canada. On the way he visits Rodriguez (Victor Rasuz), a horribly disfigured soldier in a veteran's hospital and learns that one buddy, Tommy (Joseph Gordon-Levitt), has committed suicide. Eventually, persuaded by Shriver, and aware of the devastating effects of his actions on everyone, he relents and goes back. The film's grim narrative conclusion that he can't escape becomes a kind of emblem of the country's hopeless involvement in the Iraq War.[16]

PLATE 24 *Stop-Loss* (Kimberly Peirce, 2008). Sergeant Brandon King (Ryan Phillippe) given a warm welcome home from Iraq by his parents (Linda Emond, Cierán Hinds) (Paramount Pictures/Courtesy Photofest).

## CHAPTER 8

## IWO JIMA

Known widely for his presence in genre films (Dirty Harry in crime-police dramas, The Man With No Name in Sergio Leone's spaghetti westerns), Clint Eastwood (b. 1930) first appeared in war films in 1955, with a small part in *Francis in the Navy* (1955), a service comedy; followed by *Away All Boats* (1956), a World War II film, and William Wellman's aviation film about World War I, *Lafayette Escadrille* (1958). He would later star in *Where Eagles Dare* (1968) and *Kelly's Heroes* (1970), both about fighting the Germans in World War II. The first war-related film he directed was *The Outlaw Josey Wales* (1976), in which he plays a southerner bent on avenging the deaths of his wife and son at the hands of Union soldiers just as the Civil War is ending. He directed and starred in *Heartbreak Ridge* (1986), playing a grizzled Marine commander who leads an attack in Grenada during the brief 1983 war.[1]

Eastwood's *Flags of Our Fathers* and *Letters from Iwo Jima* (both 2006) are about the bloody siege of the Japanese island that occurred from February 19 to March 26, 1945 and claimed the lives of over 6,800 Americans and 20,000 Japanese. The works are unique in the history of the genre because for the first time two separate films from one director made in different languages and released at around the same time explore the significance of a wartime campaign from the perspective of both combatants. The films offer what many critics call a "diptych," essentially two separate but related representational elements that complete and complement one another. Originally used to describe two enjoined carvings, the term now generally applies to two paintings connected by their religious or historical relationships. From the American perspective, *Flags* presents the preparations for landing on the island, aspects of the battles, the famous flag raising on Iwo Jima on February 23, and the effects of this on the three surviving flag raisers and on the morale of United States citizens. From the Japanese perspective, *Letters* shows how the soldiers prepare to resist the invasion as it concentrates on two men, a general charged with the impossible job of defending the island, and a young baker who has been drafted into the army. The flag raising and its effects on the heroes provide the narrative center of the American film. While the flag appears briefly in an extreme long shot in *Letters*, it is never mentioned by the characters.

## Flags of Our Fathers

One of the remarkable aspects of *Flags*, scripted by William Broyles, Jr., who co-wrote *Jarhead* (2005), and Paul Haggis, author and director of *In the Valley of Elah* (2007), is its connection to the earliest films, the reenactments that appeared during the Spanish-American War. While there had been short films picturing the American flag before the beginning of that war, the first film to focus on it directly is *Raising Old Glory over Morro Castle* (1899), a reenactment released several months after the end of the conflict. The Spanish flag, seen in front of an obviously painted backdrop representing the castle in Havana, is lowered and then replaced by the American flag. This reenactment documents the fall of the previously ruling country and the triumphant ascendancy of the United States, a sign of both military victory and international expansion.

The film *Flags of Our Fathers* presents two reenactments of the flag raisings on Mount Suribachi. Like that in *Raising Old Glory*, the flag raisings represent at least for the moment the ascendancy of the United States over an opponent. Since this was the first battle in which Americans actually fought on Japanese land, the symbolic value of raising a flag on top of the mountain on February 23, the fifth day of combat, was immense. In reality the fighting would continue for thirty-five more days. The first of two flag raisings on February 23 occurred when six Marines attached a small United States flag to a pipe. A

**PLATE 25** *Flags of Our Fathers* (Clint Eastwood, 2006). The flag raising on Mount Suribachi (Dreamworks SKG/Courtesy Photofest).

military photographer, Staff Sergeant Louis Lowrey, snapped a picture of this. Men around them and below on the island cheered the event, as did sailors on ships that had delivered troops. When James Forrestal, Secretary of the Navy, arrived on shore and saw the flag on top of Mount Suribachi, he asked to have it as a souvenir. According to James Bradley, the son of Doc Bradley, one of the flag raisers, the commander Colonel Johnson wanted to keep the flag for the battalion and so he sent up a larger replacement flag.[2] A runner took this up to a group of Marines carrying a telephone line on the mountain. Five Marines and a Navy corpsman raised the second flag. This is the scene captured in Associated Press photographer Joe Rosenthal's famous and iconic shot: six men struggling to raise and stabilize the flag.[3] Simultaneously, Bill Genaust, who was standing next to Rosenthal, filmed the event in color.

The first flag raising we see in *Flags* is a cinematic reenactment of the first flag raising, the original event, and shows Lowrey taking his photograph. The second flag raising sequence provides a cinematic reenactment of what is itself a physical reenactment of the first flag raising, this time with a different group of men and a larger flag. As Rosenthal's character takes his photograph, Eastwood's film freezes the action on what will become the iconic black and white shot. He makes a photograph into a cinematic freeze frame, thus foregrounding the inherent relationship and co-identity of an individual frame of film and a single photograph.

*Flags* thus contributes to a larger discourse about film and the iconic and indexical nature of historical reality raised earlier in Chapter 2. Eastwood's film is important for the genre because it is the first war film to thematize the issue of the historical reality presented by war films. In talking about this film a number of critics have cited John Ford's *The Man Who Shot Liberty Valance* (1962) as a relevant model.[4] In that film the answer to the question of who in fact shot the villainous Valance (Lee Marvin), Ransom Stoddard (James Stewart) or Tom Doniphon (John Wayne), is resolved by the revelation that the latter killed him. But Stoddard is presented as the hero because he is perceived that way, leading the town's newspaper editor to say: "When the legend becomes the fact, print the legend." In *Flags*, the narrative follows the impact of the photograph on the lives of the three surviving flag raisers who find themselves at the center of the fraudulent myth. They know they were the second team and that one of their buddies, Harlon Bloch (Benjamin Walker), who raised it with them, has not been properly acknowledged; instead another soldier, Hank Hansen (Paul Walker), receives credit for his participation; he had been one of those who raised the first flag. Eventually, the truth comes out, but that does not change the iconic status of the Rosenthal photograph.

The narrative speaks to the issues of perception and reality, beginning with the opening of the film, which sets the course for a prismatic view of the event and its effect on John "Doc" Bradley (Ryan Phillippe), Ira Hayes (Adam Beach), and Rene Gagnon (Jesse Bradford), the three surviving flag raisers. The others—Harlon Bloch, Mike Strank (Barry Pepper) and Franklin Sousley (Joseph Cross)—all die before Iwo Jima is finally taken. After some introductory credits, during which we hear Eastwood singing the first few bars of "I'll Walk Alone," a song from World War II (heard later in the film sung by Dinah Shore, who made it popular), we are thrust into the middle of what is initially a confusing welter of visual and narrative information played out across several time periods and places: 1945 (February): the battlefield at Iwo Jima, a photographer's developing room, the front page of the *New York Times*, a city scene, a neighborhood, a farm house, the White House; 1945 (May): reenactment of the flag raising on a replica of Mount Suribachi in Chicago; 1990s: Doc Bradley's home and the funeral parlor he operates, a hospital, and the living room of an old veteran.

First we see Doc Bradley, a Navy medic who is running, and hear the word "corpsman" being cried by wounded soldiers during the battle; Doc turns his anguished face towards us, looking directly into the camera in the first of what will be many similar shots. Then we realize that this has been a nightmare as Bradley, now an old man (George Grizzard), awakens in bed and is comforted by his wife. Next, the old Bradley appears climbing the stairs in his funeral parlor and then collapses, calling out, in desperation, "Where is he?" An assistant appears, promising to get him to the hospital. A young man, Bradley's son James (Tom McCarthy), runs into the hospital, and then we hear a voice-over, as it turns out spoken by an old veteran after the elder Bradley has died, talking to the son about the nature of war photographs as James does research on his father. The speaker notes that "plenty of photographs were taken that day." Eastwood cuts to a red-lighted photographic developing lab as Rosenthal takes the photograph from the bathing bin (1945), and we hear the old man's voice again, now identified as belonging to Dave Severance (Harve Presnell) as he is interviewed by James, saying: "The right picture can win or lose a war."[5] He reflects on the famous photograph by Eddie Adams from the Vietnam Era in which the South Vietnamese police chief shoots a Viet Cong, and notes that the war was in fact lost when people saw that picture.

The film then shows the flag raising photograph on the front page of the *New York Times*, from February 1945, people buying the paper, a paperboy delivering it in a suburb, and a woman picking it up from the porch of a farm house in Texas. This is Mrs. Bloch, mother of Harlon, who is sure she recognizes her son, even though she can't see his face. Then we see the paper being taken into the office of Franklin Delano Roosevelt, with the assurance by his aides that they've found the key to the next bond drive. Then we cut to a partial reenactment of the flag raising with the three survivors mounting a paper mache mountain at Soldier Field for a reenactment before thousands of citizens in Chicago. Bradley hears the cry of "corpsman" during this and turns again to the camera before Eastwood takes us back to Iwo Jima during a battle, at which time we meet Iggy (Jamie Bell), the buddy for whom the older Bradley has been calling. Bradley leaves him in a foxhole in order to respond to a call for a corpsman, finds a wounded man, kills a Japanese attacker, and returns to find that Iggy is no longer there. He asks where Iggy has gone and we then return to Soldier Field for the reenactment.

No film in the history of the genre has ever moved viewers through so many time periods and settings so quickly, purposefully, and skillfully as occurs in this astonishing sequence. As noted earlier, the flashback is not typical of war films. Eastwood bombards us with a mixture of momentary and sustained flashbacks for specific narrative reasons. Our initial confusion about what we are watching with the first ascent on Mount Suribachi presented at Soldier Field (where are we?) is central to the film's narrative focus on the nature of the reality represented in the photograph. For a while, at least, we can't quite tell the difference between the historical iconic event and the reenactment: what's real? This is, of course, one of the central concerns of the narrative. The fact that one of the flag raisers has been misidentified as Hank Hansen rather than Harlon Bloch weighs heavily on Hayes, who thinks that the real heroes of Iwo Jima are those who died there. His guilt over participating in the fraudulent story contributes to his increasing dependence on alcohol. Bradley, too, is troubled by the deception. The structure of the film, which is constantly delaying revelations about the nature of the reality we have seen or are witnessing, is of a piece with the content. That is, we must work through the various informational delays in the narrative, seeing them as kinds of textual barriers that are symptomatic of the repressions in the characters' minds of the violence and horror, of the deaths of comrades, of the shame caused by with-holding information about one of the flag raisers.

Eastwood presents another stunning montage sequence later in the most elaborate spectacle of the film. Introduced as "The heroes of Iwo Jima," the men mount the fake mountain at Soldier Field and wave. Cut back to the battlefield and the death of Mike Strank. Back to Soldier Field. A cry of "corpsman." Cut to the battlefield—this time for the death of Harlon. Soldier Field. Then shortly after, the death of Franklin. That is, at the moment of utter showmanship sponsored by the government, Eastwood returns to the deaths of the other flag raisers, including Harlon, who has yet to be publicly recognized. But Eastwood ratchets up the intensity by following this brilliant sequence with a repeat of the discovery that Iggy is missing and Bradley's question of "Where'd he go?", one like those asked earlier at the time of battle in 1945 and when the older man collapses on the stairs. Shortly afterwards Bradley comes to a cave in which he finds Iggy's brutalized remains, not shown on camera, and Eastwood once more closes in on Bradley's agonized face in a close up.

Gradually, once the revelations about Harlon begin to emerge, the confusing temporal jumps cease, and we find out through various voice-overs, including that of Bradley's son, what happened to the survivors: Hayes became an alcoholic and died of exposure, but not before he had gone to the Bloch farm and revealed the truth about Harlon to his father. Gagnon ended up a janitor, having failed to be hired by any of the prospective employers who encouraged him with phony job offers during the blitz of publicity during the bond drive. Only Bradley succeeded, running a funeral parlor and raising a family from which he kept most of the details about his heroism. We see all three men together during the ceremony at which the Iwo Jima monument is unveiled on November 10, 1954.

Thus the overall design and pattern of events in *Flags* represent a major generic innovation given the way the temporal circling back supports the thematic and narrative concerns: showing and exposing the nature of sustaining myths. As Cynthia Fuchs observes, "War, the film argues, depends on lies, on myths and beliefs that could never be sustained were the experience represented or remembered explicitly."[6] In addition, as a number of critics have observed, Eastwood and his photographer Tom Stern complement and enhance the temporal innovation with a changing color palate appropriate to each of the time frames. Events and battles on Iwo Jima appear in a greenish, sometimes almost black and white color. Scenes on the home front in 1945 appear to have the color of Hollywood films shot around 1945. The later scenes are characterized by a burnished, mellow tone emphasized with warm colors.[7]

The innovations here are matched by those connected with some of the genre conventions we have observed thus far. The unit as representative melting pot of American society is present in the make up of the flag raisers and others: Doc Bradley and Iggy from Wisconsin, the Pima Native American Ira Hayes from Arizona, Rene Gagnon from New Hampshire, Franklin Sousley from Kentucky, Harlon Bloch from Texas, and Mike Strank from Pennsylvania. Within this group, Franklin is the untried and naïve youth, a later manifestation of the new recruit tossed in a blanket in the Spanish-American War actuality. Before the landing, Mike and others play on his unsophisticated ignorance of the term "masturbation," and send him to an officer for his "masturbation papers." Mike, who initiates the prank on Franklin, is the somewhat older leader, revered by his men, especially Ira Hayes. Iggy is the feeling, somewhat nervous soldier, anxious to establish a buddy relationship with Doc, concerned that everyone's bayonets have been sharpened sufficiently, puzzled by the absence of signs of the Japanese once they land on the island, always looking for meanings in the group's positioning—first off the boat, first up the mountain—and somewhat unsettled when he learns that Doc's haircutting talent originates in his work in a mortuary. Gagnon is the handsome member, the company's own Tyrone Power: somewhat vain, wide-eyed, and receptive to the adulatory overtures of businessmen. Doc is the solid center of the group who tries as best he can to stabilize and support the increasingly unruly Ira as he gets farther out of control. Ira is the minority who experiences discrimination on different levels, from callous stereotyping (comments about his squaw on the reservation), to insults ("drunken Indian"), to outright segregation (being refused service in a Chicago bar).[8] But unlike the formulaic melting pot assemblage familiar from combat films, this one has historical validity. As such, this grouping has the effect of making us reflect back on the melting pot groups we have encountered before. That is, this is not a group "written" so as to fulfill genre expectations. Rather, their presence has the effect of validating the impulse to present such groupings in earlier war films. In other words, the convention is retroactively valorized by the historical proof of its backgrounds.[9]

Another kind of grouping in war films includes older men whose sometimes meddling attitudes or outright ignorance about how to conduct campaigns and the war are shown to be inadequate. Such types appear as civilians in Abel Gance's *J'Accuse* (1919) and Lewis Milestone's *All Quiet on the Western Front* (1930). Here the characters of Keyes Beach (John Benjamin Hickey) and Bud Gerber (John Slattery) serve a comparable function. The former is the military man who brings the men back from Japan. The latter is the civilian attaché who engineers the bond tour for the three survivors and exploits them mercilessly. The flag raisers have in fact been drafted into a new kind of campaign by these older men who continue to push them, including Beach's support of Hayes' drinking. Gerber rejects Doc's concerns about the misrepresenting of Hank Hansen for Harlon Bloch, putting patriotism and national needs for financial support above the truth. An older Beach appears briefly as one of the younger Bradley's interviewees as he conducts research for his book about his father and admits that he failed to offer Hayes a ride when he saw him thumbing a ride in New Mexico several years after the bond drive.

Some of the set generic pieces resonate precisely because we know they are anchored in the actual experiences of the men. For example, often sailors and soldiers listen to music piped over the ship's intercom or through the camp, as occurs for example in *Destination Tokyo* (1943) and *The Story of GI Joe* (1945). One of the touching moments in *Flags* occurs as the men, anxiously awaiting the landing on Iwo Jima the next day, sit pensively silent as they hear Dinah Shore's rendition of "I'll Walk Alone," the song about isolation with which Eastwood begins the film. At another point, music is followed with a typical pitch by Tokyo Rose urging the men to surrender to the Japanese. Comparable wily comments are offered by Axis Sally when the theater of war is in Europe. But here the invitation carries a special weight since in fact on the next day the men will make the first physical landing on Japan since the war began.

One relevant aspect of the music in *Flags* evokes other genres, beginning with the appearance of singers representing the Andrews Sisters (Patty, Maxene, and Laverne), who were the most popular female singing group during World War II and appeared in several war related films, including *Buck Privates* (1941) and *Hollywood Canteen* (1944). They sing twice, once in a rally at Times Square and again at a reception and dinner. Their appearance here is a reminder of how Bradley, Hayes, and Gagnon are in fact themselves engaged as performers in an extension of their combat duties as they try to raise money for the bond drive. Even more to the point, the film presents their bond drive tour with the same iconography as that used for entertainers on the road in movie musicals: numerous shots of railroad stations and arrivals and departures of trains. All that is missing is a montage of printed city names such as appears in *This Is the Army* (1943), in which we do, in fact, follow a military group whose purpose is to entertain the troops.

Depiction of the home front is another generic feature taken to new heights in the film. When Mrs. Bloch sees the photograph of the flag raising, she is certain that she recognizes Harlon, an intuitive identification denied by the cover up authorized by Beach and Gerber. Separated from her husband, years later she learns in a phone call from him that she was correct. Mrs. Hansen, who is led to believe Hank was one of the flag raisers, actually is seen twice receiving bad news about her son, once about his death and once that he is not in the picture. In contrast to the more typical scenes in which parents and loved ones receive the bad news about their sons' deaths, here the film's historical accuracy overtakes the conventions and gives a special poignancy to the responses of the mothers. This is especially true when Doc, Ira, and Rene meet the mothers of Mike, Franklin, and Hank at a reception and Doc has to point out which one of the men in the picture is Hank; of course, none of them is. Ira breaks down and sobs when he meets Mike's mother.

The mise-en-scène of the film is dominated by the photograph and various representations of the flag raising, something unique to the genre.

**PLATE 26** *Flags of Our Fathers* (Clint Eastwood, 2006). Ira Hayes (Adam Beach), Doc Bradley (Ryan Phillippe), and Rene Gagnon (Jesse Bradford) talking in front of a flag poster (Dreamworks Skg/ Courtesy Photofest).

It appears first in the photograph on the cover of newspapers, then in paintings in Gerber's and President Harry Truman's offices, then as a model in Times Square, in posters everywhere the men go, in addition to its reenactment on Iwo Jima and again at Soldier Field, incongruously in the form of an ice-cream dessert with strawberry sauce poured over it at a banquet, and, finally as the monument itself, at its public dedication in 1954. The monument serves as a commentary on the way the image has grown to such proportions in the lives of the survivors, their families, and the nation.

An inescapable presence in the background of *Flags* is Allan Dwan's *Sands of Iwo Jima* (1949), which concerns the contentious relationship between Sergeant John Stryker (John Wayne) and Private Peter Conway (John Agar), who are part of the Marine force on the island. Stryker, a troubled, divorced man, has been drinking too much, but has begun to find some meaning in his life. The flag raising itself comes just before the point at which Stryker is killed. John Bradley, Ira Hayes, and Rene Gagnon were invited by Republic Pictures to serve as flag raisers at the point at which the flag is raised. This supplies a curious added complexity to the reenactment, since the actual men who raised

**PLATE 27** *Flags of Our Fathers* (Clint Eastwood, 2006). Ira Hayes (Adam Beach), Doc Bradley (Ryan Phillippe), and Rene Gagnon (Jesse Bradford) being served a strawberry sauce over ice-cream in the shape of the flag raising site (Deamworks SKG/Courtesy Photofest).

the flag on February 19, 1945 are now joining actors in yet another restaging of the event for even wider audiences that had seen them mount the paper mache mountain at Soldier Field. It is Stryker/Wayne who gives the three of them the flag, thus intensifying the cinematic irony attending the star who was never in the military but became the one most associated with the war film. He was nominated for an Oscar for his role.[10]

## Letters from Iwo Jima

Even though Eastwood's decision to show the Japanese experience recalls films like *The Longest Day* (1962) and *Tora! Tora! Tora!* (1970), which present the unfolding of events from multiple perspectives, only *Flags* and *Letters* exist as two separate films in different languages directed by one person. Written by Iris Yamashita and Paul Haggis, *Letters* chronicles the doomed efforts by the Japanese to stave off the American attack that began on February 19, 1945. The film focuses on both historical and fictionalized characters. In the first category are General

Kuribayashi (Ken Watanabe) who is supposed to secure the island against the American attack. An earlier diplomatic assignment in the United States in the 1930s had acquainted him with Americans. Baron Nishi (Tsuyoshi Ihara) had participated in the 1932 Olympics as an equestrian, and met and visited with Douglas Fairbanks and Mary Pickford. Nishi supports Kuribayashi's decisions to defend the island by building a complex network of caves and pillboxes from which the Japanese can attack. But others at the post reject the plan and the general's leadership, thinking that digging in with traditional foxholes in the sand would be more effective.

Although tactically informed, the general's plan is hopeless because no air and sea support can be offered to sustain it by the depleted Japanese Navy or Air Force. The film offers one defeat after another, and successive deaths, some by suicide as the soldiers destroy themselves with grenades. One of the specific links to *Flags* occurs when Doc Bradley and Hayes enter a cave and discover the bodies of Japanese soldiers who have killed themselves in this manner. Mick LaSalle points out another connection between the films: "In *Flags of Our Fathers*, we saw how terrifying it was when the sleeping mountain came alive, spouting machine-gun fire. In *Letters from Iwo Jima*, we see how frightening it is to be on the inside of the mountain, as bombs dropped and American soldiers swarmed."[11] The most important narrative link between the films, the flag itself, is downplayed narratively in *Letters*. While hearing news of the progressive deterioration of their defense of the island, several Japanese soldiers are seen in a cave in the foreground while at the very back of the frame we see Mount Surbachi and, barely visible, the flag at the pinnacle.

Fictionalized characters include Saigo (Kazunari Ninomiya), a baker drafted into the army as a reluctant soldier who sees little point to the defensive actions. He befriends Shimizu (Ryo Kas), who has been exiled in disgrace from an elite corps of soldiers because he would not perform certain cruel acts. Saigo and Shimizu become buddies once Saigo recognizes that the latter is not a spy installed in the camp. Their attempts to surrender to the Americans fail, and Shimizu is shot by his captors.

The title of the film refers to the letter writing that the Japanese soldiers, particularly the general and Saigo, engage in during the narrative and to the framing device with which the film opens and closes. The film begins as excavators in the present find a leather mail pouch. Then we move into an extended flashback that comprises the rest of the film, punctuated by occasional brief internal flashbacks associated with the general, Saigo, and Shimizu. At times these are linked specifically

**PLATE 28** *Letters from Iwo Jima* (Clint Eastwood, 2006). Saigo (Kazunari Ninomiya) reading (Amblin Entertainment/Courtesy Photofest).

to the letter writing. Buried by Saigo before Americans overwhelm them at the end of the battle for the island, the letters are the last element we see as the pouch is opened and they drift through the air.

The general saves Saigo twice: first when he and another soldier are being beaten by their superior officer for using defeatist language; and again when the same officer prepares to behead him for violating a command. Their roles reverse at the end of the film, when Saigo provides support for the general by carrying out his last wish. This occurs as the wounded and defeated Kuribayashi lies bleeding. He has been unable to get his second-in-command to behead him. Now, as he prepares to shoot himself with the pistol he received in America, he asks Saigo if they are at the moment still on unoccupied land, as yet unclaimed by the Americans. If so, he wants Saigo to bury him on this Japanese soil, a task performed off screen. Saigo's burial of the letters, an act we do see, establishes complex metaphorical connections between both the general and Saigo, the chief letter writers, and between them and the letters themselves. The surviving letters found by the excavators are not just relics of the battle, but almost like relics of the men themselves. The lyrical slow-motion photography of the final outpouring of letters from the pouch seems, finally, like a way of suggesting something about them spiritually.

**PLATE 29** *Letters from Iwo Jima* (Clint Eastwood, 2006). General Kuribayashi (Ken Watanabe) standing next to the flags of his country (Amblin Entertainment/Courtesy Photofest).

Unlike *Flags*, in which no Japanese character speaks, *Letters* presents several scenes with Americans: one set in the United States in which the general is honored by his American hosts with the pistol; another in which Japanese soldiers who surrender to Americans are murdered; and one in which a wounded GI is treated humanely by Baron Nishi, who tells him about his Hollywood connections and reads a letter from the boy's mother to the Japanese soldiers. This offers an interesting use of the convention of the letter from home, since the Japanese soldiers who hear the letter realize their kinship with the American boy.

Although several critics have offered helpful commentary on the film's generic aspects, including the ways it resists treating the Japanese stereotypically, no one has positioned *Letters* generically in relation to what seems to be its most appropriate forbears.[12] Without citing a specific film, Todd McCarthy suggests: "Considered from the Japanese angle, Iwo Jima resembles the Alamo, a futile if heroic last stand against an enemy force too overwhelming to withstand, although withstand it they did, for much longer than their opponents imagined possible."[13] He thus evokes one key event treated in the western genre by Raoul Walsh in *They Died With Their Boots On* (1941) and John Wayne in *The Alamo*

(1960). Mark Sinker offers another non-war film genre association as he speaks about "a secondary . . . formal problem, call it the slasher-flick protocol. A group of people under fatal threat die one by one: how to avoid *Scream*-style over-knowing judgments about the justice of their various fates?"[14]

Viewed in relation to the war film genre, though, *Letters* clearly belongs with films like John Ford's *The Lost Patrol* (1934) and *Bataan* (1943), films in which one man after another dies. Jeanine Basinger's commentary takes us back to important representatives of the genre: "The story of the real battle of Bataan is a story of loss and defeat, as is the story of *Bataan* the movie. Although it is obvious that the battle itself inspired the movie, it is important to realize that the story the film tells is one audiences had seen before in *[The] Lost Patrol*."[15] In the earlier film, all but one of the men in the patrol are killed or die until only one man is left alive. In *Bataan*, everyone dies. In *Letters*, only one man, Saigo, is left alive from the Japanese forces, but in a narrative move that evokes the ending of *Bataan*, Eastwood has him behaving very much like Bill Dane (Robert Taylor) at that film's conclusion. Faced with certain death, Dane wields his machine gun wildly and dares the Japanese to come and get him. In *Letters*, American soldiers discover Saigo walking with a shovel after he has finished burying General Kuribayashi. As they approach Saigo, he sees the general's pistol in the belt of a soldier who found it on the ground. This incites Saigo's rage, and, like the frantic Bill Dane, he strikes out wildly against all his opponents. They do not want to kill him and finally succeed in knocking him out. We see him lying on a stretcher, framed by a shot of what is either a sunrise or a sunset. Our uncertainty as to its temporal position works effectively: is this the rising sun, emblem of the once-powerful Japan, or a setting sun, signaling its defeat?

As noted, the interest in making films about World War II in the 1990s has been explained as a result of various reasons, among them the deaths of the surviving veterans who made up "the Greatest Generation" and the need to reinvigorate American morale and ideals at a time of international uncertainty. How then should we contextualize Clint Eastwood's films, made in the first decade of the new century? Two suggestions are worth noting. Robert Sklar sees both films as "undoubtedly addressed to the present time of national crisis."[16] Richard Corliss suggests "Eastwood's compassionate, cautionary tale speaks eloquently about a time when Americans needed heroes, and does so when we are no longer sure what they look like—when the indelible photo op of the Iraq war is from Abu Ghraib."[17] In contrast,

Eastwood takes us back to a time before the overworked term "photo op" became part of our media vocabulary. His diptych, a generic first for the Hollywood war film, uses the indelible photographic image of Iwo Jima from American history and the dual perspectives on loss and death as experienced by all combatants to explore the devastating effect of war on all humanity.

# NOTES

## Introduction

1   The use of war as the subject matter
of fantasy and science fiction raises
interesting questions about the ways
one genre can incorporate conventions
of another, an issue that has engaged
attention from theorists who acknowledge affinities between the war film
and the western and those exploring the
issue of generic hybridization, a topic
explored again in this book. On the war
film and other genres, see Rick Altman,
*Film/Genre* (London: BFI, 1999): 219;
Jeanine Basinger, *The World War II
Combat Film: Anatomy of a Genre* (Middle-
town, CT: Wesleyan University Press, 2003): 239; and Steve Neale, *Genre
and Hollywood* (New York: Routledge, 2000): 126 For a discussion of
genre hybridization, see Jim Collins, "Genericity in the Nineties: Eclectic
Irony and the New Sincerity," in Jim Collins, Hilary Radner, and Eva
Collins, eds., *Film Theory Goes to the Movies* (New York: Routledge, 1993):
242–263; Janet Staiger, *Perverse Spectators: The Practices of Film Reception*
(New York: New York University Press, 2000): 61–77; and Barry Keith
Grant, *Film Genre: From Iconography to Ideology* (London: Wallflower, 2007):
22–24. As Grant explains, the issue before critics is how one can talk
about hybridization and combining of genres, as if they were pure in
and of themselves, without acknowledging that we may not be able to
conceive of genres so simply in the first place.

2   Vary, "War Movies Tanked": *ew.com*, 21 Dec. 2007; Garrett, "B.O. Battle Fatigue? War is Hell as studios try to sell conflict pics": *Variety*, 15–21 Oct. 2007: 7; Corliss, "This Means War. Why audiences aren't packing the cineplex to see Hollywood's take on the Iraq Conflict," *Time*, 26 Nov. 2007: 80–81; Toto, "Audiences Reject Iraq War at Box Office," www. washingtontimes.com, 25 Oct. 2007; Gliberman, *Entertainment Weekly* 25 Oct. 2007: 48.

3   All the films about the Spanish-American War mentioned here are viewable on the Library of Congress American Memory Website: www. lcweb2.loc.gov/ammem/sawhtml/sawhome.html.

4   Beaumont Newhall, *The History of Photography* (New York: Museum of Modern Art, 1964): 67.

5   Thomas Schatz, *Hollywood Genres: Formulas, Filmmaking, and the Studio System* (New York: McGraw Hill, 1981): 262–263.

6   "Film Projection and Variety Shows," in *The Silent Cinema Reader*, eds. Lee Grievson and Peter Krämer (London: Routledge, 2004): 35.

7   Jonathan Auerbach, *Body Shots: Early Cinema's Incarnations* (Berkeley: University of California Press, 2007): 32. See also Raymond Fielding, *The American Newsreel 1911–1967* (Norman: University of Oklahoma Press, 1973): 3–45.

8   Robert C. Allen, "Contra the Chaser Theory," in *Film Before Griffith*, ed. John L. Fell (Berkeley: University of California Press, 1983): 111.

9   Charles Musser, *Before the Nickelodeon: Edwin S. Porter and the Edison Manufacturing Company* (Berkeley: University of California Press, 1991): 135.

10  Charles Musser, *The Emergence of Cinema: The American Screen to 1907* (New York: Charles Scribner's Sons, 1990): 258–259. See James Castonguay's important study, "The Spanish-American War in United States Media Culture," *Hypertext Studies in American Studies*, www.chnm.gmu.aq/war/ index.html. He points out that people in some areas in which Spanish Americans lived were not supportive of the war.

11  Tom Gunning, "The Cinema of Attractions: Early Film, Its Spectator and the Avant-Garde," in *Early Cinema: Space Frame Narrative*, ed. Thomas Elsaesser (London: BFI, 1990): 58.

12  David Levy, "Re-constituted Newsreels, Re-Enactments and the American Narrative Film," in *Cinema 1900/1906: An Analytic Study by the National Film Archive (London) and the International Federation of Film Archives* [FIAF: Fédération d'Internationale des Archives du Film], 1982): I, 245.

13  Kristen Whissel, "The Gender of Empire: American Modernity, Masculinity, and Edison's War Actualities," in *A Feminist Reader in Early Cinema*, eds. Jennifer M. Bean and Diane Negra (Durham: University of North Carolina Press, 2002): 141–195.

14  *The Battle of the Somme*, a British documentary, appeared in 1916.

15  Andrew Tudor, "Genre," in *Film Genre Reader III*, ed. Barry Grant (Austin: University of Texas Press, 2003): 5. Compare this with Jim Kitses'

suggestion to "see the term [convention] . . . as an area of agreement between audience and artist with reference to the form which his art will take." *Horizons West: Anthony Mann, Budd Boetticher, Sam Peckinpah; Studies of Authorship within the Western* (Bloomington: Indiana University Press, 1969): 24.

16   For an exhaustive summary of conventions, see Basinger, *The World War II Combat Film*: 14–75.

## Chapter 1: Historical Overview

1   See Thomas Cripps, *Slow Fade to Black: The Negro in American Film, 1900–1942* (New York: Oxford University Press, 1973), and Robert Lang, ed., *The Birth of a Nation: D. W. Griffith, Director* (New Brunswick, NJ: Rutgers University Press, 1994).

2   Leon F. Litwack, "*The Birth of a Nation*," in *Past Imperfect: History According to the Movies*, ed. Mark C. Carnes (New York: Henry Holt, 1995): 138.

3   See Roger Ebert's query about the lack of information about the source of the quotation and also a thoughtful commentary on the film: rogerebert.com, 30 March, 2003, www.rogerebert.suntimes.com/apps/pbcs.dll/article?AID=/20030330/REVIEWS08/303300301/1023.

4   In Cecil B. DeMille's *The Little American* (1917), Mary Pickford, at the time America's most popular actress, plays a character at the center of a romantic triangle involving two men who are fighting for their native countries, France and Germany. She helps to save the life of the redeemed German American, whom she loves. In contrast to *Hearts of the World*, though, this film was not popular with American audiences because, according to Kevin Brownlow, the film displayed too much sympathy for the German soldier. In fact, DeMille was asked to recut it so that Pickford's character marries the French soldier, an indication of how strongly Americans were against Germany. See Kevin Brownlow, *The War, The West, and the Wilderness* (New York: Knopf, 1979): 134.

5   Review of *La Grande Illusion*, rogerebert.com, 3 October, 1999.

6   Cynthia Fuchs, www.popmatters.com/pm/film/reviews/38530/very-long-engagement/, 17 December 2004.

7   On genre hybridization in more recent films see Jim Collins, "Genericity in the Nineties: Eclectic Irony and the New Sincerity," in Jim Collins, Hilary Radner, and Eva Collins, eds., *Film Theory Goes to the Movies* (New York: Routledge, 1993): 242–263; and Janet Staiger, *Perverse Spectators: The Practices of Film Reception* (New York: New York University Press, 2000): 61–77.

8   Letter to Lewis Milestone, 26 June 1946, Margaret Herrick Library, Academy of Motion Picture Arts and Sciences, Lewis Milestone file. The main thrust of the letter is to provide a stinging critique of Milestone for

his most recent war film, *A Walk in the Sun*. Fuller is deeply disappointed by the film, having liked *All Quiet on the Western Front*. See Nicholas Cull, "Samuel Fuller on Lewis Milestone's *A Walk in the Sun* (1946): The Legacy of *All Quiet on the Western Front* (1930)," *Historical Journal of Film, Radio, & Television* 20, 1 (March 2000): 79–87.

9  See Guerric DeBona, "Masculinity on the Front: John Huston's *The Red Badge of Courage*," in Eberwein, ed., *The War Film* (New Brunswick, NJ: Rutgers University Press, 2004), 117–139.

10  Three more prisoner-of-war films based on actual experiences in Japanese prisoner-of-war camps are Steven Spielberg's *Empire of the Sun* (1987), about J. G. Ballard's imprisonment as a young boy in China; Bruce Beresford's *Paradise Road* (1997), about women in Sumatra; and David Cunningham's *To End All Wars* (2001). The last concludes with a sequence in which one of the actual prisoners and one of his captors are seen interacting as old men, over fifty years after the liberation of the camp.

11  American Film Institute online catalog.

12  Susan Sontag, "The Imagination of Disaster," in *Against Interpretation* (New York: Picador, 1966): 209–225. Rick Worland has noted a comparable phenomenon during World War II when "even gothic horror [films] could take on explicit war associations," specifically in *The Ghost of Frankenstein* (Earl Kenton, 1942), when "gothic trolls were nurturing Hitlerian dreams of thousand-year Reichs and world domination." Rick Worland, *The Horror Film* (Oxford: Blackwell, 2007): 71–72.

13  One Korean filmmaker has recently used that war as a way to comment on present tensions between North and South Korea. Je-Gyu Kang's *Tae-Guk-Gi* (2004) focuses on the actions of two brothers fighting for the South. In a manner that anticipates the opening of Clint Eastwood's *Letters from Iwo Jima*, the film opens with a contemporary discovery of a relic from a previous war, in this case the skeleton of the older brother. The film then flashes back to their personal histories and involvement in the war. Dave Kehr suggests perceptively that the enmity that develops between the brothers is readable in relation to the current situation in Korea, which still suffers from tensions between the North and South. Dave Kehr, *New York Times*, 3 September 2004: E20.

14  I hold to the latter view in "Ceremonies of Survival: The Structure of *The Deer Hunter*," *Journal of Popular Film and Television* 7 (1979): 352–364.

15  Doherty, "The New War Movies as Moral Rearmament," in Eberwein, ed., *The War Film* (New Brunswick, NJ: Rutgers University Press, 2004), 216–218.

16  Susan Jeffords, "The Reagan Hero: Rambo," in Eberwein, ed., *The War Film* (New Brunswick, NJ: Rutgers University Press, 2004), 140.

17  Robert Toplin, *History by Hollywood: The Use and Abuse of the American Past* (Urbana: University of Illinois Press, 1996): 172.

18  Vincent Canby, Review, *New York Times*, 24 September 1970.

19   In the restored version, a young girl who has made a garland for the sergeant's helmet is killed by a German sniper.

20   Samuel Fuller, *A Third Face: My Tale of Writing, Fighting, and Filmmaking*, with Christina Lang Fuller and Jerome Henry Rudes (New York: Applause Theatre & Cinema Books, 2002): 462–463. Lisa Dombrowski provides an analysis of the script in the Margaret Herrick Library: "Although the central conflict . . . between Zack [the Colonel] and Quan [the Vietnamese boy] could easily form a sequel to *The Steel Helmet*, the surrounding narrative is so excessive and so contradictory that it seems unimaginable that the script could ever be made." Dombrowski, *The Films of Samuel Fuller: "If You Die, I'll Kill you!"* (Middletown, CT: Wesleyan University Press, 2008): 169.

21   Eisenhower, "Farewell Address to the Nation," 17 January 1961.

22   Roger Ebert's observations are relevant: "Corporations, not commies, are the sinister force. . . . [P]oor Raymond Shaw is told by a liberal senator: 'You are about to become the first privately owned and operated vice-president of the United States.' There's a level of cynicism here that is scarier than the Red Chinese villains [in the earlier film] but the idea that corporations may be subverting the democratic process is plausible in the age of Enron." rogerebert.com, 30 July 2004.

23   I am grateful to Barry K. Grant for his suggestion that the presence of Tom Hanks has had a lot to do with the film's success, since he evokes positive military associations for both his roles in *Saving Private Ryan* and, earlier, *Forrest Gump* (1994).

## Chapter 2: Critical Issues

1   Kathryn Kane, "The World War II Combat Film," in Wes Gehring, ed., *Handbook of American Film Genres* (Westport, CT: Greenwood Press, 1988): 85.

2   *Ibid.*, 86. Her emphasis on oppositions is reminiscent of the approach to the western informing the work of Jim Kitses. He suggests that the genre is characterized by a series of antinomies or oppositions, primarily between "the Wilderness," which includes "The Individual, Nature, the West," and "Civilization," in which belong "the Community, Culture, the East." See Kitses, *Horizons West: Anthony Mann, Budd Boetticher, Sam Peckinpah; Studies of Authorship within the Western* (Bloomington: Indiana University Press, 1969), 11. The theoretical work of Claude Lévi-Strauss on myth provides an important source of this kind of thinking. He argues that upon examination, myths can be seen to resolve into basic antinomies, or categories of binary oppositions. See "The Structural Study of Myth," in *The Structuralists fom Marx to Lévi-Strauss*, ed. Richard and Fernande DeGeorge (New York: Anchor Books, 1972): 180.

3   Jeanine Basinger, *The World War II Combat Film: Anatomy of a Genre* (Middletown, CT: Wesleyan University Press, 2003): 13.

4   Steve Neale, *Genre and Hollywood* (London: Routledge, 2000): 125.

5   Neale, *Genre and Hollywood*, 126.

6   Lawrence Suid, *Guts and Glory: The Making of the American Military Image in Film* (Lexington: University of Kentucky Press, 2002): xii.

7   Lenny Rubenstein, "The War Film," in Gary Crowdus, ed., *The Political Companion to American Film* (Chicago: Lakeview Press, 1994): 455–456.

8   Thomas Doherty, *Projections of War: Hollywood, American Culture, and World War II*, revd. edn. (New York: Columbia University Press, 1999): 4.

9   Thomas Sobchak, "Genre Film: A Classical Experience," in *Film Genre Reader III*, ed. Barry Grant (Austin: University of Texas Press, 2003): 104.

10  Sobchak, "Genre Film," 105.

11  Robert Burgoyne, *The Hollywood Historical Film* (Oxford: Wiley-Blackwell, 2008): 2.

12  Some post-Vietnam films that begin with comic treatment of training camps eventually end with actual war-related activities, such as occur in the last part of *Stripes* (1981), *In the Army* (1994), and *Major Payne* (1995).

13  Joel Finler, *The Hollywood Story* (New York: Crown, 1988), 276. Profits from the film were donated to the Serviceman's Relief Fund. The only other war-themed film to earn more is *The Best Years of Our Lives* (1946) ($10.4 million), made after the war ended.

14  Bosley Crowther, "Review of *This is the Army*," *New York Times*, 29 July 1943: 11, 6.

15  Jonathan Auerbach, *Body Shots: Early Cinema's Incarnations* (Berkeley: University of California Press, 2007): 32.

16  Anton Kaes, "History and Film: Public Memory in the Age of Electronic Dissemination," *History and Memory* 2, 1 (Fall/Winter 1990): 112–113.

17  Pierre Sorlin sees a similar kind of practice at work in Russian film: *The Film in History: Restaging the Past* (Oxford: Blackwell, 1980): 16.

18  Robert Brent Toplin, "Hollywood's D-Day from the Perspective of the 1960s and 1990s: *The Longest Day* and *Saving Private Ryan*," *Film and History* 36, 2 (2006): 25.

19  Robert Brent Toplin, *History by Hollywood: The Use and Abuse of the American Past* (Urbana: University of Illinois Press, 1996): 171–175.

20  Robert Burgoyne, *Film Nation: Hollywood Looks at US History* (Minneapolis: University of Minnesota Press, 1997): 48.

21  Burgoyne, *Film Nation*, 7–8.

22  Rick Altman, *Film/Genre* (London: BFI Publishing, 1999): 189.

23  Altman, *Film/Genre*, 190. See his discussion of the Office of War Information's categorization of 1943 war-related films: 107–110.

24  Marita Sturken, *Tangled Memories: The Vietnam War, the AIDS Epidemic, and the Politics of Remembering* (Berkeley: University of California Press,

1997): 2–3. And, as Pierre Sorlin suggests, after the appearance of *The Birth of a Nation* (1915), "from now on the close relationship between war and cinema was imbedded in the memory of individuals and, throughout the twentieth century, collective celebrations made an extensive use of pictures." Sorlin, "Cinema and the Memory of the Great War," in *The First World War and Popular Cinema: 1914 to the Present*, ed. Michael Paris (New Brunswick, NJ: Rutgers University Press, 2000): 6.

25  Stephen Ambrose, "The Longest Day," in *Past Imperfect: History According to the Movies* ed. Mark C. Carnes (New York: Henry Holt, 1995): 238.

26  John Whitclay Chambers, "*All Quiet on the Western Front* (US, 1930): The Antiwar Film and the Image of Modern War," in *World War II, Film, and History*, ed. John Whitclay Chambers and David Culbert (New York: Oxford University Press, 1996): 19.

27  Peter Wollen, *Signs and Meaning in the Cinema*, 3rd edn. (Bloomington: Indiana University Press, 1973): 122–123.

28  André Bazin, "The Ontology of the Photographic Image," in *What is Cinema?*, ed. and trans. Hugh Gray (Berkeley: University of California Press, 1971): 15.

29  Caroline Brothers, *War and Photography: A Cultural History* (New York: Routledge, 1997): 18.

30  Michael Arlen, *The Living-Room War* (New York: Viking, 1969).

31  Paul Virilio, *War and Cinema: The Logistics of Perception*, trans. Patrick Camiller (London: Verso, 1989): 26.

32  Bernd Hüppauf, "Experiences of Modern Warfare and the Crisis of Representation," in *Hollywood and War, the Film Reader*, ed. J. David Slocum (New York: Routledge, 2006): 57.

33  Slocum, *Hollywood and War*, 31.

34  American Film Institute online catalog.

35  *Yankee Clipper*, 30 April 1898: 153.

36  *Yankee Clipper*, 22 April 1899: 160.

37  *New York Times*, 20 November 1925: 18, 1.

38  *Variety*, 11 November 1925.

39  *Time*, 28 September, 1942: 82.

40  *New York Times*, 12 July 1945: 8, 2.

41  *Time*, 26 February 1945: 92.

42  *New York Times*, 27 January 1945: 15, 2.

43  rogerebert.com, 20 July 1998.

44  *Entertainment Weekly*, 24 July 1998.

45  Jeanine Basinger, *The World War II Combat Film*, 14–75. See her discussion of the film, "Combat Redux," 253–262; Robert Burgoyne, "The War Film: *Saving Private Ryan*," in *The Hollywood Historical Film*, 50–73; Thomas Doherty, *Projections of War*, 300–315; and Thomas Schatz, "Old War/New War: *Band of Brothers* and the Revival of the WWII War Film," *Film and History*, 32, 1 (2002): 74–78.

46  See Albert Auster, *Saving Private Ryan* and American Triumphalism," in Eberwein, ed., *The War Film* (New Brunswick, NJ: Rutgers University Press, 2004): 205–213.

47  Studs Terkel, *The Good War: An Oral History of World War* II (New York: Pantheon, 1984); Tom Brokaw, *The Greatest Generation* (New York: Delta, 1998).

## Chapter 3: **All Quiet on the Western Front** *(1930)*

1  Every student of the film owes a debt to Andrew Kelly, who has written definitively and rewardingly on its history, production, and reception: *All Quiet on the Western Front: The Story of a Film* (London: I. B. Tauris, 1998). See also his study of World War I films: *Cinema and the Great War* (London: Routledge, 1997).

2  Letter from Ayres to Dr. Harley Taylor, Jr., 17 December 1975, in the Lewis Milestone file, Margaret Herrick Library, Academy of Motion Picture Arts and Sciences, Los Angeles.

3  On the production history, see Thomas Schatz, *The Genius of the System: Hollywood Filmmaking in the Studio Era* (New York: Pantheon, 1988): 82–87.

4  See Russell Merritt, "Roadshows Put on the Ritz," www.cinemaweb.com/silentfim/bookshelf/31_rs_1.htm.

5  For a discussion of the film and its production history, see Kelly, *Cinema and the Great War*: 65–75.

6  For more on these films, see my *Armed Forces: Masculinity and Sexuality in the American War Film* (New Brunswick, NJ: Rutgers University Press, 2007).

7  Although not given a road show exhibition, two other films deserve mention. John Ford's *Four Sons*, one of the top earners for 1928, concerns a family in which three brothers fight for Germany, and the fourth for the United States. Howard Hawks' *The Dawn Patrol* (August 1930), discussed later in this chapter, is also an anti-war film worth noting. It examines the burden of command by looking at the emotional devastation caused in commanders who have to send pilots out to certain death.

8  I do not know whether Kon Ichikawa was aware of this film when he made *Fires on the Plain* (1959). This includes a montage sequence showing a succession of Japanese soldiers trying on the same pair of boots lying in the mud on the road.

9  Robert Baird, "*Hell's Angels* above *The Western Front*," in *Hollywood's World War I: Motion Picture Images*, ed. Peter C. Rollins and John E. O'Connor (Bowling Green: Bowling Green State University Popular Press, 1997): 93.

10  *Variety*, 7 May 1930, www.variety.com/index.asp?layout=Variety100&reviewid=VE1117487991&content=jump&jump=review&category=1935&cs=1&p=0.

11  *New York Times*, 30 April 1930: 29, 1.
12  According to Kelly, at the film's premiere in Germany, before it was banned, "[Joseph] Goebbels made a speech to the audience, stink-bombs and white mice were released and there were riots outside the cinema": Kelly, *All Quiet on the Western Front: The Story of a Film*, 122. See his chapter in this book, "Reception, Condemnation and Censorship," 102–132, for a discussion of the censorship problems the film experienced in the United States and throughout the world.
13  See my essay, "Remakes and Cultural Studies," in *Play It Again Sam: Retakes on Remakes*, ed. Andrew Horton and Stuart McDougal (Berkeley: University of California Press, 1998): 15–33.
14  *Time Out London*, review, www.timeout.com/film/.
15  Schatz, *The Genius of the System*, 84–85.
16  The American Film Institute catalog includes the Foreword.
17  Michael E. Birdwell, *Celluloid Soldiers: Warner Bros.'s Campaign Against Nazism* (New York: New York University Press, 1999), 64, suggests the studio was motivated to remake the film by its desire to protect a number of British actors under contract. If war came, they would be drawn back into service with the British forces. He doesn't mention the change in plot.
18  Birdwell, *Celluloid Soldiers*, 76. See also David Welky, *The Moguls and the Dictators: Hollywood and the Coming of World War II* (Baltimore: Johns Hopkins University Press, 2008).
19  According to the American Film Institute Catalog, Selznick fired the original director, John Huston, because he wanted to focus on the war itself.

## *Chapter 4:* **Destination Tokyo *(1943)* and Retaliation Films**

1  Although Joseph I. Breen, head of the Production Code Administration, raised numerous objections to the language used by Wolf describing his actions, most of the original material in the script made it into the film.
2  Thomas Schatz, *Boom and Bust: American Cinema in the 1940s* (Berkeley: University of California Press, 1999): 467.
3  "Saga of a Pigboat," *Newsweek*, 10 January 1944: 82.
4  *Variety*, 22 December 1943, www.carygrant.net/reviews/destination. html.
5  Crowther, *New York Times*, 1 January 1944: 9, 2.
6  See Lawrence Suid for the best discussion of the inaccuracies: *Guts and Glory: The Making of the American Military Image in Film*, revd. edn. (Lexington: University of Kentucky Press, 2002): 80–82.
7  *Hollywood Reporter*, 21 December 1943.
8  *Motion Picture Daily*, 21 December 1943.

9   Publicity File No. 683 in the Warner Bros. Archives, University of Southern California.

10  Memorandum from Martin Weiser to Alex Evelove, 5 November 1943. Miscellaneous File 1943–1944, *Destination Tokyo*, AMPAS.

11  Although they aren't part of the retaliation sub-genre, two 1942 films are notable for the way in which they present the announcement of the attack on Pearl Harbor. *A Yank on the Burma Road* (1942) is the first narrative film to show a character in any American war film being informed about Pearl Harbor. According to the American Film Institute online catalogue, the film, which concerns American volunteers who are trying to help the Chinese, had been completed in November 1941, but a scene was added in which the hero learns about the attack from the Chinese. David Miller's *The Flying Tigers* (October 1942) is the next work of note to address Pearl Harbor. It concerns a force of volunteer airmen led by Jim Gordon (John Wayne, in his first war film) serving under Major General Victor Chennault in the Flying Tigers, a volunteer group that was trying to defend China from Japanese attacks before the United States entered the war. After Pearl Harbor, the force was formally reconstituted as an arm of the Air Force. Even though one of the most common elements in war films during the period was a scene in which servicemen or citizens hear about the attack, as far as I know, this film was the first to present an extended treatment of people listening to President Franklin Delano Roosevelt's speech in which he denounces the December 7 attack on Pearl Harbor as a "day which will live in infamy" and asks for a formal declaration of war. Another film about the Flying Tigers, *God Is My Co-Pilot*, was based on the autobiography of Robert Scott, one of the fliers.

12  Schatz, *Boom and Bust*, 466.

13  Jeanine Basinger, *The World War II Combat Film: Anatomy of a Genre* (Middletown, CT: Wesleyan University Press, 2003). *Bataan* is the centerpiece of her comprehensive discussion of the conventions of the combat film (46–67). She examines it along with other 1943 films: *Air Force*, *Destination Tokyo*, *Guadalcanal Diary*, and *Sahara*, and suggests that they "are all the same movie" (67). She concludes this discussion by creating the template for an imagined and unproduced film called *War Cry!* that displays all the conventions of the genre (67–70).

14  *Corregidor* (1943) opened one week before *Bataan*. Basinger does not think it belongs with *Air Force* and *Bataan* in the combat film genre. Although it has some relation to the retaliation sub-genre, I would exclude it in a similar way. The characters are fighting to get to Corregidor after the attack on Manila. Two love stories dominate this film, which received a scathing review in the *New York Times* in language that implies how the other films in the sub-genre were appreciated. The reviewer says audiences will be "fighting mad" because "such a counterfeit testament to the men and women of the 'Rock' [Corregidor] have been

perpetrated on the screen." The film lacks exactly those aspects seen in films that belong to the sub-genre: "Nothing of those grueling, harassed days, nothing of the fiber of those men and women who steadfastly clung to their duty in spite of the obvious knowledge that theirs was but a holding action until the mighty power of their country could be launched with deadly retribution ever gets on the screen. Instead it is nothing more than a couple of hackneyed love stories plus battle scenes and some hollow-sounding words about democracy and truth thrown in." L.B.F., "Review of *Corregidor*," *New York Times*, 28 May 1943: 19.

15  Schatz, *Boom and Bust*, 466.

16  *Cry "Havoc"* opened November 23, less than a week after *Guadalcanal Diary*. That day the *New York Times* displayed an advertisement for it on the same page as one for *Guadalcanal Diary*. At the top of the page, the latter had a drawing of shirtless Marines with the caption; "The picture that has captured every woman's heart." At the bottom of the page, the ad for *Cry "Havoc"* indicated it had "the greatest all feminine cast," an inaccurate claim since some males do appear.

17  American Film Institute online catalog.

18  Thomas Schatz, *Hollywood Genres: Formulas, Filmmaking, and the Studio System* (New York: McGraw Hill, 1981): 262–263.

19  I exclude Edward Ludwig's *The Fighting Seabees* (1944) from the cycle. Set in 1942, it presents an account of the creation of the Seabees. According to the American Film Institute online catalog, "The US Navy Construction Battalion, known as the Seabees, was created in Jan. 1942 to provide armed, militarily trained construction workers to erect buildings, airfields, refueling bases, etc. in support of the military during World War II." John Wayne stars as the head of a construction company working in the Pacific for the Navy. Wartime conditions result in is absorption into the service as the Seabees. Obviously, the unit's function is a result of war with Japan, but the film's narrative is not inflected by Pearl Harbor as is the case in the others discussed here.

20  Robert Burgoyne, *The Hollywood Historical Film* (Oxford: Wiley-Blackwell, 2008): 148–149.

21  Ali Jaafar, "Casualties of War," *Sight & Sound*, 18, 2 (February 2008): 20.

## *Chapter 5:* **Platoon *(1986)* and Full Metal Jacket *(1987)*

1  John G. Cawelti, "*Chinatown* and Generic Transformation in Recent American Films," in Barry K. Grant, *Film Genre Reader*, 3rd. edn. (Austin: University of Texas Press, 2003): 260

2  Cawelti, *Chinatown*, 259.

3  Cawelti, *Chinatown*, 260.

4 Jim Collins argues correctly that Cawelti doesn't really explain why such transformations occur, and suggests "we need to examine the current set of preconditions formed by the interplay of cultural, technological, and demographic factors." Collins, "Genericity in the Nineties: Eclectic Irony and the New Sincerity," in Jim Collins, Hilary Radner, and Eva Collins, eds., *Film Theory Goes to the Movies* (New York: Routledge, 1993): 245.

5 Susan White suggests "Chinatown-as-Vietnam remains allegorical in Polanski's films." White, "Male Bonding, Hollywood Orientalism, and the Repression of the Feminine in Kubrick's *Full Metal Jacket*," in *Inventing Vietnam: The War in Film and Television*, ed. Michael Anderegg (Philadelphia: Temple University Press, 1991): 221. Trevor McCrisken and Andrew Pepper argue that "other genres such as westerns (*Little Big Man* [1970]), gangster films (*Bonnie and Clyde* [1967]), film noir (*Chinatown*) and indeed war films (*M\*A\*S\*H* [1970], *Patton* [1970]) were used as allegories for Vietnam and its impact on the homefront." McCrisken and Pepper, *American History and Contemporary Hollywood* (New Brunswick, NJ: Rutgers University Press, 2005): 93.

6 Thomas Doherty, *Projections of War*, revd. edn. (New York: Columbia University Press, 1999): 282.

7 Doherty, *Projections of War*, 286.

8 Vincent Canby observes that *Platoon* "is not like any other Vietnam film that's yet been made—certainly not those revisionist comic strips *Rambo* and *Missing in Action*. Nor does it have much in connection with either Francis Ford Coppola's epic *Apocalypse Now*, which ultimately turns into a romantic meditation on a mythical war, or Michael Cimino's *Deer Hunter*, which is more about the mind of America that fought the war than the Vietnam War itself" (*New York Times*, 19 December 1986: C12). David Ansen makes a similar comment: "Watching Oliver Stone's shattering *Platoon*, it dawns on you that most previous Hollywood movies about Vietnam weren't really about Vietnam. *The Deer Hunter*, *Apocalypse Now* and *Coming Home* used the war as a metaphor to explore the American psyche, metaphysics or personal relationships" (*Newsweek*, 5 January 1987: 57). See David Halberstam, "*Platoon*," and Robert A. Rosenstone, "Oliver Stone as Historian," in *Oliver Stone's USA: Film, History, and Controversy*, ed. Robert Brent Toplin (Lawrence: University Press of Kansas, 2002): 110–119; 26–39. Stone himself is represented in this collection responding to commentary about him: "Stone on Stone's Image (As Presented by Some Historians)": 40–65.

9 Roger Ebert, Review of *Platoon*, rogerebert.com, 30 December 1986. I am grateful to Jayne Fargnoli for her suggestion that this sequence's confusion provides a kind of "condensed" version of the American experience in the Vietnam War.

10 Susan Jeffords, "Reproducing Fathers: Gender and the Vietnam War in US Culture," in *From Hanoi to Hollywood: The Vietnam War in American*

*Film*, ed. Linda Dittmar and Gene Michaud (New Brunswick, NJ: Rutgers University Press, 1990): 209.

11  I am grateful to Barry K. Grant for his suggestion that the woman's response serves as a mirror to that of the audience.

12  Mark Baker, *Nam: The Vietnam War in the Words of the Men and Women Who Fought There* (New York: Quill, 1982); Susan Brownmiller, *Against Our Will: Men, Women, and Rape* (New York: Fawcett Columbine, 1993).

13  Brian J. Woodman, "Represented in the Margins: Images of African American Soldiers in Vietnam Combat Films," in *The War Film*, ed. Robert Eberwein (New Brunswick, NJ: Rutgers University Press, 2004): 105–106.

14  The first film Kubrick ever made was about war, *Fear and Desire* (1953). He withdrew it from distribution. *Variety*'s reviewer called it "a literate, unhackneyed war drama, outstanding for its fresh camera treatment and poetic dialog" and praised it as "definitely out of the potboiler class one would expect from a shoestring budget." The reviewer summarized the film: "Story deals with four GIs stranded six miles behind enemy lines and what happens to their moral fiber as they try to escape. Kenneth Harp is a glib intellectual, grows weary with his own sophistication. Paul Mazursky, over-sensitive to violence, is a weakling who tries to befriend a captured enemy girl, Virginia Leith (a toothsome dish), shoots her, and then goes insane. Steve Coit is a level-headed Southerner who also winds up confused about his values. Frank Silvera plays the one character who fulfills himself—a tough, brave primitive, who purposely draws the fire of the enemy on himself on a river raft, so that Harp and Coitcan shoot an enemy general and escape in a captured plane." Variety.com, 1 January 1953, www.variety.com/review/VE1117790864.html?categoryid=31&cs=1&p=0.

15  Thomas Doherty suggests: "*Full Metal Jacket* exemplifies the Vietnam War film in its mature stage, a stage whose distinguishing quality is its reliance on cinematic, not historical, experience. The Vietnam film has not yet settled into the ripe generic dotage of the private eye or western genre, but it has reached the point where previous Vietnam films as much as Vietnam memory determine its rough outlines." "Full Metal Genre: Stanley Kubrick's Vietnam Combat Movie," *Film Quarterly* 42, 1 (Autumn 1988), 24. Jonathan Rosenbaum reports that Sam Fuller did not like the film: "I'll never forget escorting the late Samuel Fuller, the much-decorated World War II hero and maverick filmmaker, to a multiplex screening of *Full Metal Jacket*. . . . Though Fuller courteously stayed with us to the end, he declared afterward that as far as he was concerned, it was another goddamn recruiting film—that teenage boys who went to see Kubrick's picture with their girlfriends would come out thinking that wartime combat was neat." *Chicago Reader*, 24 July 1998, chireader.com.

16    In *Attack!* (1956), Robert Aldrich's World War II film, an inept captain whose mistakes have led to the deaths of many men is murdered by one of his junior officers.

17    Both the sniper and Pyle could be said to be the subjects of metaphorical rape: the former as she lies encircled by the men after being shot; Pyle as he's attacked during the blanket party. Cynthia Fuchs, " 'Vietnam and Sexual Violence': The Movie," in *America Rediscovered: Critical Essays on Literature and Film of the Vietnam Era*, ed. Owen W. Gilman, Jr. and Lorie Smith (New York: Garland, 1990): 126; Susan White, "Male Bonding," 212; Eberwein, *Armed Forces: Masculinity and Sexuality in the American War Film* (New Brunswick, NJ: Rutgers University Press, 2007), 127–128.

18    Michael Herr, *Dispatches* (New York: Picador, 1982).

19    Gustav Hasford, *The Short-Timers* (New York: Harper & Row, 1979): 31–32.

20    www.visual-memory.co.uk/amk/doc/0065.html.

21    See Doherty, "Full Metal Genre," 25–26.

22    Michael Anderegg, "Hollywood and Vietnam: John Wayne and Jane Fonda as Discourse," in *Inventing Vietnam: The War in Film and Television*, 28. See also James Naremore, *On Kubrick* (London: BFI, 2007): 220.

23    Michael Arlen, *The Living-Room War* (New York: Viking, 1969).


## *Chapter 6:* Glory *(1989)*

1    It is also possible to see this treatment of African Americans as anticipating a comparable kind of demonization of racial others in World War II films' depiction of the Japanese.

2    The film is viewable on the Library of Congress website: www.lcweb2.loc.gov/ammem/sawhtml/sawhome.html.

3    According to the summary in the *American Film Institute Catalog*: "At the time of the United States' entry into World War I, Amos Crow is dogcatcher in the little river town of Buford, Tennessee; he is so kind-hearted that he boards all his captive canines rather than kill them. His pal, Willie, decides to enlist after being chided for his lack of patriotism by Camilla, cook in the home of Mary Jane Robinson, daughter of an aristocratic family. Amos is rejected by the Army because of his feet, but manages to get in line with recruits bound for France, along with his dog, Deep Stuff. At a camp in France, Mary Jane, now a YMCA hostess, breaks off with Captain Davis, who is unmasked as a German spy, and Amos and Willie promise to find Ted for her. In rescuing Ted from a dugout, they learn of a surprise attack; they send Deep Stuff back with a message, but he is missing upon their return. After the war, he returns with a dachshund 'war bride' and six pups." George Marin and Charles Mack,

the stars, were well known in vaudeville and burlesque and had appeared in blackface the previous year in another film, *Why Bring That Up*, which was not war related. By 1929 the best-known example of a white actor performing in blackface was Al Jolson in *The Jazz Singer* (1927). For the fullest treatment of this practice, which is offensive to audiences today, see Michael Rogin, *Blackface, White Noise: Jewish Immigrants in the Hollywood Melting Pot* (Berkeley: University of California Press, 1996).

4   For commentary on African Americans in silent and early sound era Civil War films, see Thomas Cripps, "The Absent Presence in American Civil War Films," *Historical Journal of Film, Radio, and Television*, 14, 4 (1994): 367–376.

5   Brian Henderson, "*The Searchers*: An American Dilemma," in *Movies and Methods*, Vol. 2, ed. Bill Nichols (Berkeley: University of California Press, 1985): 429–449.

6   Robert Rosenstone, *History in Film/Film in History* (London: Pearson, Longman, 2006): 41–42.

7   See Martin H. Blatt, "*Glory*: Hollywood History, Popular Culture, and the Fifty-Fourth Massachusetts Regiment," for a painstaking account of the film's relation to actual historical detail, in *Hope & Glory: Essays on the Legacy of the Fifty-Fourth Massachusetts Regiment*, ed. Martin H. Blatt, Thomas J. Browne, and Donald Yacovone (Amherst: University of Massachusetts Press, 2001): 215–235; and Thomas Cripps, "*Glory* as a Meditation on the Saint-Gaudens Monument," for commentary on the making of the film, in *Hope & Glory*: 236–252.

8   Mulcahy and the black tentmates are all inventions. Blatt notes that one of the sons of Frederick Douglass served as a sergeant major, but he is absent from the film: Blatt, *Glory*, 220.

9   Robert Burgoyne notes that the scene duplicates the embrace in *Birth of a Nation* when lifetime friends who are fighting for different sides die in each other's arms on the battlefield. See "Race and Nation in *Glory*," in my anthology *The War Film* (New Brunswick: Rutgers University Press, 2004): 79.

10  Gary Giddens, Review of *Glory*, *Village Voice*, 19 December 1989: 98. For similar comments, see Terry Kelleher, Review of *Glory*, in *Newsday*, 14 December 1989: II, 7; Kenneth Cameron, *America on Film: Hollywood and American History* (New York: Continuum, 1997): 187–188; and Richard Combs, Review of *Glory*, *Monthly Film Bulletin*, April 1990: 105.

11  Jude Davies and Carol R. Smith, *Gender, Ethnicity and Sexuality in Contemporary American Film* (Edinburgh: Keele University Press, 1997): 74.

12  Davies and Smith, *Gender*, 75.

13  Davies and Smith, *Gender*, 78. Arguing from a different ideological perspective, Roger Ebert makes a similar point: "Watching *Glory*, I had

one recurring problem. I didn't understand why it had to be told so often from the point of view of the 54th's white commanding officer. Did we see the black troops through his eyes—instead of seeing him through theirs?" Review of *Glory*, rogerebert.com, 12 January 1990. Kevin Thomas also raises this concern: "For all that is commendable about *Glory*, you nevertheless wish you were experiencing it from the perspective of Trip." Review of *Glory*, *Los Angeles Times*, 14 December 1989, Calendar: 1. Morgan Freeman's reaction to the objection raised by Ebert is worth noting: "I don't have a problem with that. He [screenwriter Kevin Jarre] wrote it from a place he could write a story from, the only place he could get a grip on it from. You cannot reasonably ask a white writer to do it differently." Cited in Blatt, *Glory*, 221.

14  John Pym, Review of *Glory*, *Sight & Sound*, Spring 1990: 135.
15  Brian J. Woodman agrees with several critics who find this a negative conception: "Doc is still not really a doctor" but "just another in a line of non-threatening black film characters." See "Represented in the Margins: Images of African-American Soldiers in Vietnam War Combat Films," in my anthology *The War Film* (New Brunswick, NJ: Rutgers University Press, 2004): 92–93.
16  Woodman, "Represented in the Margins," 103–113.
17  Giddens, Review of *Glory*.
18  In his analysis of Ken Burns' *The Civil War* (1990), Robert Brent Toplin speaks to the post-Vietnam mood of the country: "*Glory* (1989) portrayed combat as a brutal and ugly slaughter even though it celebrated the African-Americans' commitment to fighting for the Union and freedom. Clearly, Burns shared a perspective with producers of the post-Vietnam era who intended it to reveal the darker side of war." See "*The Civil War* as an Interpretation of History," in *Ken Burns's The Civil War: Historians Respond* (New York: Oxford University Press, 1996): 27.
19  Burgoyne, "Race and Nation in *Glory*," 76. He points to the tension at work in the film between a conception of an emerging black individual nation within and one whose identity is inflected by the white nation that authorizes it from without. Trevor McCrisken and Andrew Pepper question the film's ultimate effectiveness in presenting racial issues: "*Glory* is both a success and a failure. It nominally critiques the implicit ethnocentrism of the benign meta-narrative of American history and challenges our received understandings about the significance of racial differences in Civil War America. . . . However, *Glory* also works hard to contain those really divisive racial divisions and reconcile 'black' and 'white' characters into a quite sophisticated story of national healing in which racial differences and different historical perspectives are initially emphasized, then tolerated and then managed in a complex hierarchy of command." See Trevor McCrisken and Andrew Pepper, *American History*

*and Contemporary Hollywood Film* (New Brunswick: Rutgers University Press, 2005): 68–69.

20 See Robert Burgoyne, *The Hollywood Historical Film* (Oxford: Wiley-Blackwell, 2008), especially his observations on the war film: 29–34.

21 Bruce Chadwick, *The Reel Civil War: Mythmaking in American Film* (New York: Alfred A. Knopf, 2001): 276.

22 Chadwick, *The Reel Civil War*, 279. His chapter on the film and *Gettysburg* is very informative: 276–298.

23 One famous shot that gives the impression of reality in the era before cgi occurs in *Gone With the Wind* when Scarlett O'Hara searches for a doctor and the camera pulls back in a stunning crane shot revealing hundreds and hundreds of dead or dying soldiers lying on the ground. The impressive shot was created by lining up dummies and arrangements of clothing, not human beings.

## Chapter 7: The Iraq Wars on Film

1 David Ansen suggests that Duncan's narrative is "neither knee-jerk put-down of the military nor simply a patriotic salute. He has his bones to pick with the army's duplicitous protection of its own image, but it's the critique of an insider who believes in military values. What the movie doesn't engage is the politics of the edited-for-television gulf war itself; it's just the backdrop for a story that could be told of any war." Review of *Courage Under Fire* in *Newsweek*, 15 August 1996: 59.

2 Yvonne Tasker's thoughtful assessment of this film and of *GI Jane* (1995) explores their significance in regard to gender and to action films. She suggests: "Within the current and historical context, the significance of the military woman for the codes of Hollywood cinema is that her masculinity is tied to such structures. By constructing its narrative around an exploration of whether a butch woman should be awarded the Medal of Honor, [the film] works to complexly repudiate the feminizing/superficial world of media and public relations." See "Soldiers' Stories: Women and Military Masculinities in *Courage Under Fire*," in my anthology *The War Film* (New Brunswick, NJ: Rutgers University Press, 2004): 186. Tom Tunney situates Walden in the male heroic tradition: "GI combat mythology from the Alamo to the Gulf has characteristically focused on the underdog fighting heroically against the odds. Despite its apparently groundbreaking subject matter, *Courage Under Fire* conforms to the stereotype. Karen Walden is in the same rugged tradition as either Sergeant York or Audie Murphy in her commitment to improvised, hands-on heroics." Review in *Sight and Sound*, October 1996: 38.

3 Jack Mathews points out correctly that the film has "no little courage itself, especially in a summer movie season of wholesale destruction

and cartoon violence. After all, it's going up against *Independence Day* [1996], a feel-good thrill ride whose body count is in the millions." Review of *Courage Under Fire*, *Newsday*, 12 July 1996: Part II, B2. *Courage Under Fire* earned $59,031,000 domestically, $100,860,000 worldwide. *Independence Day* earned $306,169,268 domestically, $797,900,000 worldwide.

4   Ebert, Review of *Three Kings*, *Chicago Sun Times*, 4 October 1999.
5   Todd McCarthy, Review of *Three Kings*, *Variety*, 22 September 1999.
6   Ebert, Review of *Three Kings*; Seymour, Review of *Three Kings*, *Newsday*, 1 October 1999: Part II, 83; Hoberman, "Burn, Blast, Bomb, Cut," *Sight & Sound*, 2, 2 (February 2000): 20; Gliberman, "Spoils of War," *Entertainment Weekly*, 506, 8 October 1999: 44.
7   Its ideological complexity and agenda set it apart from *Kelly's Heroes* (1970), a film about World War II also built around a heist of gold bullion. The earlier film has nothing of the political and moral critique at the center of *Three Kings*.
8   Cynthia Fuchs comments perceptively on this scene: "Swoff sits . . . a series of camera angles pairing him with the dead man, so each appears in foreground and background, as if they are conversing. The effect is more harrowing than any battle sequence, underlining *Jarhead*'s anguished point: war is not heroic or rousing. It is only devastating." "No Glory," www.popmatters.com/pm/review/jarhead-2005.
9   "The Infantryman's Creed, My Rifle," was written shortly after Pearl Harbor by Major William H. Rupertus, a Marine. It first appears in fiction in Gustav Hasford's *The Short-Timers*, the basis of *Full Metal Jacket*.
10  Owen Gliberman, "Semper High," *Entertainment Weekly*, 11 November 2005: 46.
11  A. O. Scott, "Soldiers in the Desert, Antsy and Apolitical," *New York Times*, 4 November 2005: E1.
12  J. Hoberman, Review of *Jarhead*, *Village Voice*, 25 October 2005.
13  Todd McCarthy, "Muted Winds of War," *Variety*, 31 October–6 November 2005: 47.
14  "Jarhead Full (?) of Sex & Politics," www.rogerebert.com.
15  David Denby, "Lost Boys," *The New Yorker*, 7 November 2005: 150.
16  See Richard Corliss, "Iraq Films Focus on Soldiers," *Time*, 1 September 2007; "Why the Iraq Films are Failing," *Time*, 15 November 2007; and "This Means War," *Time*, 26 November 2007: 80–81; Owen Gliberman, "The War Zone," *Entertainment Weekly*, 26 October 2007: 46–47; A. O. Scott, "A War on Every Screen," *New York Times*, 28 October 2007: Arts and Leisure Section: 1, 10; Peter Travers, "AWOL in America," *Rolling Stone*, 3 April 2008 (review of *Stop-Loss*). For commentary on documentaries, see Anthony Kaufman, "Yanks Nix Iraq Pix," *Slate*, 12 October 2006; and Philip Kennicott, "Sorting the Three Types of Iraq War Movies," *Washington Post*, 2 April 2008: C10.

## Chapter 8: Iwo Jima

1   Roger Ebert's comment on this film is worth noting: "We have seen this story in a hundred other movies, where the combat-hardened veteran, facing retirement, gets one last assignment to train a platoon of green kids and lead them into battle. But Eastwood, as the producer, director and star, caresses the material as if he didn't know B movies have gone out of style." rogerebert.com, 5 December 1986.

2   The larger flag stood for three weeks. It is not clear whether Forrestal got this one as a souvenir; he certainly didn't get the one he wanted since that was retained by Colonel Johnson. See Bradley's fascinating account in *Flags of Our Father* (New York: Bantam Books, 2000): 202–212.

3   For David Denby, "the photograph is an accidental masterpiece of classical construction, with the diagonal line of the pole supported by the surging upraised arms of the men and balanced, at the base, by a marine poised at a right angle to it." "Battle Fatigue, *The New Yorker*, 30 October 2006: 102. Stephanie Zacharek writes "the picture is virtually a silhouette, an 'action' shot in which the arrangement of the men's bodies (the composition is eerily similar to that of classical sculpture) tells us more than their faces do." Review of *Flags*, Salon.com, 20 October 2006. For other thoughtful commentary on the film, see Robert Sklar, Reviews of *Flags of Our Fathers* and *Letters from Iwo Jima*, *Cineaste*, 32, 2 (Spring 2007): 44–46; and Kenneth Turan, Review of *Flags*, *Los Angeles Times* calendarlive.com, 20 October 2006.

4   Among them Scott Foundas, "Print the Legend," *The Village Voice*, 17 October 2006, www.villagevoice.com/film/0642,foundas,74758,20.html; and Todd McCarthy, Review of *Flags*, *Variety*, 9 October 2006, www.variety.com/review/VE1117931805.html?categoryid=31&cs=1.

5   He is the older manifestation of Captain Severance (Neal McDonough), not Joe Rosenthal, as has been suggested. It is Severance who wants to promote Mike Strank to sergeant. During that conversation, they decide that Gagnon would be better as a runner. Severance gives Gagnon the second flag to take up to the top of Mount Suribachi.

6   Cynthia Fuchs, Review of *Flags*, popmatters.com, 20 October 2006.

7   James Berardinelli,, Review of *Flags*, www.reelviews.net/movies/f/flags_fathers.html; Leo Braudy, Reviews of *Flags* and *Letters*, *Film Quarterly*, 60, 4 (Summer 2007): 16–23; Richard Combs, "Tunnel Vision: Clint Eastwood," *Sight & Sound*, January 2007: 36; McCarthy, Review of *Flags*.

8   Delbert Mann's *The Outsider* (1961) presents the story of Ira Hayes, played by Tony Curtis. The film is currently unavailable on home video. In John Woo's *Windtalkers* (2002), Adam Beach plays one of the Navaho soldiers who were used by Army intelligence during World War II to prevent the Japanese from deciphering coded messages.

9    At the Cannes Festival in 2008, Spike Lee criticized Eastwood for not having any African Americans in the film. Eastwood responded in an interview: "He was complaining when I did *Bird* [the 1988 biopic of Charlie Parker]. Why would a white guy be doing that? I was the only guy who made it, that's why. He could have gone ahead and made it. Instead he was making something else." As for *Flags of Our Fathers*, he says, yes, there was a small detachment of black troops on Iwo Jima as a part of a munitions company, "but they didn't raise the flag. The story is *Flags of Our Fathers*, the famous flag raising picture, and they didn't do that. If I go ahead and put an African-American actor in there, people'd go, 'This guy's lost his mind.' I mean, it's not accurate." Jeff Dawson, "Dirty Harry Comes Clean," *Guardian*, 6 June 2008, www.guardian.co.uk/film/2008/jun/06/1. In one shot before the landing we see a group of four African-American Marines. As noted in Chapter 6, Spike Lee's *Miracle at St. Anna* (2008) concerns an African-American platoon in Italy during World War II.

10   See James Bradley's account of their experience in the film, *Flags of Our Father*, 321–322.

11   Mick LaSalle, "Once More into the Breach—Seen, this time, from the other side," SFGate.com, 20 December 2006.

12   Berardinelli, Review of *Flags*; Turan, Review of *Letters*, *Los Angeles Times* calendarlive.com, 20 December 2006; Zacharek, Review of *Flags*; Sklar, Reviews of *Flags*.

13   McCarthy, Review of *Letters*, *Variety*, 7 December 2006, www.variety.com/review/VE1117932266.html?categoryid=31&cs=1.

14   Mark Sinker, Review of *Letters*, *Sight & Sound*, March 2007: 62.

15   Jeanine Basinger, *The World War II Combat Film: Anatomy of a Genre* (Middletown, CT: Wesleyan University Press, 2003), 42.

16   Sklar, Reviews of *Flags*, 44.

17   Corliss, "On Duty, Honor, and Celebrity," *Time*, 23 October 2006: 82.

# INDEX

*Act of Violence*  23

*Action in the North Atlantic*  21

actualities  4–5, 9–10, 20, 29, 36, 142

*Adam Resurrected*  24

Adams, Eddie  51, 140

African Americans  3, 12, 16, 23,
    25–6, 86, 101–2, 110–20, 127,
    129, 163n3, 165n1, 166n4, 166n7

*African Queen, The*  29

*Air Force*  2, 20, 85, 161n13

*Alamo, The*  149

Aldrich, Robert  165n16

*All Quiet on the Western Front* (1930)  2,
    19, 28, 53, 63–72, 74, *66*, *68*, 79,
    103, 105, 143, 160n12

*All Quiet on the Western Front* (1979)
    72–3

Allen, Robert  7

Altman, Rick  52, 152n1

Altman, Robert  31, 51

Ambrose, Stephen  53

American Civil War  1, 3, 14–18, 25,
    47, 56, 85, 110–21, 136

American Revolutionary War  1,
    41

*American Soldiers*  38, 40

Anderegg, Michael  108

Andrews, Dana  *22, 84*

Andrews Sisters  144

Annikin, Ken  30

Ansen, David  163n8, 168n1

*Anybody's War*  111, 165n3

*Apocalypse Now*  32, *33*, 50, 94, 105,
    133, 163n8

*Arch of Triumph*  63

Arlen, Michael  54, 165n23

Ashby, Hal  32

*Ashes and Diamonds*  28

*Attack!*  28, 165n16

Attenborough, Richard  36

*At War with the Army*  46–7

Auerbach, Jonathan  7, 50

Auster, Alfred  62

*Away All Boats*  136

Ayres, Lew  64, *68*, 72

*Back to Bataan*   26, 90
*Back to the Future*   34
Bahktin, Mikhail   52
Baird, Robert   70
Baker, Mark   101
*Band of Brothers*   41, 158n45
*Barry Lyndon*   103
Basinger, Jeanine   43, 60, 86, 150,
    154n16, 158n45, 161n13, 161n14
*Bataan*   2, 4, 20, 25, 43, 51, *86*, 87,
    88, 91, 92, 94, 111, 150, 161n13,
    161n14
*Battle Cry*   29, 43
*Battle of Midway*   20, 57, 73, 89
*Battle of San Pietro*   57
*Battle of the Bulge, The*   3
*Battle of the Somme, The*   153n14
*Battleground*   23
*Battleship Oregon in Action*   56
Bazin, André   53
Beach, Adam   139, *145*, *146*, 170n8
*Beaufort*   1
Begnini, Roberto   24, 61
*Behind Enemy Lines*   1
Bell, Jamie   140
Bendix, William   85, 120
Berardinelli   170n7, 171n12
Berenger, Tom   97, *98*
*Best Years of our Lives, The*   22, 94,
    157n13
*Big Parade, The*   18, 57, 65
*Big Red One, The*   37, 96, 101, 121,
    128
*Big Sleep, The*   95
Bill, Tony   20
*Bird*   171n9
Birdwell, Michael   74, 160n17
*Birth of a Nation, The*   14–17, *15*,
    110–11, 113, 158n24
*Black Hawk Down*   41
*Blanket-Tossing of a New Recruit*   5, 10,
    66, 105
Blatt, Martin   166n7, 166n8, 167n13
Bloch, Harlon   139–44
Bogart, Humphrey   29, 95
*Bonnie and Clyde*   163n5
*Born on the Fourth of July*   3, 102, 119
Borzage, Frank   74

*Boy in the Striped Pyjamas, The*   24
*Boys in Company C, The*   32, 94, 116
Bradford, Jesse   139, *145*, *146*
Bradley James   138, 140, 171n10
Bradley, John "Doc"   138–46
Brady, Matthew   5
Brando, Marlon   23, 32
Braudy, Leo   170n7
*Braveheart*   1
Breen, Joseph I.   58, 160n1
*Bridge, The*   28
*Bridge on the River Kwai, The*   27–8
*Bridge Too Far, A*   36
*Bright Victory*   23, 94, 116
Broderick, Matthew   113
Brokaw, Tom   41, 62
Brothers, Caroline   54
Brownlow, Kevin   154n4
Brownmiller, Susan   101
Broyles, William, Jr.   131–3, 137
*Buccaneer, The*   1
*Buck Privates*   46, 144
Burgoyne, Robert   45, 50, 52, 92, 120,
    158n45, 166n9, 168n20
*Burial of the Maine Victims*   5, 7–8, 56
Burns, Ken   53, 167n18
Bush, George H. W.   38, 129
Bush, George W.   38, 122, 134

Cameron, Kenneth   166n10
Canby, Vincent   36, 163n8
*Casablanca*   21
Castonguay, James   153n10
*Casualties of War*   35, 119
*Catch 22*   35
Cawelti, John   95–6
Chadwick, Bruce   120–1
Chambers, John W.   53
Chaplin, Charlie   18
*Charge of the Light Brigade, The*   1
*Charlie Wilson's War*   46
children   12, 26, 37, 80, 98, 101,
    155n10, 156n19, 166n19
*China Gate*   37
*Chinatown*   95–6, 163n5
Chun, William   25–6
Cimino, Michael   32, 101, 133, 163n8
*Citizen Kane*   80, 125

*Civil War, The* 167n18
*Civilization* 18, 50
Clark, Dane 77, *81*
Clément, Réne 28
Clift, Montgomery 24, 114
Clinton, Bill 62
Clooney, George 39–40, *128*
Colbert, Claudette 29, 88
Cold War films 27–8, 30–1, 96, 101, 103, 112
Collins, Jim 152n1, 154n7, 163n4
*Colored Troops Disembarking* 111
Combs, Richard 166n10, 170n7
*Coming Home* 32, 93, 163n8
*Command Decision* 23
*Confessions of a Nazi Spy* 19, 74
Conrad, Joseph 32
Cooper, Gary 19, 75
Coppola, Francis Ford 32, 35, 163n8
Corliss, Richard 4, 150, 169n16
*Corregidor* 161n14
*Courage Under Fire* 3, 38, 110, 122–8, *124*, *126*, 169n3
Cripps, Thomas 154n1, 166n4, 166n7
Cronauer, Adrian 34
Cronkeit, Walter 109
Cross, Joseph 139
*Crossfire* 23
Crowther, Bosley 49, 82
Cruise, Tom 102
*Cry "Havoc"* 87–8, 162n16
Cull, Nicholas 155n8
Cunningham, David 155n10
Curtiz, Michael 48

Dafoe, Willem 97
Damon, Matt 60, 62, 123–4
D'Andrea, Tom *49*
Daves, Delmer 2, 77–83
David, Keith 102, 116
Davies, Jude 115
Davis, Peter 31, 58
*Dawn Patrol, The* (1930) 19, 73–4, 159n7
*Dawn Patrol, The* (1938) 73–4
Dawson, Jeff 171n9
*Day Zero* 134
Deakins, Roger 132
DeBona, Guerric 28, 155n9

*Deep Impact* 61
*Deer Hunter, The* 32, 50–1, 58, 94, 101, 133, 163n8
*Defiance* 110
DeMille, Cecil B. 154n4
Denby, David 133, 170n3
DePalma, Brian 35, 54, 119
*Desperate Journey* 21
*Destination Tokyo* 2, 20, 76–83, *78*, *81*, 90, 94, 120, 143
*Detour* 23
*Diary of Anne Frank, The* 24
*Dirty Harry* 94
Dmytryk, Edward 77, 90
Doherty, Thomas 34, 44, 96, 158n45, 164n15, 165n21
Dombrowski, Lisa 156n20
D'Onofrio, Vincent 104
Douglas, Kirk 101, 103
Douglass, Frederick 113
*Dr. Strangelove or: How I Learned to Stop Worrying and Love the Bomb* 3, 103
*Drummer of the Eighth* 14
DuBois, W. E. B. 16
Duncan, Patrick Sheene 125–6, 168n1
Dwan, Allan 145

Eastwood, Clint 3, 94, 136–51, 170n1, 171n9
Ebert, Roger 19, 59, 99, 129–30, 154n3, 156n22, 166n13, 170n1
Eden Musee 7–8, 45
Edeson, Arthur 72
*Edge of Darkness* 63
Edison, Thomas A. 7
Edwards, James 116
*84C Mopic* 33, 125
Eisenhower, Dwight D. 39–40
Emerson, Jim 133
*Empire of the Sun* 155n10
Ermey, R. Lee *104*
*Europa, Europa* 24
Evans, Gene *25*, 47

*Fahrenheit 9/11* 38
*Farewell to Arms, A* (1932) 74
*Farewell to Arms, A* (1957) 74–5, 160n19
Fargnoli, Jayne 163n9

Farrow, John 84
*Fear and Desire* 164n14
Ferguson, Charles 38, 92
Fielding, Raymond 153n7
*Fighter Squadron* 23
*Fighting Seabees, The* 30, 162n19
*Fighting 69th, The* 19
*Fires on the Plain* 159n8
*First Blood* 34, 94, 163n8
*Flags of our Fathers* 3, 41, 136–46, *138*, *145*, *146*, 147, 149, 171n9, 171n10
*Flyboys* 20
*Flying Leathernecks* 30, 48
*Flying Tigers* 30, 161n11
Fonda, Henry 20, 30
Fonda, Jane 32
*Forbidden Games* 28
Ford, John 20, 57, 73, 89, 90–1, 112, 139, 150, 159n7
*Forrest Gump* 62, 156n23
*Fort Apache* 23
*For Whom the Bell Tolls* 1
Foundas, Scott 170n4
*Four Horsemen of the Apocalypse, The* (1921) 18, 64
*Four Horsemen of the Apocalypse, The* (1962) 73
*Four Sons* 159n7
Foxx, Jamie 131
*Francis in the Navy* 136
Frankenheimer, John 26
Freeman, Morgan 113, 115, *117*
French-Indian Wars 1, 40
*Frogmen* 48
*From Here to Eternity* (1953) 75
*From Here to Eternity* (1979) 75
Fuchs, Cynthia 20, 107, 142, 169n8
*Full Metal Jacket* 3, 35, 103–9, *104*, *106*, 114, 119, 133, 164n15, 169n9
Fuller, Sam 24, 25–6, 37, 47, 96, 101, 121, 154n8, 164n15

Gagnon, Rene 139–46
*Gallipoli* 20
Gance, Abel 18, 71
Garfield, John 77, *81*, 82–3, 85
Garrett, Diana 4
*General, The* 17, 47, 112

*Gettysburg* 121
Giddens, Gary 115
*G.I. Jane* 168n2
Gliberman, Owen 4, 59, 130, 133, 169n16
*Glory* 3, 110–21, *117–18*, 167n19
*Go Tell the Spartans* 32, 93–4
*God Is My Co-Pilot* 80, 161n11
*Gods and Generals* 121
*Gone with the Wind* 1, 17, 112, 168n23
*Good Morning Vietnam* 33–4
*Good Will Hunting* 62
Goulding, Edmund 73
*Grace is Gone* 4, 38, 40, 134
*Grand-Dad* 14
Grant, Barry K. 150n1, 156n23, 164n11
Grant, Cary 77, *78*, 82–3
*Great Escape, The* 28
*Great Raid, The* 41, 50
*Green Berets, The* 31, 38, 93, 103–8, 116
Greengrass, Paul 92
Grenada 136
Grier, David Allen 116
Grievson, Lee 7
Griffith, D. W. 9, 14–16, 18, 26, 110–11
*Guadalcanal Diary* 4, 9, 51, 88–9, 111, 120, 161n13, 162n16
Guinness, Alec 27
Gulf War 1, 3, 38–40, 54, 62, 110, 122–34
*Gung-Ho!* 88–9
Gunning, Tom 8
*Guy Named Joe, A* 127
*Guys, The* 38
Gyllenhaal, Jake 131, *132*

Haggis, Paul 137, 146
Halberstam, David 163n8
Hale, Alan *49*, 77
*Halls of Montezuma* 48, 63
*Hamburger Hill* 33, 117–19
Hanks, Tom 40, 41, *59*, 60, 62, 156n23
Hansen, Hank 139, 141, 143–4
*Hart's War* 41
Hasford, Gustav 103, 107–8, 169n9
Hawks, Howard 19, 73–4, 85, 159n7

Hayes, Ira 139–46, 170n8
*Heartbreak Ridge* 136
*Hearts and Minds* 3, 31, 58, 93
*Hearts of the World* 9, 18, 26, 134
*Heaven and Earth* 3, 102
Heisler, Stuart 111
*Hell's Angels* 19, 64–5
Hemingway, Ernest 74
Henderson, Brian 112
Hepburn, Katharine 29
Herr, Michael 103, 107–8
Heston, Charlton 112
Hitchcock, Alfred 125
Hoberman, J. 130, 133
Holden, William 27–8, 112
*Hollywood Canteen* 77, 144
Holocaust, the 23–4, 58, 110
*Home of the Brave* (1949) 111, 116, 127
*Home of the Brave* (2006) 38, 40, 134
*Horse Soldiers, The* 112
Hudson, Rock 75
Hughes, Howard 19, 64
*Human Comedy, The* 21
Hüppauf, Bernd 54
Huston, John 28–9, 30, 47, 57, 160n19

Ice Cube *128*
Ichikawa, Kon 159n8
Ignatowski, Ralph "Iggy" 140–2
*I'll Be Seeing You* 23
*Immortal Sergeant* 21
*In the Army* 157n12
*In the Valley of Elah* 4, 38, 40, 134, 137
Ince, Thomas 14, 50, 110
*Independence Day* 2, 61, 169n3
*Intolerance: Love's Struggle Throughout the Ages* 16
Iraq War films 1, 3, 4, 38–40, 51, 92, 122, 134–5
Ivens, Joris 63

Jaafar, Ali 92
*J'Accuse* 18, 71
*Jarhead* 3, 38, 50, 122–3, 131–3, *132*, 137, 169n8
*Jazz Singer, The* 166
Jeffords, Susan 34, 100, 107
*Jezebel* 112

*Johnny Got His Gun* 20
Johnson, Lyndon B. 109
Johnson, Van 83, 127
Jones, James 61, 75
Jones, Jennifer 75
Jones, Tommy Lee 102
Jonze, Spike *128*
*Journey's End* 64–5
*Judgment at Nuremberg* 24
*Jumping Jacks* 46

Kaes, Anton 50
Kane, Kathryn 42
Kaufman, Anthony 169n16
Keaton, Buster 17, 47
Kehr, Dave 155n13
Keighley, William 19
Kelleher, Terry 166n10
Kelly, Andrew 159n1, 159n5, 160n12
*Kelly's Heroes* 136, 169n7
Kennedy, John F. 105
Kennicott, Philip 169n16
*King Rat* 27
*Kingdom, The* 38, 40
*Kingdom of Heaven* 1
*Kings Go Forth* 77
Kitses, Jim 153n15, 156n2
Korean War 11, 20, 24–8, 31, 35, 43–4, 46–7, 58, 63, 96
Kovik, Ron 102
Krämer, Peter 7
Kubrick, Stanley 3, 20, 35, 103–9, 164n14
Kurosawa, Akira 124

*La Grande Illusion* 19
*Ladies Courageous* 127
*Lafayette Escadrille* 20, 136
Lancaster, Burt 32
Lang, Robert 154n1
LaSalle, Mick 147
*Last of the Mohicans, The* 1, 40
*Last Samurai, The* 110
*Last Year in Vietnam* 96
Lean, David 27
Lee, Spike 111, 171n9
Leone, Sergio 136
LeRoy, Mervyn 77, 83

*Letters from Iowa Jima*   3, 136–7, 146–51, *148, 149*
Levinson, Barry   33
Lévi-Strauss, Claude   7, 156n2
Levy, David   8
Lewis, Jerry   46–7
*Life is Beautiful*   24, 61
Lincoln, Abraham   85
*Little American, The*   154n3
Litvak, Leon   16
*Longest Day, The*   3, 30, 146
*Lord of the Rings, The*   2
*Losers, The (Nam's Angels)*   31
*Lost Patrol, The*   86, 150
*Love and War*   1, *6*
Ludwig, Edward   162n19

McCarthy, Todd   129–30, 133, 149, 170n4, 170n7
McCrisken, Trevor   163n5, 167n19
*Magnum Force*   94
*Major Dundee*   112–13
*Major Payne*   157n12
Malick, Terrence   61, 75
*Maltese Falcon, The*   95
*Man Who Shot Liberty Valance, The*   125, 139
*Manchurian Candidate, The* (1962)   26–7
*Manchurian Candidate, The* (2004)   38–9
Mann, Delbert   72–3, 170n8
Martin, Dean   46–7
Marton, Andrew   30, 75
Marvin, Lee   139
*M*A*S*H*   31, 51, 163n5
Matthews, Jack   168n3
Mauldin, Bill   47
Maxwell, Ronald   121
*Memphis Belle, The* (1944)   9
*Memphis Belle, The* (1990)   41
*Men, The*   23
Mendes, Sam   122, 131–3
Merritt, Russell   159n4
*Messenger, The*   1
*Midnight Clear, A*   41
Milestone, Lewis   1, 2, 48, 53, 63–71, 77, 83, 143, 154n8
Miller, David   161n11
Minnelli, Vincent   73

*Miracle at St. Anna*   111, 171n9
*Missing in Action*   34, 94, 134, 163n8
Modine, Matthew   104, *106*
Moore, Michael   38
*Mortal Storm, The*   23
Murphy, Audie   29, 168n2
Musser, Charles   7–8, 10

*Napoleon*   1
Naremore, James   165n22
National Association for the Advancement of Colored People (NAACP)   16
Native Americans   112, 170n8
Neale, Steve   43–4, 150n1
*Negro Soldier, The*   111
Newhall, Beaumont   5
*Nibelungen, Die*   2
Nichols, Mike   40
*Night and Fog*   24
9/11   38, 76, 92, 122
Ninomiya, Kazunari   147, *148*
*9th Infantry Morning Boys' Wash*   55
Nixon, Richard M.   35, 36, 51, 96
*No End in Sight*   38, 92
Norris, Chuck   34, 94

*Objective, Burma!*   57, 59, 80
*One Million B.C.*   1
*Our Russian Front*   63
*Out of the Past*   23
*Outlaw Josie Wales, The*   136
*Outsider, The*   170n7

Pabst, G. W.   19
*Paisan*   26
*Paradise Road*   155n10
*Passage to Marseille*   2, 125
*Paths of Glory*   3, 20, 103
*Patriot, The*   1, 41, 113
*Patton*   35, 51, 116, 163n5
*Pearl Harbor*   41, 91
Peck, Gregory   23
Peckinpah, Sam   112
Peirce, C. S.   53
Peirce, Kimberly   38, 134
Penn, Sean   35
Pepper, Andrew   163n5, 167n19

Pepper, Barry   139
*Philadelphia*   62
Phillippe, Ryan   134, *135*, 139, *145*, *146*
*Pianist, The*   24
Pickford, Mary   147, 154n4
*Platoon*, 1, 3, 35, 93, 96–102, *98*, *100*, 104, 107, 112, 118, 121, 125, 163n8
Polanski, Roman   24, 95
*Pork Chop Hill*   63
*Pride of the Marines*   77
*Prisoner of War*   26
Production Code Administration (PCA) 17, 58, 74, 160n1
*Purple Heart, The*   26, 63, 83, *84*, 90, 94
Pym, John   115

*Rack, The*   26
*Raising Old Glory Over Morro Castle*   5, 137
*Rambo: First Blood Part II*   34, 94
*Rashomon*   124
*Reader, The*   24
Reagan, Ronald   26, 34, 48
*Red Badge of Courage, The*   28, 47, 112, 155n9
*Redacted*   1, 4, 38, 40, 54, 134
reenactments   5, 9–10, 29, 45, 54, 120–1, 137–8, 145–6
Renoir, Jean   19
*Rescue Dawn*   41
Resnais, Alain   24
Rogin, Michael   166n3
Rollins, Howard, Jr.   116
*Rome, Open City*   26
Roosevelt, Franklin Delano   13, 140, 161n11
Roosevelt, Theodore   5
Rosenbaum, Jonathan   164n15
Rosenstone, Robert   113, 163n8
Rosenthal, Joe   138, 140, 170n5
Rubenstein, Lenny   43
Russell, David O.   122, 128–31
Ryan, Meg   123, *126*

*Sahara*   161n13
*Sailor Beware*   46

Sandrich, Mark   77, 88
*Sands of Iowa Jima*   23, 30, 145–6, 171n10
Sarsgaard, Peter   131, *132*
*Saving Private Ryan*   1, 21, 40, 41, 58–62, *59*, 64, 130, 156n23
Schaffner, Franklin J.   35
Schatz, Thomas   7, 73, 91, 158n45, 159n3
Schickle, Richard   37
*Schindler's List*   24, 62
Scott, A. O.   133, 169n16
Scott, George C.   35
*Search, The*   24
*Searchers, The*   112
*See Here, Private Hargrove*   21, 46
Selznick, David O.   75, 160n19
*Sergeant York*   19
*Seventh Cross, The*   23–4
Seymour, Gene   130
Shaw, Robert Gould   113–15
Sheen, Charlie   97, *100*
Shore, Dinah   139, 144
*Short-Timers, The*   103, 108, 169n9
*Shoulder Arms*   18
*Siege, The*   110
Sinatra, Frank   27
*Since You Went Away*   21
Sinker, Mark   150
*Situation, The*   134
Sklar, Robert   150, 170n3, 170n12
Slocum, J. David   54
Smith, Carol   115
Smith, Kate   48
Snyder, Zack   51
*So Proudly We Hail!*   20
Sobchak, Thomas   44–5
*Soldier's Story, A*   116
*Soldiers Washing Dishes*   5, 10, 23
Sontag, Susan   30
*Sophie's Choice*   24
Sorlin, Pierre   157n17, 158n24
Sousley, Franklin   139, 141–2
Southern, Ann   87
Spanish-American War   1–2, 4–11, 14, 16–17, 20–1, 29, 36, 44–5, 47, 50, 55–6, 60, 105, 111, 120, 137
Spielberg, Steven   24, 41, 58, 61–2, 155n10

St. Jacques, Raymond 116
*Stage Fright* 125
*Stalag 17* 27
Stallone, Sylvester 34, 94
*Star Trek* 107
*Star Wars* 2
*Starship Troopers* 2
*Steel Helmet, The* 1, 25–6, 37, 47, 97,
  101, 112, 116
Steiger, Janet 150n1, 154n7
Stern, Tom 142
Stewart, James 30, 139
Stone, Oliver 3, 35, 92, 93, 96–103,
  98, 100, 121, 125, 163n8
*Stop-Loss* 38, 134–5
*Stormy Weather* 111
*Story of G. I. Joe, The* 21, 143
*Stranger, The* 24
Strank, Mike 139, 141–2
*Strategic Air Command* 29–30
*Streamers* 116
Streep, Meryl 24
*Stripes* 157n12
Sturges, John 28
Sturken, Marita 52
Suid, Lawrence 43, 160n6
*Sullivans, The* 221
Swofford, Anthony 131–3
*Syriana* 38–40

*Tae-Guk-Gi* 155n13
*Task Force* 77
Tasker, Yvonne 168n2
Taylor, Robert *86*, 150
*Tender Comrade* 21
Terkel, Studs 62
*They Died With Their Boots On* 149
*They Were Expendable* 73, 90–1
*Thin Red Line, The* (1964) 28, 75
*Thin Red Line, The* (1998) 41, 61, 75,
  130
*Thirty Seconds Over Tokyo* 89–90
*This Is the Army* 21, 48–50, *49*,
  144
Thomas, Kevin 167n13
Thorpe, Richard 77, 87
*300, The* 1, 51
*Three Came Home* 29

*Three Kings* 1, 3, 38, 122–3, 128–31,
  *128*, 132, 133, 169n7
*To End All Wars* 41, 155n10
*To Hell and Back* 29
Toplin, Robert Brent 36, 51, 167n18
*Tora! Tora! Tora!* 35–6, 91, 146
Toto, Christian 4
*Town Without Pity* 101
Tracy, Spencer 83, 127
Travers, Peter 169n16
*Tristan and Isolde* 1
*Troops Making Military Road in Front of
  Santiago* 5
*Troy* 1
Truman, Harry S. 25, 111, 145
Trumbo, Dalton 20
Tudor, Andrew 10
Tunney, Tom 168n2
Turan, Kenneth 170n3, 171n12
*Tuskegee Airmen, The* 111
*Twelve O'Clock High* 23
*Two Arabian Nights* 63
*Two Women* 101

*United 93* 38, 40, 92
*Up Front* 47
Uris, Leon 29
*US Infantry Supported by Rough Riders at
  El Caney* 5

Valentino, Rudolph 64
Vance, Courtney 117
*Verboten!* 24
Very, Adam 4
*Very Long Engagement, A* 26
*Very Thought of You* 77
Vidor, King 57, 65
Vietnam War 1–3, 20, 31–8, 41,
  43–4, 50–2, 58, 93–109, 112,
  117–19, 125, 131–4, 140
Virilio, Paul 54
Voight, Jon 32

*Wackiest Ship in the Army, The* 43
Wahlberg, Mark *128*
Wajda, Andrzej 28
*Wake Island* 84–6, 89, 92, 94
*Walk in the Sun, A* 23, 63, 155n8

Walker, Benjamin 139
Walker, Paul 139
Walsh, Raoul 65, 149
*War, The* 53
*War and Peace* (1956) 1
*War and Peace* (1967) 1
war films
  combat films *see* individual titles and
    wars
  concentration camps 23–4, 37
  and definitions 9–11, 42–50
  documentaries 3, 9, 20, 24, 30–1,
    38, 57–8, 63, 73, 89, 92–3, 169n16
  extraction films 34, 94
  and history 2, 50–5, 139
  Holocaust, the 24, 58
  home front 10, 21–2, 94
  musical 44, 48–50, 77, 144
  prisoner of war films 23–4, 26–9,
    44, 155n10
  and "realism" 53–60, 139
  remakes 72–5
  retaliation films 20, 76–7, 83–92
  service comedies 10, 21, 43–4,
    46–7, 136, 144, 157n12
war films, generic conventions
  characters 11–12, 15, 25, 37, 43, 61,
    65–6, 69, 77, 79–80, 86, 88–9,
    97, 100, 104–5, 113–16, 127, 129,
    133, 142–3
  narrative 9–13, 15, 35, 37, 43, 61,
    65–7, 78, 80–1, 85–6, 91, 93, 97,
    99, 102–3, 105, 109, 113–15, 120,
    125–6, 130–1, 133–4, 141–4,
    149–50
  *See also* African Americans, children,
    Native Americans, women
*War of the Worlds* (1953) 2
*War of the Worlds* (2005) 2
Washington, Denzel 39, 113, 115,
  *118*, 123, *124*
Watanabe, Ken 147, *149*
Wayne, John 23, 30–1, 38, 90–1,
  106–9, 112, 139, 145–6, 149,
  161n11, 162n19
*We Were Soldiers* 41
Welky, David 160n18
Welles, Orson 24, 125

Wellman, William 19, 20, 136
*Westfront 1918* 19, 72
Whale, James 64, 69
*What Price Glory?* (1926) 18, 65
*What Price Glory?* (1952) 73
*Where Eagles Dare* 136
Whisell, Kristen 8
Whitaker, Forest 117
*White Heat* 23
White, James H. 5
White, Susan 107, 163n5
Wicki, Bernhard 28, 30
Wilder, Billy 27
Williams, Robin 34
Wilson, Woodrow 16
*Windtalkers* 170n8
*Wing and a Prayer, A* 89
*Winged Victory* 103
*Wings* 1, 19, 65, 73
*Winning Your Wings* 30
Wollen, Peter 53
women 12, 21–3, 29, 67–9, 80, 98,
  101–2, 106–7, 127, 155n10
Woo, John 170n8
Woodman, Brian J. 102, 116, 167n15
Worland, Rick 155n12
*World Trade Center* 38, 40, 92
World War I 1–2, 18–20, 29, 43, 50,
  57, 63–75, 103
World War II 1, 17, 19, 20–4,
  35–7, 41, 42–4, 46–51, 57,
  60–3, 76–92, 93, 96, 119, 127,
  130, 134, 136–51
*Wounded Soldiers Embarking in Row Boats*
  5, 55
Wright, Teresa *22*, 23
Wyler, William 9, 22, 112

Yamashita, Iris 146
*Yank on the Burma Road, A* 161n11
*Young Lions, The* 114

Zacharek, Stephanie 170n3,
  171n12
Zanuck, Darryl F. 30, 36
Zemeckis, Robert 34
Zinnemann, Fred 23, 24, 75
Zwick, Edward 3, 101, 122–8